Mortality of Hispanic Populations

Mortality of Hispanic Populations

MEXICANS, PUERTO RICANS, AND CUBANS IN THE UNITED STATES AND IN THE HOME COUNTRIES

EDITED BY

Ira Rosenwaike

STUDIES IN POPULATION AND URBAN DEMOGRAPHY, NUMBER 6

GREENWOOD PRESS
New York • Westport, Connecticut • London

HB
1335
M677
1991

Library of Congress Cataloging-in-Publication Data

Mortality of Hispanic populations : Mexicans, Puerto Ricans, and
  Cubans in the United States and in the home countries / edited by
  Ira Rosenwaike.
      p.   cm.—(Studies in population and urban demography, ISSN
  0147–1104 ; no. 6)
    Includes bibliographical references and index.
    ISBN 0–313–27500–9 (alk. paper)
    1. Hispanic Americans—Mortality.   2. Mortality—United States.
  3. Mortality—Mexico.   4. Mortality—Puerto Rico.   5. Mortality—
  Cuba.   I. Rosenwaike, Ira, 1936–   .   II. Series.
  HB1335.M677   1991
  304.6′4′08968—dc20   91–2

British Library Cataloguing in Publication Data is available.

Library of Congress Catalog Card Number: 91–2
ISBN: 0–313–27500–9
ISSN: 0147–1104

First published in 1991

Greenwood Press, 88 Post Road West, Westport, CT 06881
An imprint of Greenwood Publishing Group, Inc.

Printed in the United States of America

The paper used in this book complies with the
Permanent Paper Standard issued by the National
Information Standards Organization (Z39.48–1984).

10 9 8 7 6 5 4 3 2 1

FLORIDA STATE
UNIVERSITY LIBRARIES

TALLAHASSEE, FLORIDA

Copyright Acknowledgments

The author and publisher are grateful to the following for granting permission to use
previously published materials:

Tables 3, 4, 6, 7, 28, 46, 122, 123, 125, 127, 139, 140, 144, and 156 from *La Poblacion de
Puerto Rico y su Trayectoria* by José L. Vázquez Calzada. Escuela Graduada de Salud
Publica Recinto de Ciencias Medicas Universidad de Puerto Rico, 1988.

Tables 1, 3, 5, and 14 from *The Health Revolution in Cuba* by Sergio Diaz-Briquets. Austin:
University of Texas Press, 1983.

Table 3 from "Mortality Differentials among Persons Born in Cuba, Mexico, and Puerto Rico
Residing in the United States" by Ira Rosenwaike. *American Journal of Public Health* 77
(1987): 603–606.

Table 1 from "Changes in Mortality Among Cubans in the United States Following an
Episode of Unscreened Migration" by Ira Rosenwaike and Donna Shai. *International
Journal of Epidemiology* 18 (1989): 152–157, published by the Center for Migration Studies
of New York, Inc.

"Mortality among Three Puerto Rican Populations: Residents of Puerto Rico and Migrants in
New York City and in the Balance of the United States, 1979–81" by Ira Rosenwaike and
Katherine Hempstead. *International Migration Review* 24, 4 (Winter 1990).

Extracts from "Using Surname Data in the U.S. Puerto Rican Mortality Analysis" by Ira
Rosenwaike, Katherine Hempstead, and Richard G. Rogers. *Demography* 28, 1 (February
1991).

Contents

Illustrations

Acknowledgments

This book was made possible by research support from the Center for Population Research at the National Institute of Child Health and Human Development (grant HD–20089). The manuscript has been greatly improved by critical readings of several chapters by two of the contributors, Donna Shai and Katherine Hempstead and by the editorial suggestions of Eileen Lynch who read the entire draft.

Many other individuals and agencies contributed to the preparation of this work. David McKenna made important contributions to chapter 1. Sergio Camposortega Cruz of El Colegio de Mexico read an earlier draft of chapter 2. Janusz Szyrmer and Hanna Szyrmer did computer programming of public use 1980 Census tapes and various mortality record data tapes that were used in several chapters. Bill Spears of the University of Texas School of Public Health provided a useful file drawn from a larger set of Hispanic HANES data tapes which served as the source for several tables in chapter 9. Leonard M. Gaines of the New York State Department of Commerce prepared tables from the Census Bureau's 1980 Census Summary Tape 5 which were used in developing rates in chapter 6.

The health departments of New York State and New Jersey provided mortality data used in chapters 11 and 12. The health departments of California and Texas provided data used in chapter 10. The health department of New York City provided a copy of its mortality file that was used in chapter 12. The Commonwealth of Puerto Rico health department provided a copy of its mortality file that was used in chapter 6 and chapter 8. The figures in chapter 6 were executed by Inks, Inc.

Chapter 6 was published in *International Migration Review*, Vol. 24, No. 4 (Winter 1990). Permission from the journal, which is published by the Center for Migration Studies of New York, Inc. to reprint this chapter is appreciated. A shorter version of the material reported in chapter 12 was published in *Demography*, Vol. 28, No. 1 (Feb. 1991). I am grateful to the journal's editor for permission to use much of this material in the present volume.

I am particularly grateful to all of the contributors, who share with me a strong desire to investigate the demographic characteristics of the various peoples of Hispanic descent.

Part One

Introduction

CHAPTER 1

Mortality Experience of Hispanic Populations

IRA ROSENWAIKE

Hispanics in the United States, numbering 14.6 million at the 1980 census, are the nation's second largest and fastest growing minority population. Recent studies (Tienda and Ortiz, 1986; Melville, 1988; Rosenwaike, 1987; Bean and Tienda, 1987) have increased our knowledge of the demographic characteristics and culture of this multiethnic population, yet, to date, there has been no comprehensive discussion of the Hispanic mortality experience, a potential key to assessing the relative health status of Spanish-origin subgroups in American society.

The purpose of this volume is to present a work of coherent research on the mortality patterns of the three largest Hispanic subgroups and, in the process, help dispel many anecdotal and romanticized notions about Hispanic health and illness.

The Hispanic population under consideration is young, highly urbanized, and multiracial, but it has no firm, collective identity, despite strong lingual and cultural links. It is, for the most part, a population originating in twentieth-century immigration, consisting of distinct subgroups, each concentrated in a different region of the country, each with its own socioeconomic profile.

The concept of a generalized Hispanic minority stems more from governmental agency designation and Anglo-American perceptions than from any collective initiative by the subgroups themselves (Portes and Truelove, 1987). Indeed, the very word "Hispanic" was and is a rubric used by researchers and bureaucrats to simplify dealings with the Spanish-origin subgroups. It is a term that should be used advisedly, lest unwarranted emphasis be placed on similarities between the subgroups, thereby neglecting the importance of particular histories and cultures (Melville, 1988).

Researchers have consistently pointed to problems created by analyzing Hispanics as a single homogeneous population group. In a recent study of Hispanic health care consumers in the United States, Schur and others (1987) noted that "the various Hispanic subpopulations are as different from each other as they are from white and black population groups." They concluded that each subgroup must be studied separately if health care delivery to Hispanics in general is to be evaluated accurately.

Tienda and Ortiz (1986) stated in a noteworthy study that new items and categories used in the 1980 census to elicit ethnic responses do permit a more extensive analysis of subgroups but do not "automatically establish the existence of an ethnically united group." Portes and Truelove (1987) noted that Hispanics, despite specific geographical concentrations of certain subgroups within the United States, are "a group-in-formation whose boundaries and self-definitions are still in a state of flux." Melville (1988) observed that differences among subgroups extend to immigrant status (Puerto Ricans, for instance, are "born Americans," while many Central Americans are undocumented, i.e., illegal immigrants) and to variations in use of the Spanish language.

The Hispanic population in the United States is one of diverse origin. Those of Mexican origin, which includes sizable contingents of both native-born persons and immigrants, account for 60 percent of this population. Puerto Ricans account for approximately 14 percent. Since both island and mainland-born Puerto Ricans are U.S. citizens by birth, attempts to trace Puerto Rican "immigration" present problems for researchers. Cubans, most of whom are fairly recent immigrants, account for 6 percent of the Spanish-origin population. The remaining 20 percent include a fast-growing group consisting of Dominicans, Colombians, Salvadorans, Guatemalans, and other Central and South American nationals.

The diversity of national origins creates more differences than similarities among Hispanic subgroups. As Petersen (1986) noted in a recent study, Spanish-origin subgroups in 1980 "varied greatly in median age, family type, fertility, education level, type of occupation, proportion below the poverty line, median income, and almost any other social indicator on which there are data." Mortality also should have been included on his list of indicators, as this volume will illustrate.

Understanding how the three major Hispanic subgroups differ from one another within geographical, demographic, and socioeconomic contexts is a prerequisite to discussing mortality differences among the groups themselves and in relation to the U.S. non-Hispanic population.

Mexican-Americans are concentrated in the Southwest states of California, Texas, Arizona, Colorado, and New Mexico. There is also a substantial Mexican origin population in Illinois, primarily in metropolitan Chicago, which accounted for 7.6 percent of the Mexican origin population in 1980.

Due largely to recent high levels of immigration, the Mexican-born population is slightly younger, on average, than is the native white population. At the 1980 census only 21 percent of Mexican-born adults were high school graduates compared to 66.5 percent of the general U.S. population. Only about 5 percent of employed Mexican-born males held managerial and professional positions. Families headed by Mexican-born persons had a median income some 33 percent below the U.S. average.

Most Puerto Ricans in the United States settled in New York City during the 1950s or 1960s, but, according to census data, the proportion of Puerto Rican-born living in New York declined from 58 percent in 1970 to 42 percent in 1980. Approximately 40 percent of the 5 million-plus Puerto Ricans currently live in the continental United States. Natives of Puerto Rico on the average have lived in the United States longer than Mexican-born immigrants. This fact largely explains their substantially older median age of 33.7 years.

According to the 1980 census, about 35 percent of Puerto Rican-born persons age 25 years and older had completed high school, and about 10.7 percent of employed males were in professional/managerial occupations. Despite higher educational and occupational status, the median income of Puerto Rican-born families was approximately 28 percent lower than that of families headed by a Mexican native. A reason for the lower income is that more Puerto Rican families were headed by women, owing to higher rates of separation and divorce.

Most Cubans in the United States are concentrated in Miami, Florida, the metropolitan area closest to their homeland. In 1980, 53 percent of Cubans lived in Miami, 11 percent in New Jersey, and 9 percent in New York. The Cuban-born population is considerably older than the other two migrant subgroups, with a median age of 43.9 years in 1980, compared to 29.1 for Mexican-born residents, and 30.5 for the native white population. This older median age is due in part to the large numbers of Cubans who migrated in the 1960s after Fidel Castro came to power. At the 1980 census, about 55 percent of Cuban-born persons 25 years of age and older had completed high school, close to the U.S. average of 66.5 percent and in sharp contrast to levels for Mexican-born and Puerto Rican-born persons. Of all employed Cuban males, 22.4 percent were in managerial/professional occupations, close to the U.S. average of 23.6 percent. Families with Cuban-born persons had a median income approximately 7 percent below the level for all U.S. families.

The studies in this volume illustrate the existence of Hispanic patterns of mortality that are as distinctive as the age, education, and employment patterns cited above. These mortality patterns show remarkable parallels but also major differences in the mortality experience of the three largest subgroups. Most significantly, they indicate that the death rates of all three subgroups compare favorably with those of the general population of the United States.

To date there have been no comprehensive studies of Hispanic mortality. Previous studies relied on geographically limited or incomplete data. Although Bradshaw and Fonner (1978) and Schoen and Nelson (1981) provided valuable data for the 1970 census period on Mexican origin populations in Texas and California, respectively, the authors of both studies were careful to emphasize the lack of exact correspondence between the population designated as being of Spanish surname and the population of Mexican descent. Lee, Roberts, and Labarthe (1976) used Texas vital statistics for 1969–1971 to compare lung cancer mortality among Mexican-Americans with that for other whites and blacks. Rosenwaike (1983) compared mortality among Puerto Ricans in New York with that for non-Puerto Ricans for the 1970 census period.

This volume addresses the pressing need for more accurate, current, and comprehensive data for specific ethnic groups. It uses mortality data on first-generation Hispanics born in Mexico, Cuba, and Puerto Rico in combination with selected statistics on Hispanics of all generations. The latter statistics were prepared from mortality tapes compiled in those states which code Spanish origin or surname on death certificates. It also draws on mortality data from the countries of origin, which are used as a base for the findings about migrants.

The studies presented here are divided into five basic categories: mortality in the countries of origin; comparative mortality among Spanish-origin groups in the United States; specific causes of mortality among Spanish-origin populations; analysis of mortality data based on surname statistics; and an overview of mortality among migrants to the United States as compared to patterns of death in the countries of origin.

General studies using U.S. vital statistics indicate that the mortality of both Cuban-born and Mexican-born persons at all ages under 40 years is higher than that of the total white population (with a single exception). Nativity-mortality ratios of both subgroups are lowest at ages 50–64, and the highest mortality ratios are among young males (Table 1.1).

Death rates for persons born in Puerto Rico are higher than those for total whites up to age 55, and generally higher than rates for the other two Hispanic subgroups studied. Above age 55, death rates for Puerto Ricans are generally lower than those for total whites.

The age and sex-specific rates which indicate the most marked instances of excess mortality among Hispanic migrant populations are those for Cuban-born males, ages 25–34; Mexican-born males, ages 15–24; and Puerto Rican-born males, ages 25–44. In these instances the death rates of Hispanics are approximately double (or more) those of total whites.

Table 1.1

Mortality Ratios[a] of Hispanic Subgroups According to Birthplace and Age,
United States: 1979–81

| Age | Birthplace | | |
	Cuba	Mexico	Puerto Rico
5-9 years	2.54[b]	1.27	1.37
10-14	1.22	1.00	1.39
15-19	0.73	1.67	1.12
20-24	1.31	1.79	1.41
25-29	1.70	1.57	1.80
30-34	1.67	1.39	1.77
35-39	1.07	1.22	1.76
40-44	0.89	0.90	1.42
45-49	0.77	0.78	1.29
50-54	0.69	0.67	1.15
55-59	0.69	0.71	0.99
60-64	0.64	0.72	1.02
65-69	0.68	0.83	0.91
70-74	0.73	0.92	1.00
75-79	0.76	0.99	0.96
80-84	0.92	1.08	1.04
85 and over	0.95	1.01	0.90

Source: Derived from NCHS mortality tapes and 1980 U.S census.

[a]Ratios are computed by dividing the age-specific death rate of a specified nativity group by
the death rate of the total white population in that age group.

[b]Based on fewer than 20 deaths.

It is important to reiterate that mortality patterns among the subgroups
need to be considered in their respective ethnic and socioeconomic contexts.
Migrants from Mexico, Puerto Rico, and Cuba arrived at different times,
and over different lengths of stay have attained varying educational, occupational, and economic levels. These variables and other environmental
contingencies effect inevitable differences in mortality among the subgroups
under study.

Despite these differences, there are two patterns of Hispanic population
mortality which are common to all three migrant groups. The first is that
Hispanics, especially males, show higher mortality at young adult ages than
do non-Hispanic whites. This Hispanic mortality pattern is similar to that
among blacks in the United States. The second pattern is relatively low
mortality at late middle age and the elderly ages. In this, Hispanics resemble
Asian groups in the United States, who, in fact, have low mortality at all
ages.

The studies in this volume that focus on specific causes of death show that
the male "Hispanic pattern" includes lower death rates for the three leading
causes of death—heart disease, cancer, and stroke. Although all groups of

Hispanic males do not share equally in these advantages, all three groups show markedly lower death rates for the causes which account for two-thirds of all deaths.

Conversely, all groups of Hispanic males show greatly elevated death rates from homicide, which is the only cause of death in which they show a disadvantage relative to the total male population of the United States. For all three groups, the age-adjusted death rates for homicide were about five times those for the total U.S. white population.

A female "Hispanic pattern" in causes of death is not as consistent. All groups of Hispanic females show some advantage only in deaths from cancer and suicide, and all show disadvantages in chronic liver disease and homicide.

The studies repetitive on specific causes of death give special attention to the reality of geographic variation. Among the Mexican-born, the age-standardized death rate is 17 percent higher in Texas than in California. Among the Puerto Rican-born, the age-adjusted rate for New York City residents is 20 percent higher than for those living outside the city.

Intraethnic differences for specific causes are still more dramatic. Death rates for chronic liver disease and homicide among Puerto Ricans in New York City are roughly twice those among Puerto Ricans elsewhere (chapter 6). Similarly, excess mortality among Mexicans in Texas, when compared with those in California, is substantial for almost every cause, and particularly so for diabetes, accidents, and homicide—all with differences greater than 25 percent (Rosenwaike and Bradshaw, 1989).

In contrast with the patterns observed for Puerto Ricans and Mexicans, there is little difference between the age-adjusted mortality rate for all causes between Cubans living in the Miami area and elsewhere. There are, however, some interesting differences for particular causes of death. Deaths due to stroke are substantially lower in the Miami area, but deaths due to violent causes, especially homicide and suicide, are markedly higher for Cubans in and around Miami than in the rest of the nation (Rosenwaike and Shai, 1989).

It was important to address the apparent paradox at the core of the general findings: that relatively low socioeconomic status groups have low mortality, especially among their elderly. A number of hypothetical explanations for this paradox were examined in the section on factors influencing cause-specific mortality. One such hypothesis was that Hispanic migrants might be returning to their home countries when they become elderly or ill. One piece of evidence that severely undermined this hypothesis was mortality data for 1979–1981 that indicated Cuban migrants had lower death rates at ages 55–84 than did Mexicans or Puerto Ricans. Were the repatriation hypothesis accurate, it would be expected that Cubans would have the highest death rates, since they are the least likely to return to their politically and economically troubled homeland.

It has also been suggested that substantial numbers of deaths of elderly Hispanic migrants are not registered. This, too, is highly doubtful, considering the social security, insurance, and other benefits associated with re-porting, as well as regulations that funeral directors must file death certificates.

Some observers have conjectured whether lower death rates among el-derly Hispanics could be an artifact of age misreporting on death certificates, especially exaggerated numbers at older ages. Since this seemed possible, researchers contributing to this volume examined death certificates for each place-of-birth group but found little evidence of "age heaping."

Another possibility was that the census (the denominator in our data-computing formula) had faulty age reporting. Furthermore, since numerator and denominator derive from different sources (the National Center for Health Statistics and the Census Bureau, respectively), possible discrep-ancies in reporting were suggested. However, the availability of a recent study providing death rate information produced from Medicare files, which have the advantage of consistency in numerator and denominator, since both derive from the same source, would seem to establish that the low rates are not artifactual. Recent Medicare-based data for states with high concentra-tions of Hispanics—California, Texas, Florida, and New York — showed that in each state the death rates of Spanish-surname populations are lower at age 65 and over than are rates of non-Spanish surname whites (Spencer, 1984).

There remained a more plausible explanation for the low death rates: the so-called "healthy migrant" effect. Briefly, this describes the tendency of migrants to comprise a healthy population, since those who are not healthy are not inclined to move to a new country. The classic examples of this phenomenon are the pre–1980 immigrants from Cuba, representing much of Cuba's higher social classes. Cuban immigrants of both sexes have lower age-adjusted mortality rates than the total U.S. population, a finding that is in accord with selection expectations.

However, the "healthy migrant" effect was found to be only partially responsible for the lower age-adjusted mortality rates. The finding of lower cancer mortality among all Hispanic populations relative to the U.S. aggre-gate also pointed to the persistence of lifestyle patterns—diet and other factors—and possibly to greater resistance to carcinogens. Similarly, the very low age-adjusted heart disease mortality levels among Mexican immigrants, almost as low as those among the more socioeconomically advantaged Cuban immigrants, pointed to the possibility of lifestyle factors.

Ultimately, researchers who prepared cause-specific studies for this vol-ume broadened the literature on the low mortality paradox by including discussion of statistics on U.S.-born Hispanics. Much effort was spent in assuring numerator and denominator comparability. Spanish-surname codes were determined to be superior to Spanish origin/ethnicity codes as a mea-sure and were used when available.

The major pattern that emerged when the Spanish-surname population was further distinguished into Mexican-born (first generation) and U.S.-born (second and later generations) segments was one of convergence with residence in the United States to the mortality pattern of the "mainstream" white population. In other words, both deficits and excesses in Hispanic mortality rates tend to become smaller with each generation.

For example, in both California and Texas the U.S.-born Spanish-surname population has higher (15 to 20 percent) age-adjusted mortality from the two leading causes of death, heart disease and cancer, than does the Mexican-born group. Thus heart disease and cancer mortality appear to increase as the Spanish-origin population assimilates.

Similarly, but in a favorable direction, research showed that mortality from accidents and homicide is substantially reduced (19 to 55 percent) among U.S.-born as compared with Mexican-born Spanish-surname residents of California and Texas. Less favorably, suicide among Hispanics in the second-generation groups rises sharply and more closely approaches levels in the Anglo population (Rosenwaike and Bradshaw, 1989).

A notable exception to the pattern of convergence was the death rates for diabetes, which is excessive among the Mexican-born and shows a further increase among native Spanish-surname males and females in Texas and males in California. Another was the increase in age-adjusted death rates for chronic liver disease, which is 50 percent higher among U.S.-born Spanish-surname populations than it is among the Mexican-born in those two states.

The latter pattern is puzzling because alcohol, aside from its association with mortality from chronic liver disease, has also been associated with homicide. The marked decrease in homicide rates among the U.S.-born populations seems to suggest changes in culturally defined risk-taking, independent of alcohol consumption. Similarly, the increased rates of suicide suggest changes in help-seeking behavior, symptom manifestation, stress, and social supports among the second-generation Spanish-surname populations.

The clear need for further investigation of changes in patterns of mortality led to inclusion in this volume of studies that permit comparison of the mortality rates of the three migrant populations with those in the countries of origin. By studying how the mortality of migrants changed subsequent to their arrival in the United States, researchers arrived at clues as to which environmental factors of the new country might be investigated as possible etiologies. Precedents include a study by Bradshaw, Fonner, and Wright (1979) that examined age-adjusted death rates by cause in Mexico compared with comparable rates among the Spanish-surname population in Texas. Chronic diseases (heart disease, cancer) accounted for the major share of deaths in Texas, whereas infectious diseases, influenza and pneumonia were the major causes of death in Mexico.

An important section of the volume provides an overview for the cultural and socioeconomic factors that, along with genetics, influence Hispanic mortality patterns. In this regard, some researchers noted that earlier studies had shown that Chinese Americans and Japanese-Americans have substantially lower mortality than whites (Rosenwaike, 1987). It was assumed that if environment, lifestyle and genetic influences can account for differences in mortality between the white and Asian-American populations, it is probable that similar factors account for differences between the Mexican-born, Cuban-born, and other whites.

The overview addresses this volume's major stated goal: to rectify prevalent misconceptions and misstatements concerning the mortality experience of U.S. Hispanics in their various subgroupings. As an example, a recently published research guide cited 55.6 years as the average life expectancy of Mexican-Americans despite the fact that the Schoen and Nelson study, cited earlier in this introduction, had clearly shown that in 1969–1971 Spanish-surname males in California, home of the largest Mexican-American population, had an average life expectancy of 68.3 years. The latter study had also indicated that Spanish-surname females lived on average seven years longer.

Another example of overgeneralization was a report by Becerra and Shaw (1984) stating that available research suggested "In general, the Hispanic elder suffers from poor health, lives in substandard housing and sanitation conditions, is financially depressed . . . and has access to few services that focus on his or her needs."

The studies in this volume, however, show that the mortality experience of the Hispanic elderly is generally more favorable than that of other Americans. Moreover, the findings seem to indicate that, like Chinese and Japanese residents of the United States, Latin American migrants also have retained the more favorable aspects of their original environment, thereby holding their mortality to a level lower than that generally prevailing in the United States.

It is hoped that the studies presented here will provide enough detailed empirical data to form the basis for future studies on the interrelationship of migration, acculturation, minority status, and mortality. The researchers are confident that their findings will be of use in designing and implementing future studies that might describe and explain causes and effects, provide data on the effects of cultural practices on health, and provide a better basis for programs of intervention.

PART TWO

Countries of Origin

CHAPTER 2

Mortality in Mexico

BENJAMIN S. BRADSHAW

The Republic of Mexico and the United States share a long common border, are major trading partners, and exchange millions of visitors and thousands of migrants annually, yet the two countries are probably more dissimilar demographically than any other two adjoining nations in the world. The United States has followed the western European patterns of transition toward low fertility and mortality, and consequently has a high average age, while Mexico continues to have high fertility and comparatively high mortality, and therefore a very youthful age structure. Although mortality in Mexico has improved significantly over the last 50 years, presumably the first stage in a demographic transition, fertility has only begun to decline in the past 15 years. The cause structure of Mexico's mortality also differs markedly from that of the United States, with far higher percentages of deaths attributable to preventable or manageable causes.

This report describes several of the principal features of mortality in Mexico for the period around 1980 (the year of the last national census). Historical mortality data for the decades 1910-1980 are also presented for the nation as a whole. In addition to these national level data, information is presented for selected states of Mexico: specifically, those bordering the United States as well as others from which many Mexicans have migrated. These states were selected in order to determine the degree to which the cause structure in the areas of origin resembles the cause structure of Mexican immigrants and other persons of Mexican origin in the United States. This comparison is to be addressed later.

Table 2.1

Population Size, Rate of Change and Selected Age Characteristics, Mexico: 1895 to 1980

Census	Population	Rate of Change	Median Age	Dependency Ratio	Aging Index	Crude Birth Rate	Crude Death Rate
1895	12,632,428	–	20.0	77.8	5.3	–	–
1910	15,160,369	1.22	19.8	80.0	5.7	50.5	35.5[a]
1921	14,334,780	-0.51	20.2	72.4	9.3	31.4	25.3[b]
1930	16,552,722	1.60	20.3	73.0	7.6	49.5	26.7
1940	19,653,552	1.72	19.4	79.2	7.3	44.3	22.8
1950	25,791,017	2.72	19.0	82.7	8.5	45.6	16.1
1960	34,923,129	3.03	17.8	92.3	8.5	46.1	11.5
1970	48,225,238	3.23	16.8	99.7	8.0	44.2	10.1
1980	66,846,833	3.27	18.0	89.0	9.6	35.0	6.3

Source: Mexico, 1985, p. 52.

[a]1895–1910

[b]1922

POPULATION TRENDS AND GENERAL CHARACTERISTICS

Mortality conditions in Mexico must be considered within the context of demographic features of the country and the selected states. As noted previously, Mexico only recently has begun to experience a definite decline in fertility, while at the same time experiencing a fairly rapid decline in mortality. As a result of these patterns, the country's population has increased more rapidly during this century, and at the same time become younger on average. Table 2.1 shows the total population of Mexico 1895-1980, the average annual rate of intercensal change, the median age, and the dependency ratio.

Mexico, which gained its independence from Spain in 1821, experienced only minimal in- and out-migration in the nineteenth century, hence growth largely reflected the balance of births over deaths. Natural growth fluctuated not so much from epidemics as from organized violence, often political conflict. For example, 1810–1885 was a very violent time period, and during these 75 years the population increased from 6.1 million to 10.4 million, an average annual growth rate of 0.9 percent. In contrast, the years 1885–1910 were an era of economic growth under the Diaz regime, and the population grew at an annual rate of 1.8 percent, reaching 15.2 million in just 25 years (Kicza, 1981).

The data in Table 2.1 show that, with the exception of the 1910–1921 period, during which Mexico underwent a long and violent revolution, population growth has accelerated during each intercensal period. As may be seen from the crude birth and death rates, population increases were the result of reductions in mortality, rather than increases in fertility. A more detailed list of rates would show that the decline in the crude birth rate did not begin until about the mid–1970s; the trend in the crude death rate, on the other hand, has been steadily downward for over half a century.

A striking feature of Mexico's population is the very youthful age distribution. As indicated in Table 2.1, the highest median age for the total population was 20.3 years in 1930. Previously the median had ranged around 20 years. After 1930, the median age dropped steadily to a low of only 16.8 years in 1970. With the decline in fertility in the 1970s, the median increased slightly to 18.0 in 1980. As these low medians suggest, the aging index (the ratio of persons 65 years old and over to children under age 15) has remained very low: ranging from 5.3 to 9.6 elderly per 100 children. By contrast, the aging index for the U.S. white population in 1980 was nearly 50 elderly per 100 children.

The dependency ratio (children under 15 years of age plus persons 65 and over per 100 persons ages 15 to 64) has increased steadily since 1921. The increase in the dependency ratio has been due to growth in both the young and the old segments of the population. In no intercensal period between 1895 and 1970—except for 1910–1921, when the number of children decreased by nearly 14 percent as a consequence of the Mexican Revolution— did the growth rate of the working age population (15 to 64) exceed the growth rate of the total dependent population. It was not until the 1970s, with a decline in fertility, that the dependency ratio fell, and the working age population grew more rapidly than the dependent population. Some of the implications of Mexico's age composition for potential labor force replacement, pressure on employment opportunities, and migration from Mexico to the United States have been reviewed elsewhere (Bradshaw, 1976; Bradshaw and Frisbie, 1983).

RACE

At the time of the Spanish conquest, a large Indian population resided in what is now modern Mexico, but warfare and disease greatly reduced their number. The bulk of the people of Mexico are of mixed racial origin, termed in the recent past *mestizo*. The use of this term has dwindled due to the Mexican government's de-emphasis on ethnic categories. Gradually *mestizos* and mainstream Mexicans have been considered synonymous. Race has not been a category in the national census since 1940. In 1877 it was estimated

Table 2.2
Urban and Rural Percentage of Population in Mexico: 1900 to 1980

Year	Urban	Rural
1900	28.3	71.7
1910	28.7	71.3
1921	31.2	68.8
1930	33.5	66.5
1940	35.0	65.0
1950	42.6	57.4
1960	50.7	49.3
1970	58.7	41.3
1980	66.3	33.7

Source: Mexico. Instituto Nacional de Estadistica, Geografia e Informatica, 1986: Table 1.5.

that 38 percent of the population spoke only aboriginal languages; this figure fell to 14.7 percent in 1921 and only 1.8 percent in 1970 (Rudolph, 1985).

RURAL-URBAN PATTERN

Since 1940, Mexico has evolved from a largely rural nation to one where the majority of the population lives in urban places. Between 1940 and 1980 the proportion of the population classified as urban (residing in places of 2,500 or more) climbed from 35 to 66 percent (Table 2.2). Associated with this shift is the phenomenal growth in population of the largest urban centers, particularly Mexico City. The nation's capital had a population of 345,000 in 1900, more than one million in the 1930s and 8.8 million residents by 1970. After 1950, growth of the city meant growth not only in the Federal District but within adjacent areas in the state of Mexico. By 1980, 14.5 million persons—one in five Mexicans—resided within the metropolitan zone of Mexico City. The three other major cities, Monterrey, Guadalajara, and Puebla, had a combined population of 5.6 million in their metropolitan zones (Camposortega, 1988).

LEVELS OF EDUCATION

Before the Mexican Revolution (1910) more than two-thirds of the population were illiterate. The most rapid increase in literacy has occurred since the 1930s (see Table 2.3). In 1940, 46 percent of the population over age 10 were classified as literate; this increased to almost 67 percent in 1960 and exceeded 80 percent by 1980. There are major variations in literacy by sex

Table 2.3
Percent Literate and Illiterate Among Persons 10 Years and Over, Mexico: 1900
to 1980

Year	Literate	Illiterate
1900	22.3	77.7
1910	27.7	72.3
1921	33.9	66.1
1930	38.5	61.5
1940	46.0	64.0
1950[a]	56.8	44.2
1960	66.5	33.5
1980[b]	83.0	17.0

Source: Mexico. Instituto Nacional de Estadistica, Geografia e Informatica, 1986: Table 2.3.

[a]Six years and over

[b]Fifteen years and over

and place of residence. Literacy is higher for the male population than for
the female population and higher for the urban population than for the rural.

The national educational system has greatly expanded in recent years.
According to the 1980 census, 7.6 percent of the population aged 20–24
years had never attended school; this compared with 20.6 percent among
persons 45–49 years of age. About 37 percent of Mexicans 20–24 years of
age had some instruction beyond primary school (the first six grades) compared with 12 percent among those 45–49 years of age.

LABOR FORCE

In 1980, the census indicated the labor force (persons aged 12 and over
who are working or are seeking work) totaled 22.1 million, of whom 15.9
million were male and 6.1 million were female. The rate of participation in
the labor force among males was 75 percent; among females it was 28 percent.

The structure of employment in the various sectors of the economy has
changed markedly since 1960. In 1980, 32 percent of the work force were
employed in agriculture, compared with 54 percent in 1960. Employment
in manufacturing increased from 15 percent in 1960 to almost 19 percent in
1980 and services increased dramatically from 13.5 percent to 30 percent
(Rudolph, 1985).

The Mexican government placed unemployment at 13 percent in 1983,
and underemployment affected a still larger share of the labor force. Underemployment, the underutilization of labor, was particularly endemic in

Table 2.4

Percent Change in Population, Mexico, and Selected States: 1910 to 1980

Area	1910-21	1921-30	1930-40	1940-50	1950-60	1960-70	1970-80
Mexico	-5.4	15.5	18.7	31.2	35.4	45.2	31.9
Major Immigrant Sending States	NA	14.1	17.5	29.4	37.4	50.0	36.6
Excluding Baja Calif.	-7.4	13.8	17.2	28.0	35.5	49.0	36.9
States Bordering the United States	NA	19.6	27.4	43.7	47.3	48.9	29.6
Excluding Baja Calif.	2.8	18.5	26.6	39.3	42.0	46.1	29.6
Baja California	NA	105.3	63.3	187.6	129.2	76.0	28.7
Coahuila	8.7	10.9	26.2	30.9	26.0	29.2	32.7
Chihuahua	-1.0	22.5	26.9	35.7	44.9	38.1	18.3
Nuevo Leon	-7.9	24.1	29.6	36.8	45.8	65.2	41.0
Sonora	3.7	15.0	15.1	40.2	53.4	47.5	31.1
Tamaulipas	14.9	19.9	33.4	56.5	42.6	49.5	25.7
Selected Interior States	-10.7	12.0	13.5	23.0	32.3	50.6	40.6
Durango	-30.3	20.1	19.7	30.2	20.8	29.8	19.6
Guanajuato	-20.5	14.8	5.8	27.1	30.6	37.6	25.9
Jalisco	-1.4	5.3	13.0	23.2	39.9	41.8	26.2
Mexico	-10.5	11.9	15.7	21.5	36.3	112.3	87.7
Michoacan	-5.2	11.5	12.7	20.4	30.2	31.9	17.4
Zacatecas	-20.6	21.0	23.2	17.7	22.9	22.3	13.7
All Other States	NA	16.6	19.7	32.6	33.9	41.5	28.1
Excluding Baja Calif.	-3.9	16.8	19.9	33.7	35.3	42.4	28.1

NA—Not available. Baja California was not enumerated separately in 1910.

agriculture. This lack of employment opportunities led many to seek work by migrating to the United States (Rudolph, 1985).

CHARACTERISTICS OF SELECTED STATES WITH HEAVY OUT-MIGRATION

The states of Mexico selected for particular analysis here are those which have substantial numbers of both legal and illegal immigrants to the United States since the 1920s (see Corona, 1987, for a review and summary). Certain states in particular have been major sources of immigrants throughout these several decades. In general these reflect the same patterns of rapid population growth that have characterized the Republic as a whole. Table 2.4 shows the states grouped into two broad categories: "sending states" and all others. The sending states, those from which most immigrants have come to the United States, are subdivided into those bordering the United States and those in the interior of Mexico. The figures clearly show the regional effects on population of the Mexican Revolution during the intercensal period 1910–1921. The entire country lost population (5.4 percent), but the interior sending states lost nearly 11 percent. Of these, Durango lost nearly one-third of its population, and Guanajuato and Zacatecas each lost over one-fifth. In terms of population increase, the latter states recovered rather slowly from the revolutionary period compared with the border states and the rest of the country. In general, the border states have increased in population more rapidly than other regions. However, during 1960–1980, the state of Mexico (an interior state which adjoins the Federal District) doubled its population each decade.

The age compositions of the selected states are remarkably similar to those of the entire country. This suggests that the youthfulness of the national population is shared by the states, and this is confirmed by the very low aging indexes of the states, which are quite similar to those of the nation (8.34 for males and 9.50 for females). (While the similarities in age composition indicate that there is little to be gained by standardizing death rates by age composition, we have taken that step to ensure comparability of certain measures of mortality.)

SOURCES AND QUALITY OF MORTALITY AND CENSUS DATA

Compared with many "underdeveloped" countries, Mexico's data sources are quite good. Mexico has taken national censuses since 1895 and has had national vital registration since 1926. In general, data from these sources are satisfactory for many purposes, and their quality undoubtedly has improved over the decades. Deficiencies in the censuses tend to be similar to those observed elsewhere, including the United States: underenumeration of young children (under 5) and of young adults (especially men aged 20-39), and age misreporting in old age (Benitez-Zenteno and Cabrera-Acevedo, 1967; Camposortega, 1987). If all deaths were registered, such patterns of errors in the census would lead to overestimates of death rates in childhood and young adulthood. In general, it is more feasible to adjust census data for undercount than to estimate completeness of death registration, and some authors have relied on such corrections, accepting the death data as valid (Benitez-Zenteno and Cabrera-Acevedo, 1967). Others have used model life tables to evaluate the patterns of death rates in Mexico (Camposortega, 1987). As Camposortega notes, the different adjustment procedures yield quite similar and consistent results when employed, for example, in preparing life tables. Indeed, in summary measures such as life expectancy at birth, the adjustments produce figures which are only slightly different from the unadjusted data. The latter finding suggests that the basic age and sex data are reasonably complete, at least for 1970 and 1980. For this reason, we have made no adjustments to either census or vital statistics data.

With respect to cause-of-death information, there is evidence that reporting is poor in some parts of Mexico. In 1980, for Mexico as a whole, 7 percent of deaths had no specific causes assigned or were attributed to "signs,

Table 2.5
Number of Deaths with Ill-Defined Conditions or Cause Not Specified, by State, Mexico: 1980

Area	All Causes	Deaths with Ill-Defined or Unspecified Cause			
		Symptoms & Ill-Defined Conditions	Cause not Specified	Total	Percent of All Causes
Mexico	432,518	29,015	1,075	30,090	7.0
Major Immigrant Sending States	194,055	7,759	451	8,210	4.2
States Bordering the United States	63,058	2,281	113	2,394	3.8
Baja California	6,779	108	27	135	2.0
Coahuila	9,837	253	18	271	2.8
Chihuahua	13,362	642	45	687	5.1
Nuevo Leon	12,171	546	3	549	4.5
Sonora	9,551	416	11	427	4.5
Tamaulipas	11,358	316	9	325	2.9
Selected Interior States	130,997	5,478	338	5,816	4.4
Durango	6,433	644	68	712	11.1
Guanajuato	21,960	1,029	46	1,075	4.9
Jalisco	28,670	1,166	85	1,251	4.4
Mexico	47,172	1,241	94	1,335	2.8
Michoacan	20,279	931	35	966	4.8
Zacatecas	6,483	467	10	477	7.4
All Other States	238,463	21,256	624	21,880	9.2
Aguascalientes	3,397	62	1	63	1.9
Baja California Sur	1,211	24	2	26	2.1
Campeche	2,291	170	4	174	7.6
Colima	2,448	69	7	76	3.1
Chiapas	12,602	2,202	86	2,288	18.2
Distrito Federal	49,848	511	24	535	1.1
Guerrero	12,786	1,917	34	1,951	15.3
Hidalgo	13,031	677	72	749	5.7
Morelos	5,621	188	37	225	4.0
Nayarit	3,626	166	7	173	4.8
Oaxaca	23,983	6,171	18	6,189	25.8
Puebla	31,409	3,407	85	3,492	11.1
Queretaro	5,483	236	35	271	4.9
Quintana Roo	1,136	59	2	61	5.4
San Luis Potosi	9,432	848	42	890	9.4
Sinaloa	9,265	359	45	404	4.4
Tabasco	7,523	602	20	622	8.3
Tlaxcala	3,192	78	10	88	2.8
Vera Cruz	32,332	2,685	87	2,772	8.6
Yucatan	7,847	825	6	831	10.6

Source: Mexico. Dirección General de Estadística. ND: Table 5I.

symptoms and ill-defined morbid conditions" rather than to specific causes (Table 2.5). By comparison, in the United States the percentage was 1.4 in 1980 (National Center for Health Statistics, 1985a). The lack of specificity with respect to cause of death interferes to varying degrees in making regional comparisons of the cause structure of mortality. A high percentage of deaths assigned to these categories indicates that there is likely more error in cause-of-death diagnosis even where specific causes are assigned. The range among the states was from 1.1 percent in the Federal District to over 25 percent of all deaths in the state of Oaxaca, in the southern part of the country. In Chiapas, which borders Oaxaca, the percentage was over 18 percent, and in some other states the percentage was over 10 percent. Most of the states with rather poor reporting of cause of death were concentrated in the southern or central portions of Mexico. Compared with the national average, among the selected migrant-sending states the percentage of deaths without useful cause information is quite low (3.8 percent in the border states, 4.4 percent in the other sending states, and 4.2 percent overall). The average for the remaining states is quite high—9.2 percent. Besides indicating quality of reporting of cause of death, variation in cause reporting suggests the extent to which the different areas of Mexico are integrated into the national health care system.

GENERAL TRENDS IN MORTALITY

As indicated in Table 2.1, the major mortality trend in Mexico is one of almost uninterrupted improvement during this century. More detail is presented in Table 2.6, which contains estimates of life expectancy at birth and the corresponding stationary population life table death rates. These data show clearly the effects of declining mortality rates on length of life in Mexico. There are also other points of major interest. The extremely low life expectancy for both sexes combined in 1895–1910 was less than 30 years, almost 18 years below that of the United States (47.3 years). The gap in life expectancy between the two countries actually increased between 1900 and 1940, reaching a maximum difference of 22.8 years (for both sexes) in 1930, and even in 1950 remained at 18.5 years—greater than the excess in 1900. Thus, although mortality has improved consistently in Mexico, and the percentage gains each decade after 1930 were more than in the United States, the improvements were not great enough to reduce the gap in life expectancy. Limited increases in United States life expectancy between 1950 and 1970 has considerably narrowed the gap between the two countries. However, due to the resurging mortality decline in the United States in the 1970s, the difference in years of life expectancy in 1970 was maintained in 1980.

The difference in life expectancy between the sexes in Mexico in comparison with that in the United States is difficult to assess. On first inspection, Mexican females do not appear to enjoy the marked advantage in mortality rates over males that has been observed for United States females. Mexican females have had a 4 to 6 percent advantage over males, and this advantage has not increased over time as has been the case (until the 1970s) with United States women. The sex difference in life expectancy in Mexico, however, should be considered in relation to historical development in the United

Table 2.6
Life Expectancy at Birth and Life Table Death Rates, Mexico and United States: 1900 to 1980

Country and Year	Life Expectancy at Birth (E_0)				Percent Improvement in Life Expectancy			Deaths per 1,000 Population (L_0/T_0)		
	Both Sexes	Male	Female	Ratio: Female/Male	Both Sexes	Male	Female	Both Sexes	Male	Female
Mexico										
1895-1910	29.5	-	-	-	-	-	-	33.9	-	-
1930	36.9	36.1	37.5	1.04	25.1	-	-	27.1	27.7	26.7
1940	41.5	40.4	42.5	1.05	12.5	11.9	13.3	24.1	24.8	23.5
1950	49.7	48.1	51.0	1.06	19.8	19.1	20.0	20.1	20.8	19.6
1960	58.9	57.6	60.3	1.05	18.5	19.8	18.2	17.0	17.4	16.6
1970	61.9	60.0	63.8	1.06	5.1	4.2	5.8	16.2	16.7	15.7
1980	64.9	62.3	66.1	1.06	4.8	3.8	3.6	15.4	16.1	15.1
United States										
1900	47.3	46.3	48.3	1.04	-	-	-	21.1	21.6	20.7
1930	59.7	58.1	61.6	1.06	26.2	25.5	27.5	16.8	17.2	16.2
1940	62.9	60.8	65.2	1.07	5.4	4.6	5.8	15.9	16.4	15.3
1950	68.2	65.6	71.1	1.08	8.4	7.9	9.0	14.7	15.2	14.1
1960	69.7	66.6	73.1	1.10	2.2	1.5	2.8	14.3	15.0	13.7
1970	70.8	67.1	74.7	1.11	1.6	0.8	2.2	14.1	14.9	13.4
1980	73.7	70.0	77.5	1.11	4.1	4.3	3.7	13.6	14.3	12.9

Source: Mexico, 1985, p. 52; National Center for Health Statistics, 1985a: Table 6.5.

Table 2.7
Death Rates Due to Categories of Causes of Death, Mexico: 1930 to 1980
(Rates per 100,000 population)

Year, Rate, and Percent	All Causes	Group I	Group II	Group III	Group IV	Group V
1930						
Rate	2,667	1,136	15	82	110	1,324
% of total	100.00	42.59	0.56	3.07	4.12	49.64
1950						
Rate	1,615	580	29	94	94	818
% of total	100.00	35.91	1.80	5.82	5.82	50.65
1960						
Rate	1,149	314	36	97	75	627
% of total	100.00	27.33	3.13	8.44	6.53	54.57
1967						
Rate	911	218	34	63	65	531
% of total	100.00	23.93	3.73	6.92	7.14	58.29
1980						
Rate	647	142	44	125	107	229
% of total	100.00	21.97	6.81	19.33	16.52	35.38

Group I   includes infectious and parasitic diseases, and influenza, pneumonia and bronchitis in children under 5 years old.

Group II   includes deaths due to cancers.

Group III   includes cardiovascular diseases and bronchitis in persons 5 years of age and older.

Group IV   includes deaths due to external causes.

Group V   includes all other causes of death.

Source: 1930–1967 from Alba, 1977: p. 53; 1980 based on World Health Organization, 1986: Table 11.

States. At the time (1940–1950) that the U.S. life expectancy values were comparable to the 1980 Mexico values, the percent difference between the sexes in the United States was similar—about 7 percent vs. 6 percent. Assuming that mortality in Mexico will follow a pattern similar to that in the United States, then we would expect an increasing sex differential as chronic and degenerative diseases increasingly replace other conditions in the cause-of-death structure.

CAUSES OF DEATH

Table 2.7 presents a very broad but striking view of the changing cause-of-death structure in Mexico since 1930. The crude death rate due to Group I diseases declined nearly 90 percent, from 1,136 per 100,000 population in 1930 to 142 per 100,000 in 1980. Group I causes include infectious and parasitic diseases and certain respiratory diseases in children under 5 years old. These causes are typically those which decline first and most rapidly in the epidemiologic transition. In Mexico, this has certainly been the case.

Table 2.8
Age and Sex Specific, Crude and Direct Adjusted Death Rates, Mexico: 1980
(Total population of Mexico used as standard. Rates per 100,000 population)

Age (years)	Male	Female	Ratio Male/Female
Under 1	6200.6	4935.1	1.26
1-4	393.3	367.1	1.07
5-14	97.9	68.1	1.44
15-24	272.1	105.4	2.58
25-34	448.5	173.2	2.59
35-44	638.3	308.9	2.07
45-54	1020.8	570.8	1.79
55-64	1855.2	1223.8	1.52
65-74	3679.0	2822.6	1.30
75 and over	9051.9	8701.9	1.04
All ages, crude rate	751.6	548.6	1.37
All ages, adjusted rate	762.5	539.5	1.41

As a percentage of all deaths, those in Group I decreased from about 43
percent to 22 percent. At the same time, the death rate from major chronic
diseases (Groups II and III) rose by 74 percent, from 97 to 169. Whereas
the latter conditions accounted for less than 4 percent of all deaths in 1930,
they accounted for over 26 percent in 1980. As a percentage of deaths, those
from violence and other external causes have also grown in importance; they
included about 4 percent of all deaths in 1930 but 16.5 percent in 1980.
These data suggest that Mexico has become more and more similar in cause-
of-death structure to the United States. However, enormous differences
remain, particularly in the representation of diseases in Group I vs. Groups
II and III.

Crude and age-specific death rates for males and females of Mexico as of
1980 are shown in Table 2.8. As may be seen by the ratios of male to female
age-specific rates, the peak difference between the sexes lies in early adulthood (between ages 15 and 34), while the greatest similarity is in early
childhood (between ages 1 and 4) and old age (75 years and older). These
patterns are similar to those in the United States, except, as noted before,
the sex differentials in overall mortality are not as great in Mexico. The age-
adjusted death rates for both sexes are little different from the crude rates,
suggesting the similarity of age distributions of the two sexes. However, by
removing the effects of differences in age distributions, the average difference in mortality is shown to be somewhat greater than that suggested by
the crude rates (41 percent vs. 37 percent).

Table 2.9

Age-Adjusted Death Rates, Percent of Deaths Attributed to Each Cause, and Ranking of Each Cause, Mexico: 1980

Cause of Death	Male Rate	Male Percent of all causes	Male Rank	Female Rate	Female Percent of all causes	Female Rank	Ratio: Male to Female
All Causes	762.5	100.0	--	539.5	100.0	--	1.41
Infectious and parasitic diseases	97.4	12.8	4	82.1	15.2	2	1.19
Malignant neoplasms	39.2	5.1	6	45.1	8.4	4	0.87
Endocrine, nutritional, and metabolic diseases and immunity disorders	36.8	4.8	7	38.8	7.2	5	0.95
Diseases of the circulatory system	111.7	14.7	2	102.5	19.0	1	1.09
Diseases of the digestive system	62.5	8.2	5	31.2	5.8	7	2.00
Diseases of the respiratory system	99.9	13.1	3	79.1	14.7	3	1.26
Diseases of the genitourinary system	15.5	2.0	8	13.8	2.6	8	1.12
External causes	167.1	21.9	1	37.9	7.0	6	4.41
All other causes	132.5	17.4	--	109.1	20.2	--	1.21
Preventable or manageable causes[a]	463.6	60.8		269.0	49.9		1.72
Chronic or degenerative causes[b]	151.0	19.8		147.6	27.4		1.02

[a]Includes infectious and parasitic diseases; endocrine, nutritional, and metabolic diseases and immunity disorders; diseases of the digestive system, diseases of the respiratory system, and external causes.

[b]Includes malignant neoplasms and diseases of the circulatory system.

Standardized death rates by sex for selected groups of causes of death are shown in Table 2.9. Some differences between the sexes are very large. For example, the age-adjusted death rate from external causes for Mexican males is over four times greater than that for females, and the death rate for males from diseases of the digestive system is twice as high. Excess mortality due to external causes of death account for 58 percent of the absolute difference in mortality between the sexes, and diseases of the digestive system account for another 14 percent. Among the external causes of death, motor vehicle accidents lead, but homicide is almost as important. Chronic liver disease and cirrhosis account for most of the sex difference due to diseases of the digestive system. Although, in general, male death rates by cause are greater than those for females, the reverse is true in the case of malignant neoplasms and endocrine, nutritional, and metabolic diseases, of which diabetes mellitus is most important.

Data in Table 2.9 show a ranking of causes that is quite different from that in the United States, where malignant neoplasms rank second after diseases of the circulatory system. In Mexico, external causes rank first as a cause of death among males, followed by circulatory diseases and respiratory diseases (most important of which is pneumonia), and infectious diseases. Malignant neoplasms, of second rank for both sexes in the United States, are only sixth among Mexican males and fourth among females. The leading cause of death among Mexican females is circulatory diseases, but infectious and respiratory diseases are a close second and third in rank.

The cause groups shown in Table 2.9 can be categorized further into two broad types: those that can be prevented, avoided, or managed and those that are chronic and degenerative. As societies modernize, the latter group tends to grow in importance relative to the former group. The first category will be referred to as "preventable or manageable" causes. These causes of death tend to decline rapidly when economic development is accompanied by public health measures leading to improvements in the general and personal environments (food, water, and sanitation services) and preventive medical services. With regard to the cause groups in Table 2.9, the "preventable or manageable" category includes infectious and parasitic diseases; endocrine, nutritional, and metabolic diseases, and immunity disorders; diseases of the respiratory system; and external causes.

Most deaths from these causes could be prevented, especially infectious and parasitic diseases; respiratory diseases, such as pneumonia and influenza; digestive diseases, such as chronic liver disease and cirrhosis; and external causes, such as home and industrial accidents. Other diseases, such as diabetes mellitus (and endocrine disease) may be managed so as to prevent or postpone death. Still other causes of death may be prevented or avoided, especially motor vehicle accidents (a "preventable or manageable" cause of death which rises rather than declines with economic development), homicide, and suicide. Many of the deaths due to preventable or manageable causes occur in childhood or young adulthood. For example, in Mexico in 1980, more than half the deaths due to infectious, parasitic, and respiratory diseases occurred in children under 5 years of age, and these accounted for nearly 15 percent of all deaths in the country.

There are other causes of death that tend to replace the preventable or manageable causes as the latter decline. These diseases of modern societies, the chronic and degenerative diseases, include many circulatory diseases, especially ischemic diseases of the heart, and many malignant neoplasms (although it may be noted that deaths from some sites, e.g., the lung, are largely "preventable"). Deaths from heart disease and neoplasms tend to occur at older ages.

The data in Table 2.9 indicate that preventable and manageable causes of

Table 2.10

Standardized Mortality Ratios and Indirect Adjusted Death Rates, by Selected Causes of Death, for Selected States, Mexico: 1980 (Adjusted for age and sex composition with rates for Mexico, 1980, per 100,000 population)

Cause of Death	Mexico Crude Death Rate	Major Immigrant Sending States		States Bordering the United States		Selected Interior States		All Other States	
		SMR	IADR	SMR	IADR	SMR	IADR	SMR	IADR
All Causes	649.9	98.9	643.0	93.0	604.4	102.1	663.4	100.9	655.7
Infectious and parasitic diseases	89.4	87.3	78.0	72.7	65.0	94.7	84.7	110.8	99.1
Malignant neoplasms	42.1	108.6	45.7	136.2	57.3	93.4	39.3	93.0	39.1
Endocrine, nutritional, and metabolic diseases and immunity disorders	37.8	103.9	39.3	114.1	43.1	98.5	37.3	96.8	36.6
Diseases of the circulatory system	106.8	110.9	118.4	128.7	137.5	101.4	108.2	91.3	97.5
Diseases of the digestive system	46.3	95.3	44.1	64.3	29.8	112.5	52.1	103.8	48.1
Diseases of the respiratory system	89.0	107.6	95.8	86.4	76.9	118.4	105.4	93.6	83.3
Diseases of the genitourinary system	14.5	106.1	15.4	107.2	15.6	105.5	15.3	95.1	13.8
External causes	100.8	98.7	99.5	83.3	83.9	107.3	108.1	101.1	101.9

death in 1980 accounted for nearly 61 percent of expected deaths (i.e., deaths expected in the standard population) among males and about 50 percent among females. Conversely, diseases of economic development (not adjusted for age composition) accounted for 27 percent of the expected deaths among females but 20 percent among males. In the United States in the same year, diseases of economic development accounted for 68 percent of all deaths in males and 74 percent in females, the reverse of the pattern in Mexico.

GEOGRAPHIC VARIATION IN MORTALITY

Levels of mortality and cause-of-death structure vary substantially among the states of Mexico. Table 2.10 shows standardized mortality ratios (SMR) for the major immigrant-sending states and all other states. SMRs show the ratio of the death rate in a particular area to that of the standard population. In this case, age-adjusted cause- and sex-specific rates for Mexico were used as the standard. In general, mortality is lower in the sending states. Of these, mortality is lowest in those states that border the United States. There are exceptions, of course. Chihuahua, a border state, has an SMR for all causes of 105.6. Durango and Zacatecas, two interior sending states, have SMRs of less than 85. The lowest mortality is in Nuevo Leon, a border state with an SMR of 76.5, and the highest is in the state of Mexico which adjoins Mexico City, with an SMR of 107.2.

Compared with all other states, the sending states generally have lower mortality due to certain preventable causes, for example infectious and parasitic, digestive diseases, and external causes, but higher mortality due to circulatory diseases and neoplasms. This pattern is especially notable among the states bordering the United States, suggesting either some cultural effects or economic effects consistent with their generally lower mortality. However, mortality from one group of diseases—endocrine and nutritional diseases—is highest in the border states. With the exception of Nuevo Leon, all the border states have SMRs above 114, and Baja California and Coahuila have values above 146. Whether this pattern stems from environmental or other differences in this region cannot be determined at this time. Among the other (non-border) sending states, as a group, malignant neoplasm mortality is the same as that of the non-sending states. Interestingly, the highest mortality from respiratory diseases is concentrated in two sending states, Mexico and Guanajuato, with SMRs of about 144. All other immigrant-sending states, as well as the aggregate of non-sending states, have SMRs below 100 for these causes.

CHAPTER 3

Mortality in Puerto Rico

ZORAIDA MORALES DEL VALLE

DEMOGRAPHIC HISTORY

The population of Puerto Rico has climbed at each successive census taken under U.S. rule, advancing from less than a million in 1899 to 3.2 million in 1980 (Table 3.1). Population growth in Puerto Rico during the twentieth century can be divided into three periods that differ in terms of their magnitude, velocity, trends, and causal factors. These periods of population growth, which occurred after the United States took over the rule of the island from Spain, are 1899-1940, 1940-1960, and 1960 to the present (Table 3.2). Fairly rapid mortality decline and very slight decrease in the fertility level resulted in steadily increased population growth from 1899 to 1940. Migration rates remained low during this period. During the period 1940–1960, the rate of population growth decreased due to high rates of emigration despite the attainment of rates of natural increase higher than those in any prior or later period. Since 1960, the average annual population growth rate has been increasing, with a 1.3 percent rise in the 1960s and a 1.6 percent rise in the 1970s. These increases were due to a larger return migration to Puerto Rico and a lower rate of emigration.

POPULATION DISTRIBUTION AND MIGRATION

Changes in the population distribution of Puerto Rico from 1899 to the present have led to heavy population concentration along the northeastern section of the island. In 1980, approximately 39.2 percent of the total pop-

Table 3.1
Total Population and Annual Growth Rate between Two Successive Dates, Puerto Rico: 1860 to 1980

Year	Total Population	Annual Growth Rates[a]
Spanish Government		
1860	583,308	-
1877	731,648	1.34
1887	798,565	0.88
1897	894,302	1.14
U.S. Government		
1899	953,243	-
1910	1,118,012	1.54
1920	1,299,809	1.57
1930	1,543,913	1.69
1940	1,869,255	1.94
1950	2,210,703	1.69
1960	2,349,544	0.61
1970	2,712,033	1.45
1980	3,196,520	1.66

Source: Vazquez, 1988: Tables 3, 4, and 6.

[a]Obtained by using compound interest formula.

ulation lived in this region, compared with 14.4 percent in 1899. The largest decrease was noted in Puerto Rico's western interior, declining to 5.1 percent in 1980 from 14.5 percent in 1899. The northeastern region in 1980 had the highest population density: 2,748 inhabitants per square mile.

From 1940 to 1980, municipios along the northern coast, east and west of San Juan, Puerto Rico's capital, had the highest rates of population growth. Caguas, a municipio south of San Juan, also had moderate growth during this same period. This region of high population growth around San Juan has continued to grow larger in each decade, even outstripping San Juan in the level of population growth. By the 1970s, San Juan, as well as most of the municipios that comprise the western interior region, were experiencing negative growth rates.

A critical factor in the changing population distribution from 1899 to 1940 was the declining importance of the coffee industry. Up to the end of the nineteenth century, coffee had been Puerto Rico's chief export, but a U.S.

Table 3.2
Natality, Mortality, Natural Increase, and Emigration Rates for Specific Periods,
Puerto Rico: 1899 to 1980

Period	Natality[a]	Mortality[a]	Natural[b] Increase	Emigration
1899-1910	40.5	25.3	15.2	0.0
1910-1920	40.4	24.0	16.4	0.8
1920-1930	39.3	22.1	17.2	2.6
1930-1940	39.8	19.6	20.2	0.5
1940-1950	40.7	14.5	26.2	8.8
1950-1960	35.0	8.0	27.0	19.9
1960-1970	29.6	6.8	22.8	9.4
1970-1980	24.1	6.5	17.6	1.6

Source: Vazquez, 1988: Table 7.

[a]Birth and death data have not been corrected for registration completeness. Represents rates per 1000 inhabitants.

[b]Difference between birth and death rate.

tax and destruction of coffee crops by hurricanes combined to push coffee production costs much higher than sugar and tobacco. Since the latter crops were introduced and backed by North American capital, and legislation enacted in 1907 permitted Puerto Rican tobacco to be imported into the United States practically duty-free, the coffee growers began to plant their fields in tobacco (Morales, 1982).

While the coffee industry declined, the sugar cane industry flourished due to large investments of capital from the United States which was also a sure market. As a result, numerous large-scale mills were built along the coast of the island and absentee land concentration increased (Morales, 1982). These economic changes caused thousands of persons to migrate from the coffee-growing central regions to the coastal sugar mills in the northeastern region and to Guanica and Salinas in the south, which had two important mills. San Juan, in the northeastern region, was also an attraction. It was not only the capital but also Puerto Rico's commercial, industrial, financial, and cultural center.

Beginning in 1940, the U.S. government initiated an economic development policy that had as its main objective the industralization of the island. Under this policy, agriculture diminished in importance; at present it contributes little to income and employment in Puerto Rico. Industralization has been concentrated in the northeastern region, especially near San Juan,

Table 3.3
Urban and Rural Population in Puerto Rico: 1899 to 1980

Urban Year	Urban	Rural	Total	Percent
1899	138,703	814,540	953,243	14.6
1910	224,620	893,392	1,118,012	20.1
1920	283,934	1,015,875	1,299,809	21.8
1930	427,221	1,116,692	1,543,913	27.7
1940	566,357	1,302,898	1,869,255	30.3
1950	894,813	1,315,890	2,210,703	40.5
1960	1,039,301	1,310,243	2,349,544	44.2
1970	1,575,491	1,136,542	2,712,033	58.1
1980	2,134,365	1,062,155	3,196,520	66.8

Source: U.S. Bureau of the Census, 1982: Table 1.

because of its better access to maritime and other transportation facilities.
Industrialization also generated a boom in the region's construction industry
and increased employment opportunities. As a result, migrants came to San
Juan and its outlying municipalities from all parts of Puerto Rico. In recent
years, this migration has shifted to the areas east and west of San Juan. This
changing migration pattern has made San Juan itself an area of emigration
because of geographic limitations and increase in land prices.

Available statistical data indicate that in 1899 Puerto Rico was predomi-
nantly a rural country with only 14.6 percent of its population classified as
urban (Table 3.3). At the census that year, only 17 places were classified as
urban (2,500 inhabitants or more) and none of these had 50,000 inhabitants
or more. In the twentieth century however, Puerto Rico has become pre-
dominantly urban and metropolitan. In 1980, approximately 67 percent of
the total population was urban and 56 percent lived in five metropolitan
areas (Tables 3.3 and 3.4).

Although the growth of big cities at the expense of small towns has been
the main pattern of urban growth up to 1970, a somewhat different pattern
has emerged during the last decade. Since 1970, rates of growth in the cities
and in the metropolitan areas have decreased; however, those in smaller
places located near large cities have increased. Living conditions in the big
cities and the appeal of the land may have been responsible for this move-
ment toward the outskirts of the big cities.

Table 3.4
Population of the Statistical Metropolitan Areas of Puerto Rico: 1960 to 1980

MSA	1960	1970	1980	Percentage Increase 1960-1980
Arecibo	109,856	115,303	140,608	28.0
Caguas	109,651	141,705	173,961	58.6
Mayaguez	108,203	116,100	133,497	23.4
Ponce	191,868	213,984	253,285	32.0
San Juan	695,808	936,693	1,086,376	56.1
Total	1,215,386	1,523,785	1,787,727	47.1

Source: U.S. Bureau of the Census, 1982: Table 11.

Table 3.5
Population Distribution by Broad Age Groups, Puerto Rico: 1899 to 1980

Year	Median Age	<15	15-44	45-64	65+	Total
1899	18.1	43.9	44.3	9.8	2.0	100.0
1910	18.5	42.9	45.1	9.7	2.3	100.0
1920	18.4	43.3	43.6	10.7	2.3	100.0
1930	18.3	42.1	45.0	10.3	2.6	100.0
1940	19.2	40.6	45.4	10.4	3.5	100.0
1950	18.4	43.2	41.9	10.9	3.9	100.0
1960	18.5	42.7	39.1	13.0	5.2	100.0
1970	21.6	36.5	42.0	15.0	6.5	100.0
1980	24.6	31.6	44.9	15.6	7.9	100.0

Source: U.S. Bureau of the Census, 1963: Table 14; 1983b: Table 17.

AGE STRUCTURE

In 1899 the median age of the population was only 18.1 years and remained fairly constant until 1960. Since the 1960s, however, the median age in Puerto Rico has continued to rise and in 1980 reached 24.6 years. This trend is illustrated by changes in the percentages of the population in broad age groups. Table 3.5 indicates that the percent of persons under 15 years decreased markedly between 1960 and 1980. The percent of the population 65 years and over doubled between 1899 and 1950, then doubled again between 1950 and 1980.

The data for the 1980 census indicate that the urban population is older than the rural one, with a difference of three years in the median age (25.6 versus 22.7 years). There is a direct association between the median age and the degree of urbanization. That is, big cities have a higher median age than small towns.

RACE

Puerto Ricans have been described as of mixed racial origin (Bullough and Bullough, 1982). The Spanish conquerors who came to the island in the sixteenth century virtually decimated the native Indian population. By the end of the eighteenth century, only about 2,000 remained (Costas et al., 1981). The present inhabitants are largely descendants of the Spanish settlers and their black slaves, with some slight Indian mixture. Unlike the United States, there was considerable intermarriage of blacks and whites from the earliest times. After slavery was abolished in 1873, blacks obtained legal and political equality. Rogler has observed that over time there has been a strong tendency to define light mulattoes as white (Rogler, 1972). This is borne out by census data: in 1860, 48.5 percent of the population was classified as nonwhite; in 1887, 40.5 percent; in 1910, 34.5 percent; in 1930, 25.7 percent; and in 1950, 20.3 percent (Rogler, 1972; U.S. Bureau of the Census, 1953). As Rogler remarks, "it is apparent that race mixing is changing the racial character of the Puerto Rican population with comparative rapidity." In view of the differences in categorization of race between Puerto Rican and mainland U.S. society, the item on race was deleted from the decennial census in Puerto Rico after 1950.

MARITAL STRUCTURE

The marital structure of the Puerto Rican population has changed significantly since 1899. The percentage of single persons has decreased greatly, and the married population has increased. These changes have been different for females and for males. By 1980, approximately 25 percent of the total female population over 14 years of age was single, and 59 percent was married. For males, the proportions were 31 and 63 percent respectively (Table 3.6).

The proportion of persons that are widowed, on the other hand, has consistently decreased since 1899 due to the decline in mortality levels. By 1980, this proportion was lower for males than for females, because men have higher mortality and remarry more frequently than women.

Divorce, which was not allowed in Puerto Rico during the Spanish regime, has increased significantly during the present century. By 1985, Puerto Rico had one of the highest divorce rates of the world with 48 divorces per 100 marriages (Departamento de Salud, 1985).

Table 3.6

Percentage Distribution of the Population 15 Years or More by Marital Status and Sex, Puerto Rico: 1899 to 1980

Sex and Year	Single	Married[a]	Widowed	Divorced	Total
Males					
1899	48.4	46.9	4.7	b	100.0
1910	43.7	52.3	3.9	0.1	100.0
1920	41.9	53.5	4.3	0.3	100.0
1930	43.2	52.6	3.9	0.3	100.0
1940	42.4	53.3	3.8	0.5	100.0
1950	38.6	57.0	3.6	0.8	100.0
1960	34.6	61.1	3.1	1.2	100.0
1970	33.6	61.7	2.9	1.8	100.0
1980	31.3	62.5	2.7	3.5	100.0
Females					
1899	43.7	44.0	12.3	b	100.0
1910	38.0	51.1	10.7	0.2	100.0
1920	34.0	53.4	12.0	0.6	100.0
1930	33.8	54.0	11.3	0.9	100.0
1940	31.4	55.4	11.6	1.6	100.0
1950	27.3	59.4	11.2	2.1	100.0
1960	25.6	61.4	10.3	2.7	100.0
1970	26.8	60.0	9.3	3.9	100.0
1980	24.7	58.7	9.3	7.3	100.0

Source: Vazquez, 1988: Table 28.

[a]Includes legally and consensually married and separated persons.

[b]Divorce was not permitted during the Spanish government.

HOUSEHOLD AND FAMILY STRUCTURE

Household size has changed significantly since 1950, decreasing from 5.1 members to 3.7 members in 1980. This has been due to a decrease in the average number of children per household and in the number of relatives and nonrelatives living in the household. Similar trends have been noted in the family structure. The average number of persons per family decreased from 5 in 1960 to 4 in 1980 because of a reduction in the average number of children, of relatives, and of nonrelatives.

The percent of two-parent families has also decreased from 79 percent in 1970 to 77 percent in 1980 because of the increase in the numbers of divorces. In 1980, nearly one of every five Puerto Rican families was headed by a woman (U.S. Bureau of the Census, 1984a).

LEVEL OF EDUCATION

Up to the end of the nineteenth century, most of the Puerto Rican population was illiterate. Data from the 1887 census indicate that only 14 percent of the total population (5 years or more) could read and write. Only 7 percent of the population aged 5-19 years attended school, and of these, women

Table 3.7
Proportion of the Population 10 Years and Over Able to Read and Write, Puerto
Rico: 1899 to 1980

Year	Males	Females	Total Both Sexes
1899	24.1	16.8	20.4
1910	37.7	29.3	33.5
1920	49.3	40.9	45.0
1930	63.0	54.3	58.6
1940	72.3	64.7	68.5
1950	78.2	72.4	75.3
1960	84.8	81.4	83.0
1970	90.3	88.2	89.2
1980	90.3	89.1	89.7

Source: U.S. Bureau of the Census, 1963: Table 43; Vazquez, 1988: Table 41.

comprised 58 percent. Since 1899, the proportion of illiterates in the island
has decreased significantly, with the greatest changes occurring during the
first decade of the century and from 1950 to 1980. By 1980, only 10 percent
were illiterate.

The median years of school completed increased dramatically from 2.7 in
1940 to 9.4 in 1980. In spite of these positive changes, it is a matter of great
concern that some 10 percent of the island's population are still illiterate,
and that, from 1970 to 1980, this proportion decreased only slightly (Table
3.7).

ECONOMIC ACTIVITY

Up to the end of the nineteenth century, almost all Puerto Rican men
aged 16 years and over were employed, largely in the agricultural sector.
During this same period, only a small percentage of the women were employed outside the home. Since 1920, labor force rates for males have steadily
declined, reaching 60.7 percent in 1980, while rates for women have risen
somewhat, reaching 27.8 percent in 1980. As a result of these opposing
trends, the total labor force participation rate decreased from 55.4 percent
in 1920 to 43.3 percent in 1980 (Table 3.8). The labor force activity rates
for Puerto Rican males in all age groups were among the lowest in the world
in 1980. Even for those aged 25-34, generally the group expected to have
the highest labor force participation, the Puerto Rican rate was only 86

Table 3.8

Labor Force Participation Rates for the Population 16 Years and Over by Sex, Puerto Rico: 1899-1980

Year	Both Sexes	Males	Females
1899	54.5	96.6	15.4
1910	58.3	96.0	22.1
1920	55.4	89.5	22.3
1930	56.1	86.1	26.7
1940	54.9	84.3	25.6
1950	59.5	83.8	32.8
1960	48.9	76.4	24.5
1970	48.0	70.8	28.0
1980	43.3	60.7	27.8

Source: Vazquez, 1988: Table 46.

percent compared with 95 percent and over for most other countries. High unemployment rates over many years (e.g., 19.5 percent among males in 1980) have resulted in men becoming "voluntarily idle persons" or legally incapacitated when they realized that no jobs were available. This is evident in the increases since 1966 in the percentage of males classified as incapacitated or "voluntarily idle." These percentages approximately doubled among males in all age groups between 1966 and 1981. Some critics say that the government promotes idleness and underemployment by providing economic assistance and welfare to the unemployed without insisting on adequate controls (Vazquez, 1987).

Female labor force participation, on the other hand, increased from 1899 to 1950 in all age groups except those aged 65 years and over. Since 1950, female labor force activity rates have continued to increase for those aged 25 to 64 years, while decreasing for all other age groups. Female activity rates, although lower than those for men, are high compared with those in developing countries. In 1940, 11 percent of the women in the labor force were unemployed; in 1960, 9.9 percent; and in 1980, 12.3 percent (Vasquez, 1987).

Unemployment has been a persistent problem for young men and women in Puerto Rico that has exacerbated over time. From 1970 to 1980, unemployment rates for men aged 20–24 and 25–34 roughly doubled, reaching 35 percent and 20 percent respectively in 1980. During the same period, women aged 20–24 years were most affected by unemployment (23 percent unemployed).

Puerto Rico has not had uniform growth in employment. There was only minimal growth in the 1940s and negative growth in the 1950s due to sharply reduced employment in agriculture and the closedown of the home needle-work industry. In the 1960s, employment again increased, and the 1970s showed a fluctuating trend. Since 1982, a rising trend has been observed.

The employment trends previously discussed have been due to changes in Puerto Rico's economy and its inability to keep employment growth and population in balance. From 1940 to 1985, the population increased 76 percent, but employment increased only 48 percent, despite the migration of over a million residents to the United States.

During the first 40 years of American rule, Puerto Rico's economy was geared to increased agricultural production, chiefly coffee, tobacco, and sugarcane. Cultivation of each of the three major crops took place in a different region. Industrialization was generally limited to expansion of the needlework industry, processing of agricultural products, and manufacturing of fertilizer, furniture, and metal products.

During the Spanish regime, the agricultural industries, especially sug-arcane, were largely family enterprises, but in the twentieth century they gradually became large corporate holdings, characterized by ownership of vast amounts of land as a means of assuring greater productivity. This ex-pansion occurred at the expense of smaller farm owners. As a result, many persons were displaced from their land and were unable to find work with the corporate farms.

From 1940 to the present, Puerto Rico's economy has taken new direc-tions. There has been implementation of a major industralization program, which initially focused on the establishment of light industries employing mostly women. However, since the middle of the 1960s, capital-intensive industries have assumed greater importance in manufacturing. As a result of those trends, the proportion of the population employed in agriculture decreased from 63 percent in 1899 to 46 percent in 1940, and 5 percent in 1980. This decline affected mainly males, since they were the chief source of agricultural labor. The proportion of persons employed in the industrial sector, however, increased from 10.4 percent in 1899 to a peak of 37 percent in 1970. Since then, the rate has decreased greatly due in part to changes in types of industry and in part to the economic crisis of the 1970s that affected the construction industry.

The service industry, which had employed more than 25 percent of the population in 1899, declined to 20 percent in 1920 because of reductions in domestic service. Since then, the rate has greatly increased, and in 1980, over three-fifths of Puerto Rico's labor force were employed in the service sector. Most women (62 percent) are employed in white collar occupations, especially as clerks and as professionals, while male employment is divided almost equally between white and blue collar occupations.

At current prices, per capita personal income increased from $121 in 1940 to $4,369 in 1985—an annual increase of 8.3 percent during the period. The greatest increase—a 9.5 percent annual change—occurred in the 1970s. At constant prices, however, the annual increase was only 3.9 percent, and the per capita personal income increased from $115 in 1940 to just $648 in 1985.

Despite the increased personal income since 1940, income distribution has been inequitable. The percent of total income received by families who were below the median income decreased from 24 percent in 1953 to 21 percent in 1977. When income from the Nutrition Program is excluded, this proportion drops to 18 percent. The Nutrition Supplementary Program has significantly affected the income distribution of the Puerto Rican family. In 1977, this program accounted for 7 percent of family income. Families with less than $2,000 received 38 percent of their income from this program, while families with $10,000 or more received only 2 percent. It is likely that more low-income families are currently dependent upon this program since unemployment has grown and the dependency ratio has increased.

Poverty levels in Puerto Rico, as officially defined, did not change significantly during the 1970s. In 1970, 60 percent of Puerto Rican families were below poverty level; in 1980, 58 percent. The dependency of these families on government assistance has increased over time; in 1963, 84 percent of family income came from work while in 1977, this proportion decreased to 63 percent (Departamento del Trabajo, 1967; Departamento del Trabajo y Recursos Humanos, 1981). By 1980, 30 percent of all Puerto Rican families did not obtain their income from employment (U.S. Bureau of the Census, 1984a).

FERTILITY

Analysis of fertility trends for Puerto Rico indicates that fertility has been declining since the beginning of the present century, except for the period just after World War II. This declining trend in fertility, which was slow during the first decades of the century, has accelerated since the 1950s. By 1987, the crude birth rate was 19.6 while the total fertility rate was 2.4 births, compared with a crude birth rate of 41.0 and a total fertility rate of 6.4 in 1932. Fertility reduction has been highest among older women and among those with highest parity.

The factors that identify the best predictors of fertility group differences in Puerto Rico are marital status, duration of marriage, years of age, and years of school completed (Vazquez, 1987). On the other hand, the factors identified as responsible in part for the fertility reduction in Puerto Rico are sterilization and Cesarean births. In 1982, 38.7 percent of ever-married Puerto Rican women aged 15–49 years were sterilized while 27 percent of the births that occurred to mothers 15–49 years were Cesarean. Although more frequent among women with higher fertility levels, sterilization has reduced overall fertility in Puerto Rico by an average of about one child per woman (Vazquez and Morales, 1982; Warren et al., 1986).

Cesarean births also seem to have contributed to reduced fertility in Puerto

Rico, especially in recent years, because women who deliver by this method usually choose to become sterilized at the third birth. Data for 1982 indicate that mothers whose first child was a Cesarean birth have fewer children, on the average, than women with vaginal births. This relationship was independent of the mother's age, duration of marriage, and other socioeconomic variables (Vazquez, Parrilla, and Leon, 1986).

SOURCES OF MORTALITY INFORMATION

Puerto Rican mortality data prior to the twentieth century are very scarce. Although information for that period is available from parish records which existed at that time, the parish registers were very incomplete and data were published only for some years. In 1885, the Civil Register was established in Puerto Rico and data have been published since 1888.

Before 1931, vital statistics in Puerto Rico (including deaths) were collected by the municipal governments. The local registrar at each municipality was responsible for recording the event, classifying deaths by cause, preparing statistical tabulations, and forwarding the data to the Department of Health where the information was analyzed and published. In 1931, the Law of the Demographic Registry established a centralized system of vital events in the island. In accordance with this law, the General Registry of Puerto Rico was established at the Department of Health and local registers were established in the municipalities. The local registrar records the event and related information and sends the original within one month to the Central Registry. Information is revised, coded, tabulated, and published at the Department of Health (Rivera de Morales, 1970).

Centralization of the system improved the quality of the data and at present they are considered highly reliable. Studies by the Department of Health regarding the classification of cause of death indicate that categorization by cause is not altered significantly by the elements of judgment introduced by the classifier (Carnivali and Torres, 1986). As shown in Table 3.9 mortality trends in Puerto Rico may be divided into four phases: pre-twentieth century, 1900–1939, 1940–1959 and 1960 to the present. These are discussed in the following section.

MORTALITY TRENDS AND CAUSAL FACTORS

Mortality Prior to the Twentieth Century

What little information that is available indicates that mortality was high in Puerto Rico before the present century. Estimates by Vazquez (1987) give a crude mortality rate of 40 deaths per 1,000 inhabitants for 1765, 33 deaths per 1,000 in 1818, and 34 deaths per 1,000 in the period 1895–1899. However, the decline in mortality was extremely slow and by the end of the

Table 3.9
Crude Death Rates, Puerto Rico: 1890 to 1984 (Deaths per 1,000 population)

Period	Rate	Period	Rate
1890-94	28	1940-44	16.6
1895-99	34	1945-49	12.4
1900-04	28.1	1950-54	9.0
1905-09	22.6	1955-59	7.2
1910-14	22.0	1960-64	6.9
1915-19	26.0	1965-69	6.4
1920-24	21.2	1970-74	6.5
1925-29	23.1	1975-79	6.4
1930-34	20.4	1980-84	6.5
1935-39	19.0		

Source: Vazquez, 1988: Tables 122 and 123.

nineteenth century, mortality levels in Puerto Rico were similar to those in Europe during the eighteenth century. Mortality rates also fluctuated abruptly because of hurricanes, epidemics, and crop failures.

Another factor affecting nineteenth-century mortality trends in Puerto Rico was the growing importance of manufacturing. This indirectly stimulated education, and literacy increased from 10 percent in 1860 to 20 percent in 1899. Some public health measures were also introduced but they were not of sufficient magnitude to have any real effect on mortality levels.

Toward the end of the nineteenth century, the responsibility for providing general, medical, and hospital care was still in municipal hands. The central government provided services to those with mental conditions, leprosy, and tuberculosis, and was in charge of licensure and epidemiological surveillance (Arbona and Ramirez, 1971).

Mortality During the Period 1900–1939

From the early 1900s to the end of the 1930s, mortality levels in Puerto Rico decreased slowly. The average death rate was 28 per 1,000 population in the period 1900–1904 and 19 per 1,000 for the period 1935–1939, a 32 percent reduction. At the same time, life expectancy increased from 33 years in 1903 to 46 years in 1940, an increase of more than 33 percent (Table 3.10).

The downward trend in mortality during this period is primarily due to preventive and public health measures initiated by the government. These measures included vaccination, inspection and control of food, development of aqueduct and sewage disposal systems, and improvements in the trans-

Table 3.10
Life Expectancy at Birth, Puerto Rico: 1894 to 1980

Year	Life Expectancy
1894	32.1
1903	33.3
1910	38.2
1920	38.5
1930	40.6
1940	46.0
1950	60.8
1960	69.4
1970	71.9
1980	74.1

Source: Vazquez, 1988: Table 127.

portation and communication systems. These measures were implemented as a result of a 1902 law which required that a Council on Health be established within the Ministry of the Interior. Among its duties, the Council on Health was to investigate the causal factors of morbidity and to establish regulations concerning the requirements, inspection, and functioning of public hygiene on the island; of the aqueduct system; of the admission of persons to medical practice and other health professions; and on the safety of food, alcoholic beverages, and medicines (Morales and Carnivali, 1985).

Beside preventive and health measures, there was also a marked change in Puerto Rico's public health system during the period 1900–1939. In 1926, a new modality of health care was initiated when the first public health unit opened in Rio Piedras, a suburb of San Juan. These units were to provide environmental surveillance, public health education, control of communicable diseases, maternal and infant health, and school health. Despite political objections to this new concept of health care, there was a public health unit in every municipality by 1938 (Ramirez, 1981).

Mortality During the Period 1940–1959

During the 1940s and 1950s, mortality rates declined rapidly and consistently. By 1960, the rate had declined by 62 percent (from 19.0 deaths per 1,000 inhabitants in 1935–1939 to 7.2). Life expectancy at birth also had its greatest increase during this period, from 46.0 years in 1940 to 69.4 years in 1960.

During this period, there were significant changes in Puerto Rico's socioeconomic conditions which markedly improved the quality of life for the population. For example, education, personal income, nutrition, housing conditions, transportation, and communication all improved greatly, which helped to reduce susceptibility to disease.

These socioeconomic changes were initiated by the political party that came to power in 1940. The government's program was geared toward industrialization of the island. To attain this objective, the government created new agencies that would direct, implement, and facilitate the industrialization process and expanded the infrastructure to support the industrialization process (Morales, 1982).

This government policy effectively changed the economy of the island during the period 1950–1957 from one based primarily on agriculture and related trades and services to one that relied primarily on manufacturing for economic growth.

In the first phase of industrialization, light and labor-intensive industries were mainly established. After 1963, heavy and capital-intensive industries began to gain impetus. These new industries were primarily in petrochemicals, pharmaceuticals, and electronics.

Mortality: 1960 to the Present

Since 1960, the crude death rate in Puerto Rico has generally remained stationary, fluctuating between 7.3 and 6.4 deaths per 1,000 inhabitants. Average life expectancy increased by five years during this period, from 69.4 years in 1960 to 74.1 years in 1980. Since 1980, it has remained stationary.

The modest improvement in Puerto Rican mortality since 1960 was due mainly to reductions in infant and childhood mortality rates. By 1980, the mortality rates at ages 25–44 years were already at very low levels and any further improvement is unlikely. In fact, the mortality rates for this age group actually increased in the period 1980–1985. Lifestyles in Puerto Rico have changed greatly since 1960. Consumption of cigarettes and alcohol, as well as environmental pollution, have increased markedly. Deaths due to external causes, especially homicides, have increased among males at ages 15–44. These factors have tended to counterbalance the reductions in total mortality in Puerto Rico during this period.

MORTALITY DIFFERENCES BY SEX AND AGE

Mortality by sex in Puerto Rico shows the expected pattern of higher death rates among males. In the early 1900s, male mortality was slightly higher than that of females, but since 1930 this difference has increased. At present the mortality rate for males exceeds that of females by 46 percent.

Mortality rates among the Puerto Rican population show the expected pattern by age for all years for which data are available, that is, high in the

Countries of Origin

Table 3.11
Mortality Rates by Age, Puerto Rico: 1903 to 1980ª (Deaths per 1,000 population)

Age Group	1903	1940	1950	1960	1970	1980
Under 1 yearᵇ	186.9	114.1	66.6	44.4	28.6	19.2
1-4	36.5	30.6	10.6	3.1	0.9	0.6
5-9	12.5	5.5	2.1	0.8	0.4	0.3
10-14	9.6	2.7	1.1	0.6	0.5	0.3
15-19	12.0	4.8	2.2	0.9	0.9	0.8
20-24	20.1	8.6	4.0	1.5	1.4	1.2
25-29	19.8	10.4	4.9	1.9	1.5	1.4
30-34	20.5	11.0	5.4	2.2	1.8	1.7
35-39	22.7	11.9	6.3	3.0	2.5	2.2
40-44	26.0	12.6	7.2	4.1	3.7	2.9
45-49	31.4	15.6	8.9	5.1	5.3	4.4
50-54	37.6	18.7	10.8	8.0	7.8	6.9
55-59	42.0	24.3	14.8	11.1	10.6	9.7
60-64	49.0	31.3	21.0	16.1	16.0	14.9
65-69	66.3	43.7	31.8	24.8	23.7	21.3
70-74	88.4	63.4	46.5	37.6	38.2	34.0
75 and over	127.2	137.8	103.4	99.5	94.7	88.4

Source: Vazquez, 1988: Table 125.

ªRates refer to the average for the triennial which has as its midpoint the indicated years, except for the 1903 rate which refers to that fiscal year.

ᵇInfant mortality rate is based on deaths per 1,000 live births.

youngest ages, declining to its lowest level between ages 5–14, and increasing to high levels at the oldest ages.

In the early 1900s, mortality levels were high in all age groups (Table 3.11). Since then, mortality has been reduced significantly in all age groups among both sexes. By 1980, the levels of mortality by age compared closely to those of developed countries. The rates for mortality reductions since the beginning of the century have been greatest among those aged 1–14 years. These reductions decrease with age and reach their lowest levels in the oldest age group. Reductions in infant mortality have been very substantial but not as great as for those aged 1–14 years.

Data for 1930, the first year for which information by age and sex are available, indicate that death rates among males were higher than those for females in all age groups except at the reproductive ages (15–39). Since then,

Table 3.12
Life Expectancy by Sex for Selected Ages, Puerto Rico: 1902–03, 1940, 1960, and 1980

				Exact Age				
Year and Sex	0	10	20	30	40	50	60	70
1902–03								
Males	29.8	35.6	29.6	25.5	20.5	15.8	12.0	8.8
Females	31.0	36.1	30.3	26.7	22.9	18.5	14.2	10.4
Difference	1.2	0.5	0.7	1.2	2.4	2.7	2.2	1.6
1940								
Males	45.1	48.5	40.1	33.4	26.8	20.3	14.4	11.6
Females	47.1	50.2	41.9	35.7	29.5	23.0	16.6	13.4
Difference	2.0	1.7	1.8	2.3	2.7	2.7	2.2	1.8
1960								
Males	67.1	61.7	52.5	43.2	34.5	26.1	18.6	12.2
Females	71.9	66.0	56.4	47.0	37.9	29.2	21.0	13.3
Difference	4.8	4.3	4.2	3.3	3.4	3.1	2.4	1.6
1980								
Males	70.5	62.2	52.7	43.8	34.9	26.5	19.1	12.8
Females	77.6	69.1	59.3	49.6	40.0	30.7	22.1	14.6
Difference	7.1	6.9	6.6	5.8	5.2	4.2	3.0	1.8

Source: Morales and Carnivali, 1985.

mortality rate declines by age and sex have been similar to trends for the total population. Reductions in mortality rates by age for both males and females were highest during the 1940–1960 period. However, reductions in mortality were greater for females in all but one age group during the same period.

There are interesting differences in mortality trends by age and sex for the period 1960–1980. Death rates for males under 15 years show a clear decreasing trend of 50 percent or more, while rates for some older groups decreased less than 10 percent and increased in others. Death rates among females, on the other hand, show a decreasing trend in all age groups.

Whereas female life expectancy at birth has always been higher than that of males, this difference has increased over time. As Table 3.12 indicates, female life expectancy at birth in 1902–03 was 1.2 years higher than that of males. By 1980, this difference had increased to 7.1 years. Significant increases in the sex differential can be observed also at older ages.

The sex differential in life expectancy has accelerated since 1940 due to changing patterns in the causes of death which reflect the epidemiological transition. As will be described in a subsequent section, a higher proportion of deaths in Puerto Rico are now due to chronic and degenerative diseases, illnesses which are more common among males.

INFANT MORTALITY

Despite dramatic declines, infant mortality remains high in Puerto Rico compared with most developed countries. In 1985, the infant mortality rate was 14.9 deaths per 1,000 live births. Most of these deaths occurred in the first month of life. The neonatal mortality rate was 12.1 per 1,000 as compared to a post-neonatal mortality rate of 2.8.

Studies have indicated that the probability of an infant dying during his first year of life is greatly affected by the number of weeks of gestation, and by birth weight. Infant survival is also highly dependent on the care received by the mother during pregnancy and childbirth. The decision to seek prenatal care, on the other hand, is closely related to age, parity of the mother, and socioeconomic conditions of the parents. Thus, it seems that infant mortality could be further reduced if all mothers received adequate prenatal care.

CAUSES OF DEATH

Infectious and parasitic diseases predominated as causes of death in Puerto Rico until the 1940s, and accounted for more than 50 percent of all deaths (Table 3.13). Since then, this proportion has decreased, reaching its lowest level—7 percent—in the 1980s. In the period 1931–1934, the mortality rate for infectious and parasitic diseases was 1238.5 deaths per 100,000 inhabitants; in the period 1980–1984, it was 46.7 (Table 3.14).

From 1900–1939, the main infectious and parasitic diseases were: diarrhea-enteritis, tuberculosis, malaria, tetanus, pneumonia, and influenza. In the period 1980–1984 mortality rates for most of these causes were very low. By far the highest rate was due to pneumonia: 32.8 per 100,000 in 1970–1974 and 35.0 per 100,000 in 1980–1984.

Paralleling the decline in infectious and parasitic diseases, the percent of all deaths due to chronic and degenerative diseases has increased from 10 percent at the end of the 1920s to 63 percent in the period 1980–1984. The proportion of deaths due to external causes (accidents, homicides, and suicides) increased to 9 percent in the period 1970–1974 and has declined only slightly since then.

As these trends indicate, the pattern of causes of death has changed drastically since 1940. That year three infectious diseases—diarrhea-enteritis, tuberculosis, and pneumonia—were the leading causes of death, accounting for 45 percent of all deaths in Puerto Rico (Table 3.15). Heart disease was the fourth leading cause of death, with cancer, arteriosclerosis, and cere-

Table 3.13
Percentage Distribution of Registered Deaths by Cause of Death, Puerto Rico:
1921 to 1984

Years	Infectious and Parasi- tic[a]	Main Chronic and Degenera- tive Diseases[b]	External Causes[c]	Other Causes	Total
1921-25	51.5	7.7	2.0	38.8	100.0
1926-30	54.6	9.6	2.3	33.5	100.0
1931-34	58.5	10.5	3.4	27.6	100.0
1935-39	59.5	12.5	4.0	24.0	100.0
1940-44	56.2	14.7	4.0	25.1	100.0
1945-49	46.9	18.2	5.3	29.6	100.0
1950-54	34.0	27.0	5.6	33.4	100.0
1955-59	23.2	38.4	6.7	31.7	100.0
1960-64	17.4	45.9	7.9	28.8	100.0
1965-69	12.4	52.7	8.8	26.1	100.0
1970-74	8.1	58.6	9.1	24.2	100.0
1975-79	8.8	62.0	8.0	20.3	100.0
1980-84	7.2	62.9	8.0	21.9	100.0

Source: Vazquez, 1988: Table 139.

[a]Includes all the infectious and parasitic diseases, diarrhea-enteritis, pneumonia, and influenza.

[b]Includes heart diseases, cancer, cerebrovascular diseases, diabetes mellitus, arteriosclerosis, hypertension, and hepatic cirrhosis.

[c]Includes accidents, homicides, and suicides.

brovascular diseases ranked seventh, ninth, and tenth respectively. By 1960, all three leading causes of death were degenerative diseases, and by 1980 seven of the ten leading causes of death were in this category. The increase in chronic and degenerative diseases as causes of death (Table 3.15) is due to the significant reduction in mortality from infectious and parasitic diseases, and to the aging of the population.

The population of Puerto Rico has aged during the present century, especially since 1960, and chronic and degenerative diseases are more common at older ages. The fact that age-specific death rates for the three major degenerative diseases have decreased in Puerto Rico whereas the crude death rate for these diseases has increased indicates the effect of the aging of the population on the importance of chronic and degenerative diseases as causes of death.

Heart disease has been the most important cause of death in Puerto Rico since 1960. Other important causes of death have been diabetes mellitus, cancer, cerebrovascular disease, arteriosclerosis, cirrhosis, and hypertension (Table 3.16). For these seven diseases combined, males have a mortality

Table 3.14
Mortality Rates for Three Main Cause-of-Death Groups[a], Puerto Rico: 1931 to
1984 (Rates per 100,000 population)

Years	Infectious and Parasitic	Major Chronic and Degenerative	External Causes
1931-34	1,238.5	209.0	70.6
1935-39	1,131.1	228.8	75.2
1940-44	930.2	233.9	73.0
1945-49	583.5	221.1	65.8
1950-54	303.0	235.0	50.2
1955-59	166.2	268.4	47.3
1960-64	120.6	310.1	54.6
1965-69	82.2	348.7	58.1
1970-74	53.2	388.1	60.3
1975-79	56.5	399.6	57.5
1980-84	46.7	409.9	52.4

Source: Vazquez, 1988: Table 140.

[a]For definitions, see Table 3.13.

rate that is 30 percent higher than that for females. Females have a higher
mortality rate for only diabetes mellitus and arteriosclerosis (Table 3.17).

Mortality rates for chronic and degenerative diseases increase with age.
Most of these diseases are more frequent among persons 75 years and older.
In 1980, more than half of the deaths due to heart disease, arteriosclerosis,
and cerebrovascular diseases were of persons at the older ages. Deaths due
to cancer, diabetes, hypertension, and especially cirrhosis, occur at somewhat younger ages.

The leading external cause of death since 1930 has been accidents. In
1980, accidents accounted for 51 percent of all external deaths; homicides,
25 percent; suicides, 15 percent; and undetermined external causes, 9 percent. The death rate for accidents has fluctuated between 28 and 39 per
100,000 population since the 1930s. In 1980-1984, it was 28 deaths per
100,000 persons (Table 3.18).

The risk of dying from automobile accidents increased up to the period
1970-1974, and then decreased in the following decade. The mortality rates
for all other accidents (e.g., falls, drowning) have decreased since the 1930s.
Automobile and other accidents are more frequent among males than among
females. Automobile accidents are more common at ages 15-44 while accidents such as falls and choking on food are more common among older
people.

Table 3.15
Ten Leading Causes of Death, Puerto Rico: 1940, 1960, and 1980

Cause of Death and Year	Percent of Total Deaths
1980	
Heart Disease	25.3
Cancer	16.0
Cerebrovascular diseases	6.2
Pneumonia and Influenza	5.9
Accidents (All)	4.8
Diabetes Mellitus	4.4
Cirrhosis of Liver	4.1
Arteriosclerosis	3.9
Hypertension	3.2
Homicide	2.5
Number of deaths, all causes: 20,486	
1960	
Heart Disease	17.2
Cancer	12.5
Cerebrovascular diseases	6.9
Diarrhea-enteritis	5.9
Accidents (All)	5.6
Pneumonia	4.8
Tuberculosis	4.4
Perinatal Conditions	2.5
Congenital Malformations	2.5
Arteriosclerosis	2.1
Number of deaths, all causes: 15,841	
1940	
Diarrhea-enteritis	22.1
Tuberculosis	14.2
Pneumonia	9.2
Heart Disease	6.8
Nephritis	5.9
Malaria	5.3
Cancer	2.1
Accidents (All)	1.9
Arteriosclerosis	1.5
Cerebrovascular diseases	1.5
Number of deaths, all causes: 34,477	

Source: Vazquez, 1988: Table 156; Departamento de Salud de Puerto Rico, 1981: Table 5.

Mortality rates due to homicide began to decrease in the 1940s and reached their lowest level of 6 per 100,000 in the late 1950s. Since then, the rate has increased, and in 1980–1984 it was 15. Puerto Rico's homicide rate is 50 percent higher than that of the United States and 15 times higher than those of France, Sweden, and England and Wales (Carnivali and Martinez, 1986). Homicide rates among males are several times higher than among females. Mortality rates for homicides increased from 1940 to 1980 at all ages from 15–54 years, with the highest increases occurring among persons aged 25–34 years.

Before the 1970s, suicide was more frequent in Puerto Rico than homicide. Suicide rates began to decrease in the 1930s and reached their lowest level

Table 3.16
Mortality Rates for the Major Chronic and Degenerative Diseases, Puerto Rico:
1931 to 1984 (Rates per 100,000 population)

Period	Heart Disease	Cancer	Cerebro-vascular	Diabetes Mellitus	Hyper-tension	Arterio-sclerosis	Cirrhosis
1931-34	103.8	44.7	23.3	2.9	0.1	23.4	10.8
1935-39	111.6	50.7	25.2	3.5	0.3	27.0	10.5
1940-44	111.9	52.7	29.4	4.7	0.9	23.4	10.9
1945-49	100.6	54.1	31.2	4.9	2.0	17.5	10.8
1950-54	107.2	63.0	34.0	5.1	2.0	14.1	9.6
1955-59	112.1	76.9	43.6	7.9	4.0	12.6	11.3
1960-64	125.7	85.5	50.4	13.0	4.8	16.7	14.0
1965-69	143.6	90.2	53.1	19.3	4.8	18.3	19.0
1970-74	154.7	93.6	49.6	25.1	2.4	34.1	24.5
1975-79	170.6	98.0	51.2	23.1	4.8	27.6	24.3
1980-84	166.6	103.7	42.6	29.0	22.9	21.1	24.0

Source: Vazquez, 1988: Table 144.

Table 3.17
Mortality Rates by Sex for the Seven Leading Chronic and Degenerative
Diseases, Puerto Rico: 1980 (Rates per 100,000 population)

Cause	Males	Females	Ratio: Males to Females
Heart Disease	179.9	144.2	1.24
Cancer	125.1	81.1	1.54
Cirrhosis of Liver	42.8	10.2	4.20
Cerebrovascular Diseases	39.7	39.7	1.00
Diabetes Mellitus	23.5	32.6	0.72
Hypertension	23.0	20.6	1.12
Arteriosclerosis	22.8	26.9	0.85
All Causes	760.9	524.5	1.45

Source: Departamento de Salud de Puerto Rico, 1981: Table 5.

in the early 1960s. Since then, the suicide rate has fluctuated between 8
and 11 deaths per 100,000 persons. Mortality rates for suicide were lower
in 1980 than in 1940 for both sexes and in all age groups. But in 1980, as
in the past, the rate was much higher for males than for females (16 per
100,000 as compared to 3). Data for 1985 indicate that suicide rates are

Table 3.18
Mortality Rates for Accidents, Homicides, and Suicides, Puerto Rico: 1931 to
1984 (Rates per 100,000 population)

Years	Accidents			Homicide	Suicide
	Total	Motor Vehicle	All Other		
1931–34	36.7	7.8	28.9	12.8	21.1
1935–39	30.8	8.7	22.1	15.3	28.9
1940–44	33.0	10.4	22.6	15.6	24.3
1945–49	29.5	9.9	19.6	13.8	22.4
1950–54	28.1	10.6	17.5	8.2	13.0
1955–59	30.2	11.7	18.5	6.3	11.2
1960–64	30.4	15.5	14.9	8.0	10.3
1965–69	39.2	18.6	20.6	8.0	10.9
1970–74	36.6	20.1	16.5	13.3	9.2
1975–79	32.5	17.4	15.2	15.6	10.1
1980–84	28.1	16.2	11.9	15.0	9.3

Source: Vazquez, 1988: Tables 149, 152, and 154.

highest at ages 55 and over. This age pattern differs from that for 1940 when
those aged 20–34 had the highest mortality rates for suicide.

Currently, significant differences can be observed in the pattern of cause
of death by sex and age. Heart disease and cancer are the leading causes of
death for both sexes, but accidents and homicides rank higher for males than
for females. Females have higher death rates due to diabetes and arteriosclerosis than do males (Table 3.16).

With regard to age, external causes, especially accidents and homicide,
were the leading cause of death among males aged 1–44 years and among
females aged 1–34 years. From 45 years of age on, heart diseases and cancer
were the two leading causes of death for both males and females.

CHAPTER 4

Mortality in Cuba

SERGIO DIAZ-BRIQUETS

Cuba's demographic history in the 20th century has differed from that of most Latin American and Caribbean nations. Declines in mortality and fertility began relatively early in Cuba, and during the early 1900s, Cuba attracted many international migrants. Cuba had its highest population growth earlier in the century, while most of Latin America experienced its highest rates of population growth after the end of World War II. Cuba's highest annual population growth rates occurred during the 1899-1907 and 1907-1919 intercensal periods when they approached or exceeded 3 percent (Table 4.1). Migration was largely responsible for these high growth rates, although a major increase in fertility following the 1895–1898 War of Independence and an early onset of mortality decline were also factors.

According to the census of 1899, the Cuban population totalled nearly 1.6 million and by the 1919 census, had nearly doubled to 2.9 million people. At the time of the 1931 census, there were four million Cubans. Between 1899 and 1931, net international migration added some 700,000 people to the national population (Diaz-Briquets and Perez, 1981). In Latin America, only Argentina and Uruguay exceeded Cuba in the share of population growth attributed to international migration.

After World War II, Cuba, like most other developing countries, experienced increased population growth rates, although the annual growth rates in the 1943–1953 intercensal period barely exceeded 2 percent. Such relatively low growth rates were due largely to earlier mortality and fertility declines. A more recent period of accelerated population growth, but from even lower rates of natural increase, took place during the 1960s. This recent

Table 4.1
Intercensal Population Growth, Cuba: 1899 to 1981

Census Year	Enumerated Population	Annual Growth Rate
1899	1,572,797	-
1907	2,048,980	3.3
1919	2,889,004	2.9
1931	3,962,344	2.6
1943	4,778,583	1.6
1953	5,829,029	2.1
1970	8,569,121	2.2
1981	9,723,605	1.1

Source: Comite Estatal de Estadisticas, 1984: Table 1.

spurt in population growth rates was produced by a steep but temporary fertility rise. Since the 1970s, population growth rates have been declining due to a very rapid fertility decline. Since 1959, emigration has also contributed to the decline in population growth rates. Overall, between 1959 and 1980, Cuba lost over 800,000 people through emigration. At the last census in 1981, Cuba had 9.7 million people.

Mortality began to fall in Cuba by the turn of the century, much earlier than in most developing nations, and the mortality decline had gained momentum by the 1920s. Life expectancy at birth for both sexes combined rose from 33 years in 1900 to almost 42 years in 1930 (Table 4.2). By the end of World War II, average life expectancy had risen to 51 years and continued to rise rapidly. By 1952–1954, the average life expectancy for Cubans was 62 years (Comite Estatal de Estadisticas, 1981; Hollerbach and Diaz-Briquets, 1983).

By the 1980s, the Cuban population had attained one of the most favorable mortality levels in the developing world, on a par with many industrialized Western countries. The 1980 Cuban average life expectancy for both sexes combined was estimated at 72 years.

As expected with extensive gains in life expectancy, there have been very substantial declines in infant mortality. Crude estimates of the infant mortality rate suggest that it dropped from 167 infant deaths per 1,000 live births in 1930 to 97 in 1950, and to 40 in 1960 (Hollerbach and Diaz-Briquets, 1983:26 and 30). The 1960 figure, however, is an underestimate since at that time some infant deaths were not reported. By 1970, when death registration was more complete, the rate had dropped to 39, while in 1980 it had fallen to 20 infant deaths per 1,000 births. In 1986, the infant mortality rate was at its lowest level, 13.6 infant deaths per 1,000 live births (De la Osa, 1987).

Table 4.2
Estimated Life Expectancies at Birth, Both Sexes Combined, Havana and Cuba:
1900 to 1980

Year	Estimated Life Expectancy (Years)	
	Havana	Cuba
1900	–	33.2
1901	37.2	–
1905	36.4	34.2
1907	39.1	–
1910	–	35.3
1915	37.2	36.3
1919	41.3	–
1920	–	37.4
1925	39.2	38.5
1930	–	41.5
1931	50.8	–
1935	–	44.6
1937	46.4	–
1940	–	47.5
1943	54.0	–
1945	–	51.0
1950	–	55.8
1953	62.7	–
1955	–	60.7
1960	–	64.0
1965	–	67.2
1970	–	70.0
1980	–	71.8

Source: Diaz-Briquets, 1983: Table 3.

As expected with a significant decline in mortality, there has also been a major shift in cause of death patterns. Infectious diseases no longer are the leading causes of death, as they were five or six decades ago. Today, the degenerative diseases dominate, with cancer and cardiovascular diseases accounting for most deaths.

The fertility trend in Cuba during the twentieth century has also been atypical for Latin America. Previously, the 1895–1898 War of Independence had had a strong dampening effect on fertility but in the early 1900s, fertility rose abruptly (the birth rate reaching above 40 per 1,000 population, and the total fertility rate 6 children per woman). By the 1920s and 1930s however, fertility had begun to decline, earlier than in most Latin American countries. By World War II, the total fertility rate had dropped to 4 children per woman, and the birth rate was in the low 30s. The decline in fertility continued into the late 1950s, when the total fertility rate was below 3.8 children per woman and the birth rate was hovering between 27 and 30 per 1,000 population (See Table 4.3).

In the 1960s, a short-lived "baby boom" raised the total fertility rate to 4.7 children per woman, but since then the fertility rate has continued its rapid decline, with a particularly steep decline in the early 1970s. Since 1978, fertility has been below replacement, when the total fertility rate

Table 4.3
Average Annual Birth Rates in Cuba: 1953–57 to 1978–82

Years	Birth Rate
1953-57	27.0
1958-62	30.1
1963-67	33.8
1968-72	28.9
1973-77	21.1
1978-82	14.9

Source: Derived from Comite Estatal de Estadisticas, 1984: Table 19.

reached 2 children per woman (Diaz-Briquets and Perez, 1982). According to a recent estimate the total fertility rate appears to have stabilized at 1.8 children per woman (Comite Estatal de Estadisticas, 1984). This cycle of "boom-and-bust" fertility has produced a rather distinctive bulge in the country's population age structure, highly noticeable between ages 5 and 19 in 1980. The persistence of below-replacement fertility in combination with high life expectancies are leading to a rapid aging of the Cuban population. The median age, which rose from 22.3 years in 1970 to 25.8 years in 1985, is expected to reach 32 years by the year 2000 (United Nations, 1986).

Between 1950 and 1980 Cuba's population density increased from 51 to 85 persons per square kilometer, reaching 88 by 1985. This population density is relatively high with respect to most Central and South American countries but lower than those generally found in other Caribbean countries.

Cuba, despite its heavy reliance on agriculture, has long been a highly urbanized nation. By 1931, over 50 percent of the population were classified as urban, increasing to 57 percent in 1953. In 1981, almost 70 percent of all Cubans lived in urban areas (Table 4.4). Havana, the capital city, dominates the urban landscape. Throughout most of this century, Havana has accounted for between 16 and 21 percent of the urban population. In recent decades, the growth rate of the capital city has declined: in 1981 Havana accounted for a lower percentage of the urban population than it had in 1953. This has been the result of several factors, including high emigration rates from the city, the substantial decline in fertility, a lessening of rural-to-urban migration, and a long-established urban grid that over time has helped channel the growing population to secondary cities (Luzon, 1987).

Ethnicity is another distinctive demographic characteristic of the Cuban population. Colonialism, slavery, and heavy European (mainly Spanish) immigration in the early 1900s led to a society marked by social and economic cleavages between blacks and whites. Throughout this century, as well as earlier, Cuban censuses reported skin color. Overseas immigration probably

Table 4.4
Urbanization Trends in Cuba: 1899 to 1981

Census Year	Percent Population Urban	Percent of the Population in Metropolitan Havana
1899	44.3	-
1907	39.6	18.3
1919	41.3	16.5
1931	44.2	18.5
1943	46.2	20.0
1953	54.0	21.3
1970	60.4	20.8
1981	69.0	19.8

Source: Cuban censuses.

Table 4.5
Percentage Distribution of the Cuban Population by Race: 1899 to 1981

Census Year	White	Black	Mestizo	Asian
1899	66.9	14.9	17.2	1.0
1907	69.7	13.4	16.3	0.6
1919	72.2	11.2	16.0	0.6
1931	72.1	11.0	16.2	0.7
1943	74.3	9.7	15.6	0.4
1953	72.8	12.4	14.5	0.3
1970	na	na	na	na
1981	66.0	12.0	21.9	0.1

Source: Cuban censuses.

was responsible for increasing the percentage of the population classified as white from 66.9 percent in 1899 to 72.2 percent in 1919. In the 1953 census, 72.8 percent of the population was classified as white and 12.4 percent as black. Cuban censuses also record separate categories for Mestizos (mixed blood) and Asians. In 1953, the former accounted for 14.5 percent; the latter, 0.3 percent of the total population. The 1981 census showed a substantial decline in the white proportion (66 percent); blacks were 12 percent of the total and Asians a much reduced 0.1 percent. Mestizos, however, increased to 21.9 percent of the total population (Table 4.5). These changes were due to the disproportionate emigration of whites, especially since the 1959 revolution (prior to the 1980 Mariel boat lift relatively few blacks had emigrated

Table 4.6
Literacy of the Population Over Ten Years of Age, Cuba: 1899 to 1970

Census Year	Percent Literate
1899	43.2
1907	56.6
1919	61.6
1931	71.7
1943	77.9
1953	76.4
1970	87.1

Source: For 1899-1953 from Cuban censuses; for 1970, Mesa-Lago, 1981, p. 164.

from Cuba), and, according to an official report, to increased numbers of interracial unions (Comite Estatal de Estadisticas, 1983a).

Since the 1959 revolution, Cuba has not published mortality statistics by race. However, prerevolutionary data of questionable quality show greater mortality and poorer health standards among blacks than among whites. Such a pattern was consistent with the relatively disadvantaged socioeconomic status of blacks, a situation comparable to that observed in the United States. It is likely that mortality differentials by race have been reduced with the expansion of medical services to the more disadvantaged social groups during the 1960s and 1970s, and with the overall decline in mortality. Nevertheless, it is reasonable to assume that some differentials persist, since blacks continue to be disproportionately concentrated in some of the most backward and rural regions of eastern Cuba where mortality levels continue to be above the national average and somewhat higher than in the more developed urban regions of the country.

LITERACY

The literacy of the Cuban population rose steadily over the first four decades of this century (Table 4.6). By 1943, over 75 percent of all Cubans over ten years of age were literate, this percentage holding steadily throughout the 1950s. Nine of every ten Cubans were literate by 1970. In 1981 the vast majority of Cubans could read and write, and educational attainment levels had risen significantly above the levels reached in earlier decades. As Table 4.7 shows, in 1981, 59 percent of the population six years of age or older had not received more than a primary education, as compared to 89 percent in 1953. The percentage of the population with some secondary education (but not higher education) substantially increased from 10 percent

Table 4.7
Percentage Distribution of the Population Six Years of Age and Over by
Educational Attainment, Cuba: 1953 to 1981

Educational Attainment	Census Year		
	1953	1970	1981
Total	100.0	100.0	100.0
Sixth Grade or less	89.0	84.5	59.2
Secondary Education	9.9	14.0	37.6
Higher Education	1.1	1.1	3.2
Not Stated	-	0.4	-

Source: Oficina Nacional del Censo, Comite Estatal de Estadisticas, 1983a, p. clxxv.

Table 4.8
Economically Active Population (Ten Years of Age and Over) by Economic
Sector, Cuba: 1950 to 1980

Year	Agriculture	Industry	Services
1950	42.7	20.5	36.8
1960	36.7	23.7	39.6
1970	30.2	26.6	43.1
1980	23.8	28.5	47.7

Source: International Labour Office, 1986: Table 3.

in 1953 to almost 38 percent in 1981. In this intercensal period, the relative number of people with some higher education had nearly tripled to 3 percent in 1981 from 1 percent in 1953. Cuban educational attainment levels in the 1980s, in general terms, compare rather well with those found in other Latin American countries at similar levels of development.

EMPLOYMENT/INDUSTRY PATTERNS AND TRENDS

In 1980, less than 25 percent of the Cuban economically active population was engaged in agricultural activities, down from over 40 percent in 1950 (Table 4.8). Almost half were employed in the service sector, and about 28 percent in industrial activities. Among women in 1980, 68 percent were in the service sector as compared to 39 percent of the men, while 10 percent were in agriculture as compared to almost 30 percent of the men.

The activity rate for the combined male and female economically active population in 1980 was 36.6 percent, 50.4 percent for men and 22.4 percent for women (Table 4.9). The 1980 value for both sexes combined exceeded

Table 4.9
Activity Rates of the Economically Active Population (Ten Years of Age and
Over) by Sex, Cuba: 1950 to 1980

Sex	1950	1960	1970	1980
Both Sexes	35.4	34.0	30.0	36.6
Males	59.4	56.0	48.8	50.4
Females	9.2	10.6	11.7	22.4

Source: International Labour Office, 1986: Table 2.

that recorded 30 years earlier, partly because of drastic changes in age
structure, and partly because of notable changes in sex-specific activity rates.
Between 1950 and 1980, while the male activity rate declined, the female
rate rose significantly—more than doubling in the interval—as more and
more women entered the work force.

Another major development in the Cuban labor force over the 1950–1980
period has been a significant decline in the open unemployment rate. In
1981, according to census data, the open unemployment rate stood at 3.4
percent, or about a third (8.4 percent) of that recorded in the 1953 census.
Both census rates severely understate a problem that has historically plagued
Cuba: high levels of underemployment. Underemployment in 1953 and 1981
differed in some very important respects, however. The 1981 underemployment is typical of that in many socialist states in which the underemployed, although gainfully employed, have very low productivity. Under
socialism the state guarantees full or nearly full employment, even if it entails
low output per worker. The underemployment of 1953, on the other hand,
was similar to the underemployment found today throughout Latin America.
In these economies the underemployed worker earns very low and uncertain
wages, holds unstable occupations, and often experiences unemployment.
The end result of these differences is that under socialism the underemployed
worker has an income security absent under more market-determined conditions characteristically found in underdeveloped Latin American economies.

MORTALITY HISTORY

Prior to the twentieth century, Cuba exhibited a characteristic pre-modern
mortality pattern. Infectious epidemic diseases, such as cholera, yellow fever, and smallpox, were frequently rampant, as shown in Table 4.10. Epidemics produced substantial fluctuations in the death rate. The degree of
variability in the death rate from year to year can be seen in the annual
cause-specific death rates for the city of Havana from 1895 to 1902 (Table

Table 4.10
Average Crude Death Rates Each Decade, City of Havana: 1801 to 1900
(Deaths per 1,000 population)

Decade	Crude Death Rate	Recorded Epidemics and Wars
1801-1810	38.0	
1811-1820	46.7	Yellow fever: 1816-1820
1821-1830	36.2	
1831-1840	32.2	Cholera: 1833-1836
1841-1850	23.3	Yellow fever: 1844
1851-1860	26.2	Asiatic cholera: 1850-1854
1861-1870	42.0	Asiatic cholera: 1867-1868 Yellow fever: 1861
1871-1880	45.0	Yellow fever: 1873-1877 Smallpox: 1871-1872, 1874-1875, 1878-1881 Ten Years' War: 1868-1878
1881-1890	34.2	Smallpox: 1887-1888
1891-1900	43.8	Yellow fever: 1885-1898 Smallpox: 1891, 1894-1898 War of Independence: 1895-1898

Source: Diaz-Briquets, 1983: Table 1.

4.11). Reliable data by cause of death for the whole country are not available for that period. As indicated, the death rate was greatly affected by epidemic outbreaks over the period, reaching extraordinarily high levels between 1896 and 1898. At that time, Cuban nationalist irregular forces were fighting the Spanish colonial army in the War of Independence. The war not only destroyed the national economy but also uprooted the rural population, who were forced to relocate in the cities. Lack of food led to severe malnutrition. These conditions greatly increased the risk of contagion.

After the U.S. victory in the 1898 Spanish-American War, American military forces occupied Cuba from 1898 to 1902. The earlier decline in Cuban mortality coincided with the U.S. occupation. The military government instituted major sanitary reforms that sharply reduced the incidence of many infectious diseases, as indicated in Table 4.12. A major factor in the decline in the death rate was the success of an anti-mosquito campaign that was launched after mosquitoes were proven to be carriers of yellow fever, the scourge of both the occupation forces and the local population.

The anti-mosquito campaign, the cessation of hostilities, and improvements in nutrition and sanitation had very noticeable effects (Diaz-Briquets, 1983). By 1902, the crude death rate in Havana was at an all-time low. After 1901, no deaths from yellow fever were ever again recorded in Cuba.

Table 4.11
Cause-Specific Death Rates for Certain Infectious Diseases, City of Havana:
1895 to 1902 (Deaths per 100,000 population)

Year	Infectious Diseases								Crude Death Rate (All Causes)
	Yellow Fever	Smallpox	Malaria	Diphtheria	Infantile Tetanus	Typhoid Fever	Tuberculosis	Total	
1895	242.3	79.3	90.3	11.0	78.9	80.2	711.3	1293.3	3226.3
1896	553.4	433.4	194.2	8.2	100.2	210.2	681.2	2180.8	5077.5
1897	364.9	597.1	344.9	15.3	91.4	288.8	819.2	2521.6	7713.1
1898	57.0	70.4	799.3	9.6	72.5	423.3	1171.1	2603.2	8907.5
1899	42.6	1.6	375.5	16.1	38.0	57.8	405.3	936.9	3368.2
1900	124.5	0.8	138.2	6.0	55.8	36.2	341.8	703.3	2451.2
1901	7.0	0	59.0	9.8	50.0	32.4	351.8	510.1	2235.8
1902	0	0	29.3	9.5	25.9	33.1	361.2	459.0	2219.9

Source: Diaz-Briquets, 1983: Table 5.

Table 4.12
Age-Sex-Standardized Cause-Specific Death Rates, Municipality of Havana: 1901
to 1953 (Per 100,000 population)

	Census Years					
Cause of Death	1901	1907	1919	1931	1943	1953
All causes	2,481.2	2,449.7	2,370.5	1,702.6	1,434.3	957.1
Respiratory tuberculosis	360.8	379.0	344.1	164.3	177.0	41.3
Other infectious and parasitic diseases	262.3	222.4	119.9	58.5	74.8	10.6
Malignant and benign tumors	105.7	139.0	186.9	147.8	170.2	176.2
Cardiovascular diseases	675.2	778.7	760.0	536.6	406.3	359.1
Influenza, pneumonia, bronchitis	176.4	178.1	168.8	145.6	113.0	35.4
Diarrhea, gastritis, enteritis	350.8	181.0	227.6	135.0	82.5	23.2
Certain degenerative diseases	126.5	112.8	173.0	143.4	100.7	65.5
Complications of pregnancy	17.7	20.4	23.0	14.4	6.5	1.7
Certain diseases of infancy	36.8	55.7	29.5	18.3	21.0	25.4
Accidents and violence	66.0	81.6	101.7	97.5	60.2	58.9
All other and unknown causes	303.0	301.0	236.0	241.2	222.1	159.8

Source: Diaz-Briquets, 1983: Table 14.

65

Smallpox mortality was dramatically reduced, except for one severe outbreak reported during the early 1920s. This outbreak was associated with high and largely unregulated immigration from countries such as Haiti where the disease was endemic. The last death from smallpox occurred in Cuba in 1925. Malaria remained a persistent but gradually less important health problem well into the 1960s. Today only cases of the disease contracted outside the country are reported.

As indicated in Table 4.12, data on trends in cause-specific mortality show that rates from all major causes of death, except malignant and benign tumors, declined substantially in Havana between 1901 and 1953. The declines were particularly significant for tuberculosis, other infectious and parasitic diseases, cardiovascular diseases, influenza, pneumonia and bronchitis, and diarrhea, gastritis, and enteritis. Between 1901 and 1953, the age-sex standardized death rate for the city was reduced by more than 60 percent and for some causes of death, the decline approached or exceeded 90 percent. On the other hand, mortality from malignant and benign tumors increased almost 70 percent. As the relative importance of infectious diseases in overall mortality declined, the importance of degenerative diseases rose. Tumors and cardiovascular diseases, which in 1901 accounted for 17 percent of all deaths in Cuba, were responsible for 48 percent of all deaths in 1953 when they were the leading causes of death. In Havana, the percentages were 25 and 58 respectively. The differences between the percentages for Havana and Cuba reflect the city's greater success in conquering infectious diseases, and Havana's relatively older age structure due to lower urban fertility and rural-to-urban migration. The marked decline in tuberculosis mortality probably resulted from gradual improvements in education and nutrition (Diaz-Briquets, 1983).

Mortality trends in Cuba since the 1960s are shown in Tables 4.13 and 4.14. Table 4.13 presents age-specific death rates by sex and by age and Table 4.14 shows cause-specific death rates by sex for the five leading causes of death for the years 1965, 1972, 1975, 1978, and 1983. As these tables indicate, mortality has continued to decline since the 1950s. The major declines in age-specific mortality were among children under age 5 and for those aged 45–54 and older. Age-specific death rates were lower for females, a sex differential also evident with the estimated life expectancies by sex.

In terms of cause-specific mortality, the data in Table 4.12 reveal the overwhelming importance of degenerative diseases in overall mortality already observed in the 1950s. In 1965 and 1972, diseases of the heart, neoplasms, and cerebrovascular diseases were among the five leading causes of death, a position they have retained. Up to 1972, a leading cause of death was perinatal mortality, but after 1974, it was no longer ranked as a major cause. This reflects the advances made by Cuba in reducing infant mortality. Since 1974, mortality from accidents and violence and from influenza and pneumonia joined diseases of the heart, neoplasms, and cerebrovascular

Table 4.13
Age-Specific Death Rates per 1,000 Population, by Sex, Cuba: 1965 to 1978

Sex and Year	Age Group (years)									Crude Death Rate	Age-Adjusted Rate
	Under 5	5-14	15-24	25-34	35-44	45-54	55-64	65-74	75+		
Total											
1965	9.7	0.5	1.3	1.5	2.5	5.4	13.6	31.9	135.2	6.6	5.6
1971-72	7.1	0.5	1.1	1.4	2.0	4.2	11.6	30.7	119.0	5.9	4.8
1974-75	5.8	0.4	1.1	1.3	2.1	4.5	10.6	27.8	108.2	5.6	4.5
1978	3.8	0.4	1.2	1.3	2.3	4.9	10.9	28.7	103.5	5.7	4.3
Male											
1965	10.5	0.6	1.5	1.6	2.6	5.9	15.9	38.9	143.5	7.4	6.2
1971-72	7.9	0.5	1.2	1.6	2.1	4.6	12.7	36.6	128.7	6.6	5.4
1974-75	6.4	0.5	1.2	1.4	2.3	4.8	12.2	31.4	114.2	6.2	4.9
1978	4.1	0.5	1.3	1.6	2.6	5.6	12.4	31.2	111.9	6.3	4.8
Female											
1965	8.9	0.4	1.1	1.3	2.3	4.8	10.9	23.9	126.7	5.7	4.9
1971-72	6.2	0.4	0.9	1.2	1.8	3.8	10.3	24.1	109.4	5.1	4.2
1974-75	5.2	0.4	0.9	1.1	1.9	4.2	9.0	23.3	102.1	5.0	4.0
1978	3.5	0.3	1.1	1.1	1.9	4.2	9.2	25.6	94.9	5.0	3.8

Source: Pan American Health Organization, 1974, 1978, 1982.

Table 4.14

Mortality Rates for Leading Causes of Death, Cuba: 1965 to 1983
(Deaths per 100,000 population)

Sex and Cause	1965	1972	1975	1978	1983
Both Sexes					
Diseases of the heart	125.6	137.5	148.6	169.2	171.6
Malignant neoplasms	102.1	102.1	99.3	99.3	113.2
Accidents and violence	-	34.9	35.1	63.9	66.9
Cerebrovascular diseases	62.2	53.7	50.9	53.6	56.5
Influenza and pneumonia	37.6	-	38.8	44.8	38.0
Causes of perinatal mortality	68.4	37.4	-	-	-
Males					
Diseases of the heart	-	152.3	163.1	190.0	190.7
Malignant neoplasms	-	119.7	114.3	117.2	132.2
Accidents and violence	-	48.6	47.9	81.9	85.7
Cerebrovascular diseases	-	54.6	52.1	52.7	56.5
Influenza and pneumonia	-	-	42.0	49.0	41.6
Causes of perinatal mortality	-	44.4	-	-	-
Females					
Diseases of the heart	-	122.2	133.3	147.5	151.7
Malignant neoplasms	-	83.7	83.5	80.7	93.3
Accidents and violence	-	20.7	21.6	45.1	47.4
Cerebrovascular diseases	-	52.6	49.6	54.5	56.4
Influenza and pneumonia	-	-	35.4	40.4	34.1
Causes of perinatal mortality	-	30.0	-	-	-

Source: Pan American Health Organization, 1974, 1978, 1982, 1986.

disease as the dominant determinants of the national death rate. The previously noted sex differential in mortality is also evident by cause of death.
Overall, the contemporary Cuban mortality profile by age, sex, and cause
of death resembles that of the more developed nations, including the United
States.

In the following section, the characteristics of Cuban mortality in 1981,
the year of the last national population census, are examined in detail.

MORTALITY PROFILE IN 1981

The latest censal year is pivotal for the analysis of the structure of mortality
in Cuba. To assess the age-, sex-, and cause-specific mortality profile, the
ideal method would be to derive average rates with data from the three
years around the census date (1980, 1981, and 1982) to reduce the proba-
bilities of chance fluctuations. Unfortunately, the required detailed data for
1980 and 1982 are not readily available, so average rates could not be computed. However, the effects of random fluctuations in the trend of annual
deaths can be roughly evaluated by comparing the total number of deaths
recorded in 1981 with the average for all deaths occurring in the three-year
period. The comparison can also be made by sex. This procedure suggests

that 1981 was a year in which the number of deaths was somewhat above the average for the three-year period. In 1981 the total number of deaths for both sexes exceeded the three-year average by about 2 percent. The relative excess was approximately the same for both sexes (2.0 percent), although slightly higher for males (2.1) than for females (1.9). The differences between 1981 and the three-year average, while not inconsequential, are not sufficiently large to significantly bias the presentation of Cuba's mortality profile, although they tend to inflate somewhat the true mortality picture. The data to be discussed were provided by Cuba to the World Health Organization (1985) and tabulated according to the Ninth Revision of the International List of Causes of Death.

Cause-specific death rates by age and sex, and for both sexes combined, are shown in Table 4.15. The age-specific death rates for males for all causes of death combined are consistently higher than are those for females. As expected, the age-specific death rates are lowest between ages 1–4 years and 15–24 years. Age-specific death rates begin to rise gradually at ages 25–34, increasing more rapidly by ages 55–64. The infant mortality rate is quite low, particularly for a developing country.

In 1981, infectious and parasitic diseases were responsible for 2.1 percent of all deaths registered in Cuba. Most deaths attributed to these causes occur in early infancy and in the advanced elderly ages. The age-specific rates tend to be quite low between infancy and the older ages. The principal specific causes of death within this broader category are intestinal infectious diseases, septicemia, and other viral diseases. Unlike intestinal infectious diseases and septicemia, death rates from viral diseases are relatively constant throughout the age distribution.

Malignant neoplasms accounted for 18.5 percent of all deaths. Not surprisingly, the age-specific mortality rates for neoplasms are much higher at the older ages. The male death rate for all ages combined is approximately 48 percent higher than the female rate. Quantitatively, the two cancers that account for the greatest number of cancer deaths are neoplasms of the respiratory system—the bronchus and lung (23 percent of all cancer deaths)—and cancers of the gastrointestinal tract (22 percent of all cancer deaths). The cancer mortality rates, with the exception of colon cancer, are higher among males. The death rate for cancer of the trachea, bronchus, and lung is at least three times higher for males than for females at all ages; the sex differences are even higher in the elderly population. Three other neoplasms with high mortality rates in the Cuban population are breast cancer, uterine cancer, and malignancies of the prostate.

The 1981 statistics show low mortality rates from causes associated with poor nutritional status. The most acute effects of these conditions are found with anemias, especially among the elderly population. Diabetes mellitus, a cause of death of some importance in low mortality populations, is re-

Table 4.15
Age-Specific Death Rates for Selected Causes, Cuba: 1981 (Rates per 100,000 population)

Sex and Cause of Death	All Ages	0	1-4	5-14	15-24	25-34	35-44	45-54	55-64	65-74	75 & +
							Age Group (Years)				
All causes											
Total	595.9	1850.1	105.5	50.0	114.4	144.0	229.1	482.7	1090.6	2708.5	8548.7
Male	672.7	2050.8	107.8	56.6	120.8	171.2	273.1	545.2	1269.7	3172.0	9145.3
Female	517.4	1637.1	103.1	43.1	107.9	117.2	185.1	420.0	907.8	2231.2	7915.0
Infectious and parasitic											
Total	12.8	197.5	23.4	6.8	3.8	4.8	4.7	7.1	14.0	28.7	74.8
Male	13.4	211.1	23.2	6.9	3.7	4.3	4.0	7.6	16.0	32.8	80.1
Female	12.1	183.1	23.6	6.6	3.9	5.4	5.3	6.5	12.0	24.5	69.3
Cancer											
Total	110.0	5.9	8.4	6.7	6.1	14.3	40.1	116.7	297.9	675.8	1339.1
Male	130.8	10.0	7.1	7.2	7.1	12.0	31.6	106.9	329.0	850.2	1746.5
Female	86.7	1.5	9.9	6.2	5.0	16.6	48.7	126.4	266.2	496.2	906.3
Stomach cancer											
Total	7.3	–	–	0.1	0.1	0.6	1.6	9.0	17.8	43.7	102.7
Male	9.9	–	–	0.2	0.1	0.7	1.7	11.9	26.2	57.5	140.8
Female	4.5	–	–	–	0.1	0.4	1.6	6.0	9.2	29.6	62.2
Cancer of the large intestine											
Total	7.6	–	–	0.0	0.2	0.3	1.6	6.7	20.2	47.9	111.9
Male	7.2	–	–	0.1	0.1	0.4	1.6	6.7	18.4	46.4	103.8
Female	7.9	–	–	–	0.2	0.1	1.6	6.7	22.1	49.5	120.5
Lung cancer											
Total	25.8	–	–	0.1	0.2	1.8	5.8	24.6	74.1	187.4	311.2
Male	39.2	–	–	0.2	0.4	2.3	7.9	34.4	106.6	292.7	479.2
Female	12.1	–	–	–	–	1.3	3.6	14.8	40.9	79.0	132.3

Breast cancer Female	100.0	68.0	47.3	32.6	14.5	2.5	0.1	–	–	–	14.2
Prostate cancer Male	364.2	93.6	10.1	3.3	0.3	–	–	–	–	–	16.3
Diabetes Total	156.2	79.3	33.9	9.4	5.1	2.3	1.4	0.1	–	–	12.5
Male	104.5	62.0	22.9	8.6	5.3	2.3	1.1	0.1	–	–	9.5
Female	211.0	97.2	45.2	10.3	4.8	2.3	1.7	0.2	–	–	15.6
Heart disease Total	4867.9	1346.1	495.4	185.5	58.2	19.7	7.3	2.5	4.5	31.6	260.4
Male	4911.8	1533.7	583.7	213.4	68.6	21.2	7.9	3.0	5.4	29.9	283.7
Female	4821.3	1153.0	405.2	158.0	47.8	10.2	6.8	1.9	3.5	33.3	236.7
Myocardial infarction Total	1391.4	551.0	237.9	86.9	24.1	5.6	0.8	0.1	0.2	1.5	92.4
Male	1533.7	681.9	305.2	117.2	33.4	7.4	0.8	0.1	0.3	1.4	112.0
Female	1240.2	416.3	169.1	56.5	14.8	3.8	0.8	0.1	–	1.5	72.4
Cerebrovascular disease Total	934.7	309.0	119.1	53.0	17.6	5.7	1.4	0.4	0.3	4.4	56.6
Male	897.7	319.4	127.6	48.7	19.7	6.1	1.8	0.6	0.3	4.3	57.2
Female	974.0	298.4	110.4	57.2	15.5	5.4	0.9	0.3	0.4	4.5	55.9
Atherosclerosis Total	682.3	68.5	10.0	1.9	0.1	0.1	0.1	–	–	0.7	22.8
Male	650.9	77.6	12.0	3.1	0.2	0.1	0.1	–	–	1.4	23.1
Female	715.7	59.2	8.0	0.7	–	–	–	–	–	–	22.5
Pneumonia Total	868.7	160.1	36.8	12.0	5.4	2.5	2.7	1.9	10.8	154.2	39.8
Male	946.6	184.7	42.1	12.4	6.4	2.9	3.8	1.8	9.4	156.9	44.5
Female	765.8	134.8	31.4	11.5	4.5	2.1	1.6	1.9	12.4	151.3	35.0
Chronic obstructive pulmonary disease Total	92.0	34.8	15.5	8.0	3.5	2.3	1.0	0.4	2.8	0.7	7.2
Male	109.0	39.8	16.9	6.4	3.3	2.3	0.4	0.2	2.0	1.4	7.7
Female	74.0	29.6	14.1	9.6	3.8	2.3	1.5	0.6	3.5	–	6.7

Table 4.15 (*continued*)

Sex and Cause of Death	All Ages	Age Group (Years)									
		0	1-4	5-14	15-24	25-34	35-44	45-54	55-64	65-74	75 & +
Symptoms, signs and ill-defined conditions											
Total	1.7	6.6	0.3	0.4	0.5	1.5	1.7	1.9	1.1	2.3	21.4
Male	2.0	8.6	0.3	0.4	0.4	1.9	3.1	3.1	1.5	2.9	18.5
Female	1.4	4.5	0.4	0.5	0.6	1.1	0.3	0.7	0.8	1.6	24.4
Accidents											
Total	67.3	62.4	24.4	20.2	71.9	73.6	72.4	72.7	77.7	114.3	339.8
Male	87.3	55.6	30.2	25.3	76.1	102.0	113.6	111.2	118.9	154.4	368.4
Female	46.7	69.0	18.4	15.0	67.6	45.5	31.2	34.0	35.7	73.1	309.4
All others											
Total	84.2	1391.2	31.1	11.0	19.7	23.0	38.0	69.4	118.3	267.1	768.8
Male	93.7	1577.1	30.2	11.7	20.3	22.3	37.2	75.6	138.7	311.5	859.9
Female	74.5	1193.8	30.4	10.2	19.0	23.7	41.7	63.0	96.4	221.2	713.8

Source: World Health Organization, 1986: Table 13.

sponsible for 2.1 percent of all deaths. Most mortality from this cause occurs among the old, the age-specific rate rising rapidly after ages 35–44. At all ages, the death rates are higher for females.

Diseases of the circulatory system, as a group, account for as many deaths as all other conditions combined. In 1981, 44 percent of all deaths were due to diseases of the heart, particularly acute myocardial infarction and other ischemic heart diseases. At all ages men exhibit higher mortality, although the rates for the two sexes tend to converge at the older ages. Heart attacks accounted for 36 percent of all deaths from diseases of the circulatory system, with the overall death rate among males from this cause being 50 percent higher than the rate among females. The sex differentials in age-specific death rates from other ischemic heart diseases are less pronounced and rates are almost identical at some ages. At the older ages, however, female rates exceed male rates. These patterns, in general, are very similar to those found in most industrialized countries.

Cerebrovascular diseases continue to be one of the principal causes of death in Cuba and account for 9.5 percent of all deaths. Sex differences in the patterns of mortality by age for this cause are not substantial. Rates are higher among males at the younger ages but not among the elderly.

Deaths from pneumonia, influenza, and bronchitis are relatively high in the Cuban population. These diseases accounted for 8 percent of all deaths in 1981. Within the group, pneumonia was the cause of 40 percent of all deaths. The age-specific death rates are generally higher for males than for females. In both sexes, the age-specific death rates for pneumonia are much higher toward the extremes of life. Mortality from chronic liver disease and cirrhosis, which are frequently associated with the excessive consumption of alcohol, is rather moderate in Cuba. Without exception, in every age group, deaths from these causes are higher for males than for females. Mortality rates from these causes, as from other degenerative diseases, rapidly increase with age. The patterns of mortality from nephritis, nephrotic syndrome, and nephrosis are very similar to those observed for chronic liver disease and cirrhosis.

Congenital anomalies and other prenatal conditions are jointly responsible for 3.2 percent of all deaths. Mortality from these conditions occurs primarily among infants under one year of age and is higher among males than females.

A principal cause of death in Cuba that accounted for 11 percent of all mortality in 1981, is accidents and violence. This category includes all violent deaths, ranging from accidents to suicides and homicides. For this cause-of-death category, the overall mortality rate is higher for males than for females, the sex differential narrowing substantially toward the oldest ages. Since the late 1970s, Cuba has not provided detailed statistics for subgroups in the accidents and violence classification. However, Cuba has reported that of the 6,117 accidents and self-inflicted deaths registered in 1981, 65.5 percent were accidents and 34.5 percent suicides or homicides. In 1977, the last year with detailed information, of 6,112 violent deaths, 24.3 percent were due to motor vehicle accidents; 37.8 percent to all other accidents, 27.7 percent to suicides; 6.0 percent to homicides; and 4.2 percent to injuries in which it could not be determined whether they were accidental or purposeful. In that year, the overall death rates from suicide and homicide were higher for males, although up to ages 25–34 women had a higher suicide rate. After ages 35–44, males had a suicide rate that was generally at least twice as high as the female rate. The death rates from homicide are almost invariably higher for males.

In comparison to other Western Hemisphere nations, Cuba had death rates from suicides and self-inflicted injuries that were among the highest until the late 1970s. Between 1961 and 1984, the Cuban crude suicide rate rose from 14.4 to 20.9 per 100,000 population. In 1965 the rate was 11.4; in 1970, 11.8; in 1975, 17.2; and in 1980, 21.6 (Comite Estatal de Estadisticas, 1984:15 and 85–86). Some fluctuations observed in the trend can be attributed to changes in age structure. In 1970, however, the Cuban age-sex standardized suicide rate was nearly double and in some cases, higher, than the rates for Argentina, Costa Rica, Chile, Panama, Uruguay, and Venezuela, which are among the Latin American countries with the most complete and dependable death registration (Pan American Health Organization, 1974, 1978). In 1975, the age-sex standardized suicide rate for Cuba was the highest in the Western Hemisphere (Pan American Health Organization, 1978). Underreporting of suicide in other nations, however, may bias the comparison.

Finally, the percentage of all deaths allocated to signs, symptoms, and other ill-defined conditions in 1981 was very low, only 0.2 percent of all deaths. Such a low percentage is a tribute to the fact that most deaths registered in Cuba are accompanied by a medical certificate.

QUALITY OF THE DATA

Occasional examinations by foreign analysts and routine evaluations conducted by domestic statistical agencies suggest that Cuban demographic data are of exceptionally high quality in comparison with those of other developing countries (Comite Estatal de Estadisticas, 1981; Hill, 1983). The following discussion briefly reviews several indicators of the quality of both the census data and the death registration data for 1981.

1981 Census

The 1981 Census conducted on September 11th on a *de jure* basis, enumerated a total population of 9.724 million inhabitants, 4.915 million of whom were males. The population totals (not adjusted to the mid-year point) were used by the World Health Organization to calculate the total and cause-specific death rates by sex and age (Table 4.15). According to a ten-day post-enumeration survey which began on September 16 to estimate the coverage of the census, the 1981 census had included 99.4 percent of all inhabitants of the nation. Approximately 1.58 percent of all residential dwellings (2.8 percent in rural areas and 1.06 in urban areas) were sampled. The survey found that only 0.11 percent (2,577 units out of a total of 2,363,364) of all residential units were not covered by the census, although the deficit was partly compensated by the inclusion of nonresidential units. As these figures suggest, the coverage of the census was more than adequate (Comite Estatal de Estadisticas, 1983b).

Further analysis of the quality of the data confirms that the census succeeded in collecting highly satisfactory age data. Standard indices used to gauge the extent of digit preference in age reporting show the 1981 census did considerably better than earlier Cuban censuses. In the United Nations index, a value under 20 is generally considered to be indicative of good age reporting. The United Nations index provides a score of 14.8 for the 1981 census, as compared to earlier values of 34.1 in the 1953 census and of 22.4 in the 1970 census. The same index for the United States in 1970, in comparison, was 13.7. The Myers index, another commonly used indicator of digit preference, provides equally good results: a value of 2.4 (2.4 for males and 2.5 for females) in 1981 compared with a value of 9.3 in 1953 (9.7 and 9.0 for males and females, respectively). The lower the score, the less the digit preference. The 1970 United States Myers index stands at 1.1 (1.1 for males and 1.2 for females). The values for both Cuba and the United States fall within the range of good age reporting. Finally, the Whipple index shows that digit preference for ages ending in zero and five was not a problem in the 1981 census. The scores on this index were, for both sexes, 99.3, and for males and females, 99.5 and 99.1, respectively. Scores close to 100 represent an absence of reporting preferences for ages ending in zero and five in the population between 23 and 62 years of age (Comite Estatal de Estadisticas, 1983a). The 1970 United States score was very close to but in the opposite direction from Cuba.

Death Statistics

According to a number of measures, Cuban vital statistics, and in particular death statistics, have been of relatively good quality for several decades and have been consistently improving (Collver, 1965; Gonzalez and Debasa, 1970; Comite Estatal de Estadisticas, 1981; Hill, 1983). Cuba's birth and death registration, for example, was considered to be virtually complete by the early 1970s (Hill, 1983). One measure of the high quality of Cuban mortality data is the very high percentage of death registrations accompanied by a medical certificate. In 1981, only 0.2 percent of all causes of death were ill-defined (0.2 percent for males and 0.1 percent for females). Another indication of the quality of the data is that the age of the deceased was unknown in only 0.02 percent (0.03 for males and 0.02 for females) of all deaths in 1981. In addition, the cause of death can generally be assumed to be reported since almost every registered death is accompanied by a medical certificate. Common errors in diagnosis, however, may be undetected in the statistics.

The contemporary Cuban health system has been praised for its scope and coverage. The country has been able to attain a very favorable ratio of physicians to population, and hospitals and other medical facilities can be found throughout the national territory. The general consensus is that Cuban mortality statistics are extremely reliable for a developing nation. Such a conclusion also applies to the quality of the census data.

Special Considerations Pertaining to the Analysis of Cause-Specific Mortality Rates in Cuba

In evaluating cause-specific mortality rates in Cuba, three issues may be relevant: diet, smoking, and drastic social changes. With regard to diet it appears that most Cubans are relatively well-fed, although the diet is monotonous and leans heavily toward the consumption of carbohydrates and animal (pork and lard) fats (Benjamin, Collins, and Scott, 1984). According to Cuban health authorities, too many Cubans are overweight (Janofsky, 1987). Egg consumption is quite high, fish consumption is rising, and consumption of milk and milk products is generally restricted, although children have access to assured supplies. Gordon (1982), who sampled 1980 Cuban refugees, found that about 20 percent of the children he examined suffered from first-degree malnutrition. However, cases of second-degree malnutrition were rare and no cases of kwashiorkor were present. Gordon's sample showed a low prevalence of vitamin deficiencies although low dietary iron intakes were apparently related to a relatively high incidence of anemia. Fruit and vegetable consumption was low. These findings generally correspond with Jolliffe's findings in a study conducted during the 1950s (Jolliffe et al., 1958). However, the latter study also reported some vitamin deficiencies and concluded that anemia and low hemoglobin were not major problems among Cuban children.

Smoking is a second issue of concern in evaluating cause-specific mortality. Many Cubans, particularly males, are heavy smokers of both cigars and cigarettes. As recently as 1987 it was reported that some 48 percent of all adult Cubans smoked. The use of nonfiltered cigarettes is believed to be high (Janofsky, 1987).

Finally, the relationship between a higher-than-average suicide rate and a series of drastic socioeconomic and political changes over the course of the last quarter-century must be considered. These changes led to the separation of many families because of emigration, abrupt modifications in traditional social norms, and an unusually high level of social alienation among members of those social sectors who found it most difficult to adapt to the new society. Theoretically, these developments may be linked to the high suicide rate observed in the country.

PART THREE

Immigrant Groups in the United States

CHAPTER 5

Mortality of Mexican-Origin Persons in the Southwestern United States

BENJAMIN S. BRADSHAW AND KAREN A. LIESE

In recent years, interest in the study of the Hispanic population in the United States has been increasing, for this is a rapidly growing population, which already numbered 14 million at the time of the last census in 1980. Among the Hispanic population, the Mexican-origin population, which numbers 8.7 million or 60 percent of the total Hispanic population, has increased in size by 93 percent over the past decade. This group is concentrated in the Southwestern United States, with the majority residing in Texas and California.

The paucity of research on the mortality and morbidity of the Mexican-origin population has recently been noted in the *Report of the Secretary of Health and Human Services Task Force on Black and Minority Health* (U.S. DHHS 1985). That there have been so few mortality studies of the Hispanic population in the Southwestern United States may be due to the unavailability of vital statistics that define Hispanic ethnicity in a manner consistent with that of the decennial census. Although Arizona, California, Colorado, New Mexico, and Texas include a question about ethnic origin on the death certificate, the wording varies among the states and differs from that in the 1980 Census. As a result, data derived from death certificate information regarding decedents of Hispanic origin are inconsistent to varying degrees with census data. Moreover, there are no national data on Mexican-origin mortality, though death certificates in an increasing number of states now include a question on Hispanic origin of decedents.

For these reasons, researchers have had to rely on vital statistics and census data classified according to Spanish or non-Spanish surname, as these are the only death and population data that are consistently defined for the Hispanic population. Virtually all studies of Mexican-American mortality have used this definition, despite its inherent disadvantages.

The study of mortality patterns among racial and ethnic minorities is important for two reasons: (1) demographic relevance and (2) analysis of ethnic mortality may contribute to our understanding of the genetic and environmental development of disease. The purpose of this review of literature of Spanish-surname mortality in the Southwestern United States is to describe certain patterns in the estimated mortality of white Spanish persons of Spanish surname. The findings of all major studies since the 1950s are reviewed and discussed. Age-specific and cause-specific mortality patterns for Spanish-surname males and females are described and compared to those of the non-Hispanic white population.

In one of the first descriptions of Spanish-surname mortality differentials, Ellis (1959) reviewed mortality data for Houston, Texas, for the years 1949–1951 and calculated standardized death rates using the U.S. white population in 1940 as the standard. (Prior to 1950, reliable population data upon which to base death rates were not available.) He found that Spanish-surname males had total mortality rates that compared favorably with those of other white males. Spanish-surname males had death rates that were higher than those for other white males at most ages under 45 years but were lower for all ages over 45 years. Spanish-surname females, however, had death rates that were 40–60 percent higher than those for white females for all ages except 40–44 years and 75 years and over, and their total mortality was considerably higher.

An examination of the ten leading causes of death showed that Spanish-surname males had standardized death rates only slightly above those of other white males, but much higher rates for tuberculosis, pneumonia, accidents, and homicide, and strikingly lower rates for heart disease and malignant neoplasms. Spanish-surname females compared to other white females had significantly higher standardized death rates due to higher mortality rates for tuberculosis, pneumonia, malignant neoplasms, diseases of the heart, nephritis, accidents, and homicide. Only mortality due to suicide and vascular lesions was lower among Spanish-surname females. The mortality differential between male and female Spanish-surname persons was much less than that between other white males and females.

In a subsequent study, Ellis (1962) tested the findings of his Houston research against a larger urban Spanish-surname population. Death rates were calculated for San Antonio, Texas, for 1950 and were standardized using the age-sex distribution of the white population of the U.S. as a standard. Life expectancies were also calculated. Age-specific death rates showed that Spanish-surname females had higher death rates than other white women at every age except 75 years and over. Spanish-surname males, however, had lower death rates than other white males at several ages, and exhibited lower total death rates (probably as a result of the younger age of the group).

Standardized death rates for selected leading causes of death showed significant mortality differentials. Spanish-surname females had lower mortality rates than other white females for non-disease causes only (accidents, homicide, suicide), while Spanish-surname men had lower rates than other white men for malignant neoplasms and diseases of the heart. Standardized mortality rates for all causes showed that the Spanish-surname population had a very unfavorable mortality experience relative to that of other whites, largely due to the high mortality of Spanish-surname females.

At birth, the life expectancy of the Spanish-surname population was lower than that of the comparison group, especially for females. The lower life expectancies continued for every age group in both sexes, except for males aged 55–59, when Spanish-surname males had a slightly higher life expectancy than that of Anglo males.

The results of this study confirmed the mortality pattern that Ellis had previously noted in his Houston study. Roberts and Askew (1972) also reported similar findings for Houston in 1950 and 1960.

Subsequently, Schoen and Nelson (1981) examined mortality patterns of Mexican Americans by age, sex, and cause of death in California for 1969-1971, and presented the first life table ever published for a large Spanish-surname population. They concluded that life expectancies for Spanish-surnamed males and females did not differ significantly from those of other whites. Although at ages 40 and 65, Spanish-surnamed males had longer life expectancies than other white males, Spanish-surnamed females had shorter life expectancies than did other white females at those ages.

The standardized death rate for the Spanish-surnamed males was slightly lower than that of other white males, and the standardized death rate for Spanish-surname females was higher than that of the comparison group. When mortality was examined by selected causes of death, the authors concluded that Spanish-surnamed males had higher death rates for all causes except cardiovascular diseases and neoplasms. Spanish-surnamed females exhibited similar patterns, except for a decreased advantage in deaths due to neoplasms and no advantage in cardiovascular diseases. Spanish-surnamed males and females had higher mortality from infectious and communicable diseases.

Bradshaw and Fonner (1978) calculated standardized death rates for all causes of death combined and for several categories of primary causes for Texas for the years 1969–1971. The 1970 Texas non-Spanish-surname white female population was used as the standard. They found that the age-adjusted death rates of Spanish-surname males, compared to those of other white males, were almost identical, while the Spanish-surname female death rate exceeded that of other white females by 19 percent. The difference between male and female age-adjusted death rates for the Spanish-surname population was smaller than the difference in the other white population, due to the higher mortality of Spanish-surname females.

An examination of age-specific death rates showed that Spanish-surname male mortality was substantially higher below the age of 30, but lower above the age of 45 when compared to those of other white males. Spanish-surname females had a higher mortality than other white females at every age group; the greatest difference occurred below the age of 15.

Adjusted death rates for selected causes of death showed that Spanish-surname males, compared to other white males, had higher mortality due to infectious and parasitic disease, diabetes, influenza, accidents, and violence. Spanish-surname males had lower death rates due to neoplasms and circulatory diseases. Spanish-surname females, compared to other white females, had higher mortality rates for most causes of death except neoplasms and circulatory diseases.

The results of this study generally agreed with those of Schoen and Nelson. In both California and Texas, standardized death rates for Spanish-surname males were slightly lower than those for other white males, and adjusted death rates for Spanish-surname females were somewhat higher than those for other white females. Spanish-surname persons had relatively high death rates from infectious disease, diabetes mellitus, and accidents (preventable and manageable causes), and generally relatively low death rates (especially for males) from the major chronic diseases—cardiovascular disease and cancer.

Samet et al. (1980) investigated respiratory disease mortality in several ethnic groups in New Mexico during the period 1969–1977. They examined deaths due to infectious respiratory diseases, chronic respiratory diseases, and cancer of the respiratory tract. Average annual ethnicity- and sex-specific mortality rates were calculated and compared with the 1973 U.S. total mortality rates.

Mortality from all causes for male and female Hispanics was found to be less than that of the New Mexico Anglo and total U.S. population. However, age-specific mortality rates for lung cancer and chronic obstructive pulmonary disease (COPD) among Hispanic females over 65 years of age were considerably higher than those for Anglo females. In addition, excess mortality from tuberculosis, influenza, and pneumonia was noted among both Hispanic males and females. Hispanic males in the study population enjoyed a reduction in mortality risk due to lung cancer and COPD when compared to New Mexico Anglos and the total U.S. population. The authors explained their low-risk status as a function of a low prevalence of cigarette smoking.

The conclusion that "overall mortality rates for Hispanics of both sexes were less than Anglo and U.S. rates" differed from the conclusions of Schoen and Nelson (1981) (California) and Bradshaw and Fonner (1978) (Texas). It is possible that these findings did not agree because New Mexico's Hispanic population differed markedly from that in other states or that state vital statistics offices used slightly different procedures for associating ethnicities with surname.

More recently, Bradshaw et al. (1986) contrasted patterns of excess mortality by cause in the Spanish-surname male population of Texas with those observed among other white males for the years 1970 and 1980. The impact on life expectancy of changes in cause-specific death rates during the 1970s was also examined. Excess and deficit mortality were computed by multiplying the difference between age and cause-specific death rates for the two groups of males in 1969-1971 and 1979-1981 by the 1980 population age distribution of Spanish-surname males.

The authors concluded that the mortality rates in 1980 for both groups of males were lower than those for 1970. The "crossover" pattern for Spanish-surname males (higher death rates at younger ages and lower death rates at older ages) that had been previously reported for 1970 (Bradshaw and Fonner, 1978; Schoen and Nelson, 1981) and 1950 (Ellis, 1959, 1962) was also present for 1980. Spanish-surname males, however, differed markedly from other white males in their mortality patterns by cause. They experienced much higher mortality due to diabetes, pneumonia and influenza, external causes, and "all other" causes, while other white males had higher death rates due to cancers and major circulatory diseases. This pattern was observable for both 1970 and 1980.

An examination of excess deaths showed that if Spanish-surname males had benefited from having death rates equal to those of other white males in those ages and causes in which the rates of the latter group were lower, about 14 percent fewer deaths would have occurred in the Spanish-surname male population. However, the Spanish-surname male population enjoyed a substantial advantage due to deficit deaths compared with other white males for several causes in which they had a mortality advantage over other white males.

An analysis of life expectancies showed that lower Spanish-surname life expectancy at birth was due almost entirely to excess mortality from a limited number of causes of death (diabetes, motor vehicle accidents, homicide), some of which may be controlled or prevented.

Markides (1983) also examined life expectancies in the Spanish-surname population in a report that discussed recent patterns and trends of mortality among the nation's largest disadvantaged ethnic minority groups, including blacks, Hispanics, and Native Americans. According to the 1970 life expectancy values for Texas, the life expectancy of Spanish-surname persons was only slightly lower than that of other whites, but was considerably higher than that of blacks. For Spanish-surname males, life expectancies were very similar to those of other white males, and by the age of 65, slightly higher. On the other hand, Spanish-surname females had deficits of 3.1 years at birth which gradually decreased 1.5 years at age 65, when compared to other white females. Markides concluded that mortality rates and life expectancy values for the Spanish-surnamed population in Texas were more favorable than expected.

In the most recent study of Mexican-American mortality to date, Rosen-waike and Bradshaw (1989) presented cause-specific age-adjusted death rates by sex for the Spanish-surname populations of Texas and California in 1980, and compared mortality data for the white native-born and Mexican-born Spanish-surname populations. This was a seminal study on two counts: (1) it is the only study to date to include information for both California and Texas (where over 85 percent of the Spanish-surname population reside), and (2) it is the first study to present data for both the U.S.-born and Mexican-born portions of this population.

Striking mortality patterns were evident among white Spanish-surname males. When compared to other white males, the Spanish-surname males showed relatively low death rates for heart disease and malignant neoplasms, but significantly higher mortality rates for deaths due to accidents, chronic liver disease, homicide, and diabetes.

Spanish-surname females from Texas and California differed in their mortality patterns when compared to other white females. The age-adjusted death rate for heart disease was slightly higher for Spanish-surname females in Texas, but lower for those in California. The mortality rate for chronic liver disease was slightly higher for Hispanic females in Texas. In both states, death rates for cancer and mortality due to accidents were lower among Spanish-surname females than among other white females. Spanish-surname females in Texas and California had higher death rates for homicide and diabetes than did other white women.

When the Spanish-surname population was categorized as Mexican-born or U.S.-born, the major pattern that emerged was one of convergence: The mortality pattern of the U.S.-born population approached that of the other white (mainstream) population, and deficits and excesses in mortality tended to decrease. The U.S.-born Spanish-surname male population experienced higher mortality from heart disease, cancer, and suicide, and lower mortality from accidents and homicide than did the Mexican-born population. Two exceptions to the pattern of convergence were mortality due to diabetes and chronic liver disease. Death rates for these causes increased in the U.S.-born Spanish-surname population relative to the Mexican-born population.

The authors concluded that mortality patterns in the Spanish-surname population differed significantly from those in the Anglo population of Texas and California, although the mortality patterns were not the same for Spanish-surname males and females.

Markides and Coreil (1986) reviewed cause-specific mortality studies and found that a "Mexican-American pattern" of causes of death emerged from the cumulative findings. Specifically, Spanish-surname males tend to have death rates that are low for heart disease, cancer, and suicide, but high for infectious disease, diabetes, pneumonia and influenza, accidents, and homicide. Spanish-surname females, however, compared to other white women, tend to have death rates that are similar for heart disease and cancer, lower for accident and suicide mortality, and higher for infectious disease, diabetes, and homicide. This finding corroborates the recent findings by Rosenwaike and Bradshaw.

The evidence presented thus far in this review of the literature indicates a substantially different mortality pattern between the Spanish-surname and other white populations, one which has changed little, except in the degree of difference, since the first studies of Mexican-American mortality in the 1950s.

Striking differences in cause-specific mortality patterns have been noted for the Spanish-surname population compared with other white populations. To explore and document more fully these mortality differentials, researchers have cited numerous studies that examine trends in specific causes of death such as cancers, circulatory diseases, and violence, among the Mexican-American population. The Mexican-American population overlaps extensively with the Spanish-surname population in the Southwest so that the results of these studies are considered to be directly applicable. A detailed review of cause-specific mortality is presented below.

Shai and Rosenwaike (1988) analyzed national and regional mortality rates for violent causes of death among first-generation Hispanic Americans (Mexican-, Puerto Rican-, and Cuban-Americans) around 1980. Age-, sex-, and cause-specific death rates were computed and standardized using the age distribution of the United States as the standard.

The authors concluded that mortality from violence among first generation Hispanic Americans considerably exceeded the U.S. average, and that each Hispanic group had an elevated risk from one form of violent death. Of the three groups, Mexican-Americans experienced the highest mortality due to accidents (mostly motor vehicles) and the lowest mortality due to suicide. Whereas mortality from major chronic diseases such as cancer is somewhat lower in the Hispanic population, patterns of violent death have produced higher mortality rates among Hispanic adolescents and young adults, and lower mortality rates among the Hispanic elderly, compared with those of the white non-Hispanic population.

In an early study of Mexican-American mortality from lung cancer (Buechley et al., 1956), average annual death rates for California were computed for the period 1949–1953. Using 1950 Census Bureau procedures for defining and enumerating persons of Spanish surname, the authors calculated death rates for 10-year age groups (beginning with age 25) for each sex for both the entire population of California and the Spanish-surname population.

The researchers found that beginning at age 45, women with Spanish surnames had a definite excess of lung cancer mortality compared to all women in California. The age-adjusted death rate for Spanish-surname women was more than twice that of the state's female population. In contrast, the age-adjusted rates for men with Spanish surnames were almost equivalent to those for all men in California. The authors presented evidence that the excess mortality due to lung cancer was confined to Spanish-surname women of Mexican origin (foreign-born) and appeared to be nonexistent among U.S.-born women with Spanish surnames.

In an attempt to explain the threefold excess of lung cancer mortality among Mexican-born Spanish-surname women described by Buechley et al., Buell, Mendez, and Dunn (1968) surveyed surviving members of families of Mexican-American women who had died of lung cancer during the period 1950–1962. Information on early home environment, cooking practices, migration, illness, and use of tobacco and alcohol was elicited. The authors initially concluded that excess lung cancer mortality risk was significantly associated with the unusual smoking histories of the deceased Mexican immigrant women.

Another survey was then undertaken to study smoking patterns of Mexican-American women in Los Angeles County from 1963 to 1964. (The comparison data for all California women were obtained from the California Health Survey, 1960–1961). Again, results from the second survey revealed that older Mexican immigrant women had unusual smoking patterns when compared to all California women.

The researchers concluded that, although a larger proportion of Mexican immigrant women than other women were cigarette smokers and a much larger proportion began smoking before age 15, cigarette smoking was not solely responsible for the increased number of deaths due to lung cancer among these women. Rather, excess mortality due to lung cancer was the result of a smoking experience unique to one birth cohort, females born in Mexico prior to 1900, and the trend of excess deaths due to lung cancer among Mexican-Americans appears to be diminishing.

Lee, Roberts, and Labarthe (1976) examined patterns of lung cancer mortality among three ethnic groups in Texas from 1969 through 1971 in an effort to determine whether the lung cancer mortality patterns of Mexican-Americans, documented earlier by Buechley et al. (1956), still persisted around 1970. As reported in previous studies, lung cancer mortality was higher for Hispanic males than females. However, Spanish-surname males experienced a lower age-adjusted mortality rate than did other white or black males. Spanish-surname females had only slightly higher mortality rates due to lung cancer than did females in the two comparison groups. However, age-specific rates for these females revealed significant excess lung cancer mortality in the group aged 70 years and over which was masked by a striking mortality deficit among women aged 40 to 60 years.

The authors concluded that the differential reported for females in earlier studies was no longer evident, as excess mortality is confined to the older foreign-born women, and that Hispanic males do, in fact, experience a substantially lower number of deaths from lung cancer when compared to other whites and blacks.

More recently, Holck et al. (1982) examined lung cancer mortality among Mexican-American women in Texas in an effort to update information on lung cancer mortality and smoking habits in this population in 1970, 1974–1976, and 1979. Mexican-American women were identified by Spanish surname and compared to other white women in Texas. Age-specific lung cancer mortality rates were calculated in 10-year age groups for all women over the age of 35, as was an overall age-standardized rate, using the age distribution of the combined population groups as the standard.

The authors found that the age-standardized lung cancer death rate for Spanish-surnamed women remained at approximately the same level for each of the three time periods analyzed. During the same period, the mortality rate for other white women increased by 73 percent. Spanish-surnamed women consistently demonstrated lower mortality for all age groups (in all three time periods) except for 75 years and above, where they experienced significantly higher lung cancer mortality. The total age-standardized rates were lower for Spanish-surname females when compared to those of other white females. The difference in rates, though insignificant in 1970, was considerable in 1974–1976 and increased again in 1979.

Previous reports by Buell (1968) and Buechley (1956) indicated an excess in lung cancer mortality among Spanish-surname women when compared to other white women. However, this excess declined from 1950 to 1970, and has continued to decline into the 1970s, so that the mortality rate among Spanish-surname women is substantially lower than that for other white women. Holck et al. (1982) believe that these results support Buell's hypothesis that the decline in Mexican-American lung cancer mortality is a consequence of the pre–1900 cohort of Mexican-born women aging out of the population.

Martin and Suarez (1987) examined cancer mortality patterns of Spanish-surnamed (primarily Mexican-Americans) persons in Texas for the period 1969–1980. Age- and sex-specific population counts were used to generate standardized mortality ratios for 33 cancer sites and for total cancers; the number of deaths among Mexican-Americans was compared to the expected number of deaths of other whites.

Data analysis revealed that overall cancer mortality for Spanish-surnamed males was 25 percent lower than that for other whites. The decreased mortality rate was considered to be due to lower risks for smoking-related cancers and for colon, rectal, and prostate cancer. Mexican-American females experienced a total cancer mortality rate that was only slightly lower than that for other white females. Although mortality risk due to breast cancer is significantly lower among Mexican-American females, the risk of death due to cervical cancer is more than twice that of other females. All Mexican-Americans experienced more than twice the mortality risk for cancer of the stomach, liver, and gallbladder.

Analysis of cause-specific mortality in the Spanish-surname population has not been limited to cancers. Several researchers have directed their efforts toward examining deaths due to cardiovascular disease in the Hispanic population, because the study of mortality in minority groups whose economic and cultural patterns differ from those of the majority of the population may offer clues about genetic and environmental factors in the development of disease.

Stern and Gaskill (1978) examined age-adjusted mortality rates by sex, ethnic group, and cause of death in Bexar County, Texas, for the period 1970–1976 in an effort to describe cardiovascular disease trends among Mexican-Americans. They noted declines in ischemic heart disease (IHD) mortality for Spanish-surname women. Total cardiovascular disease mortality also decreased for all Mexican-Americans and for other white males. The authors noted that declines in mortality due to acute myocardial infarction were not substantial for Spanish-surnamed men, nor was there any trend for cerebrovascular disease. These findings were not considered significant.

The researchers discounted the theory that changes in personal health habits were the sole cause of the observed declines in IHD mortality, and presented evidence that fluctuations in other diseases, such as diabetes and pneumonia and influenza, and improvement in medical care, contributed to the decreased mortality due to IHD.

Although Stern and Gaskill's research had been based on a sizable local Mexican-American population, there previously had been no studies of trends in Mexican-American mortality for larger populations. Because the size and composition of the Texas population make it ideal for studying ethnic trends in mortality, Kautz, Bradshaw, and Fonner (1981) examined whether the three major ethnic groups (Spanish-surname, other white, and black) in that state had comparable changes in cardiovascular mortality during 1970–1975. Standardized proportional mortality ratios were computed for Texas and the United States for each sex and ethnic group. Causes of death examined were cardiovascular disease, acute myocardial infarction, chronic ischemic heart disease, and cerebrovascular disease.

Declines in total cardiovascular mortality in Texas were consistent with U.S. trends for whites and blacks, but Spanish-surnamed males experienced a much smaller decrease, which may be due to the lower initial level of total cardiovascular mortality in this group. Mortality from acute myocardial infarction declined dramatically, with a smaller decline in the Spanish-surnamed population than in the other populations.

Mortality due to chronic ischemic heart disease rose in all groups except among Spanish-surname females, who showed a relative decline. Cerebrovascular disease mortality declined significantly in other white and black males, but barely declined among Spanish-surname males. The change in cerebrovascular mortality was negligible for Spanish-surname and other white females.

The authors concluded that the changes in mortality imply that the overall differences in rates by ethnicity observed in 1970 are diminishing, and that the Spanish-surnamed population of Texas shows different trends in cardiovascular mortality, that is, a less dramatic decline than do the other ethnic groups of Texas. As these results differed substantially from those of Stern and Gaskill (1978), Kautz, Bradshaw and Fonner (1981) indicated that the previous study may have been adversely affected by population estimation errors, a problem that might have been critical in estimating age-standardized rates for small geographic areas such as San Antonio.

Since the two earlier studies of cardiovascular disease reached somewhat divergent conclusions, and since they were both carried out before the 1980 U.S. Census data became available, Stern et al. (1987) conducted another study to describe the trends in ischemic heart disease death rates in the Mexican-American (Spanish-surname) population of Texas from 1970 to 1980. The non-Hispanic white population of Texas was the comparison group. Age-, sex-, and ethnicity-specific death rates were computed for all causes of death, total IHD, acute myocardial infarction, and chronic ischemic heart disease. The percent changes in age-adjusted mortality rates from 1970 to 1980 for all causes were highly statistically significant, except for the rate for chronic IHD in Spanish-surnamed males. Consistent declines of 11.1–13.5 percent in mortality were noted in each age, sex, and ethnic group during this time period; a steep decline of 21.7 percent occurred in Spanish-surnamed women.

The results of this study showed both similarities and differences when compared with the earlier studies. All studies reported declines in total ischemic heart disease and acute myocardial infarction mortality in Mexican-Americans of both sexes, with Spanish-surname men showing less steep declines. However, in contrast to earlier studies, Stern et al. (1987) concluded that the declines among Mexican-Americans of both sexes were highly statistically significant. This suggests that the differing patterns of change in death rates from ischemic heart disease have diminished one of the most important differences in cause-specific mortality between Hispanic and non-Hispanic males. These results, however, indicate that the Mexican-American population has shared in the national decline in ischemic heart disease mortality.

The rate of decline in infant mortality in the United States, one of the most notable health accomplishments of the century, has not been uniform for all racial and ethnic groups. Studies documenting ethnic differentials in infant mortality have indicated that nonwhite babies have a higher risk of dying than do white babies. At the time the following study was conducted, few other studies had directed attention to the Mexican-American infant mortality rate, and the vast majority of published research was descriptive in nature, rather than analytic.

Gee, Lee, and Forthofer (1976) analytically studied ethnic differentials in neonatal and postneonatal mortality among three ethnic groups, including Spanish-surname, other white, and nonwhite populations in Houston, Texas, for births occurring in 1958 and 1959. Their results indicated that the Spanish-surname neonatal mortality rate was comparable to the other white experience, despite the population's less favorable socioeconomic conditions. The low neonatal death rate was attributed to better birthweight distributions and full-term gestation periods. The postneonatal mortality rate was, however, higher than that of other whites, indicating the negative influence of low socioeconomic status, poor nutrition, and inadequate access to health care.

In light of the unexpected findings of Gee, Lee, and Forthofer (1976), Markides and Hazuda (1979) analyzed infant mortality rates in Texas counties for 1968 to 1972, excluding those counties along the Mexican border which are thought to have artificially low infant death rates. They attempted to document the impact of the border counties on the correlations between ethnicity, socioeconomic status, and infant mortality. The results of the study indicated that, compared to other whites, Spanish-surname infants were advantaged during the neonatal period because of their more favorable birthweight distribution, but were disadvantaged during the postneonatal period which is more influenced by environmental factors. An overall negative association between Spanish surname and infant mortality was supported by the data.

Because the unexpectedly low neonatal mortality rates for Spanish-surname babies have generally been viewed with suspicion and attributed to unreliable data, Powell-Griner and Streck (1982) attempted to determine the extent to which neonatal mortality rates represent the true health status of the Hispanic newborn population. They examined neonatal mortality for the Spanish-surname population of Texas during 1979 and found that the neonatal death rate for this population was very similar to that of the Anglo population. The validity of these findings was doubted, however, due to the known effects that socioeconomic disadvantage has on infant mortality. The authors investigated possible explanations for the unexpectedly low death rates, including unreliable data attributable to overreporting of births and/or underrepresentation of deaths. They concluded that the low neonatal mortality rates observed in the Spanish-surname population in Texas may have been due, in part, to the underreporting of neonatal deaths.

Considering all research for all causes of death combined, the death rates of persons of Spanish surname compare favorably with those of other white persons. A "Hispanic pattern" of mortality includes advantages in diseases of the heart, malignant neoplasms, and chronic obstructive pulmonary disease, and disadvantages from homicide, diabetes mellitus, chronic liver disease, and pneumonia and influenza. This pattern is not as evident in Spanish-surname females, yet Hispanic females do have a mortality advantage for malignant neoplasms and suicide, and a disadvantage for diabetes mellitus and chronic liver disease. This striking pattern of Hispanic mortality, first suggested in studies as early as the 1950s, has consistently been identified in research since then.

The "Hispanic pattern" of mortality may be due to cultural or biological differences such as diet, cigarette smoking, or resistance to carcinogens. Differences in lifestyle are undoubtedly reflected in the high mortality due to homicide, accidents, and chronic liver disease, and in the low mortality due to suicide. Elevated diabetes mortality may be biological in origin, with cultural factors contributing significantly. However, available data do not permit attributing mortality variation to specific environmental, social, cultural, or genetic factors.

The fact that the Spanish-surname population is disadvantaged mainly from deaths due to conditions which may be successfully managed, prevented, or avoided, suggests that life expectancy at birth might be fairly easy to improve. However, if interventions succeed in lowering the Spanish-surname death rate for manageable or preventable causes, a greater number and proportion of the population might survive to older ages, and deaths from cancer, circulatory diseases, or other chronic and degenerative conditions might increase.

Mortality data only indirectly indicate the health and distribution of disease in a population. Differences in levels of mortality and causes of death among racial and ethnic groups in the United States may indicate, to some extent, the relative survival among these groups. A more complete examination of data pertaining to those conditions and practices which may affect mortality levels and the cause structure of mortality is warranted to discern more clearly those factors affecting mortality that are of genetic or cultural origin.

CHAPTER 6

Mortality Among Three Puerto Rican Populations

IRA ROSENWAIKE AND KATHERINE HEMPSTEAD

BACKGROUND

Mortality studies of immigrant groups are an important way to assess the relative significance of environmental and genetic factors on mortality. In general, the convergence of an immigrant group's mortality profile with that of the host population suggests environmental influences on mortality, while the persistence of differentials suggests that genetic factors and/or lifestyle differences may be significant. The effect of migration on health and mortality may be mixed, since migration may bring with it an increase in socioeconomic status, yet at the same time expose migrants to a new environment and a new set of health risks. The process of migration itself is stressful, and migrants may adjust in ways that affect their health adversely (Evans, 1987). Hispanic groups living in the United States are of increasing interest to researchers, since their mortality profile is unexpectedly favorable, given their socioeconomic status (Markides and Coreil, 1986; Rosenwaike, 1987).

The present study examines the mortality experience of three Puerto Rican populations: residents of Puerto Rico, Puerto Rican-born residents of New York City, and all other Puerto Rican-born residents of the U.S. mainland. The effects of socioeconomic, cultural, and environmental factors on mortality as well as selective migration are considered.

The Hispanic population in the United States, which has been growing rapidly, is ethnically diverse. The three largest Hispanic origin populations are (in order) Mexicans, Puerto Ricans, and Cubans. Until quite recently, vital statistics on these groups have been inadequate, but recent changes in

coding practices (in particular, the coding of place of birth on death certificates by the National Center for Health Statistics as of 1978) have made it
possible to study Hispanic mortality more comprehensively (Trevino, 1982).
For the Puerto Rican population this change in coding procedures (which
coincided with the 1980 Census) is significant, since no mortality statistics
were previously available for the Puerto Rican-born population in the United
States living outside of New York City.

Previous mortality studies of Hispanics in the United States have found
that, relative to the total U.S. population, Hispanic groups have lower mortality rates for certain major causes of death, particularly heart disease and
cancer, but higher mortality rates for lifestyle-related causes such as cirrhosis, accidents, and homicide. This "Hispanic pattern" of differences between
Hispanic and non-Hispanic mortality is more pronounced among males (Markides, 1983; Rosenwaike, 1987).

While all three major Hispanic groups in the United States have mortality
advantages in heart disease and cancer, there are significant differences in
rates for other causes by group. The Mexican-born population has much
higher mortality due to accidents than is the case for other Hispanic groups
but substantially lower mortality due to suicide. Death rates among Cubans
due to pneumonia and influenza, cirrhosis of the liver, and diabetes mellitus
are markedly lower than rates among Puerto Rican- and Mexican-born persons. The death rate among Puerto Ricans from cirrhosis of the liver is about
twice that among Mexicans and nearly three times that among Cubans (Rosenwaike, 1987). In general, the Puerto Rican-born have the least favorable
mortality profile. A mortality study of Puerto Ricans in New York City for
1969–1971 indicated that, although this population had low rates for heart
disease and cancer relative to those of other whites, Puerto Rican-born New
Yorkers, particularly males, had excessive rates from several other causes
(e.g., cirrhosis of the liver, homicide) (Rosenwaike, 1983).

Data on the mortality of the Puerto Rican-born population outside of
New York City, which first became available at the 1979–1981 census period,
come at an appropriate time, given that the proportion of the U.S. mainland
Puerto Rican-born population living outside of New York City has been
rising since 1950. Between 1970 and 1980, the proportion of the Puerto
Rican-born population living in New York City fell from 58 to 42 percent.
In 1980 there were 1,002,863 Puerto Rican-born persons on the U.S. main-
land, 418,642 in New York City and 584,221 outside New York City, compared with 3,196,520 persons living in Puerto Rico (U.S. Bureau of the
Census, 1983a, 1983b, 1984b).

The Puerto Rican-born outside of New York City are largely clustered in
urban areas of five states: New Jersey, Illinois, Florida, California, and
Pennsylvania (Fitzpatrick, 1987). Some of these migrants previously lived
in New York City and left due to shortages of housing and jobs. Others have
come directly from the island, and increasing numbers of new Puerto Rican

migrants are settling outside of New York City (Ortiz, 1986). Unfortunately, this dual migration of Puerto Ricans from both Puerto Rico and New York City to areas outside of New York City complicates any simple attempt to separate the effects of environment, assimilation, and population characteristics on mortality. Yet distinctions can be drawn between the Puerto Rican-born population of New York City and those residing elsewhere in the United States. Those residing outside of New York City, in general, have higher family income and higher levels of educational achievement than do the Puerto Rican-born residents of New York City (U.S. Bureau of the Census, 1983c).

The major objective of this study is to examine the extent to which the Hispanic mortality pattern discussed above is found among each of the three Puerto Rican populations. For this purpose, mortality rates for the three groups are compared to those for the U.S. white population. This comparison will enable us to see to what extent the three Puerto Rican populations have assimilated to the mortality pattern of U.S. whites, and how this level of assimilation varies among the three groups. In doing so, we will discuss how genetic, environmental, and socioeconomic variables interact to affect mortality.

The relative importance of these effects would be expected to vary significantly by cause of death. Genetic characteristics may influence susceptibility to heart disease and cancer, but lifestyle-related behaviors such as smoking, diet, and alcohol use are important as well. Death rates from causes such as cirrhosis of the liver and homicide are influenced primarily by nongenetic factors, behaviors stemming from some combination of socioeconomic status, lifestyle, and characteristics of the environment.

These considerations should help to frame our expectations as we consider the relative mortality of the two mainland Puerto Rican-born groups. The move to the mainland may affect behaviors related to mortality as Puerto Rican migrants assume dietary and other practices of the U.S. population. Yet there are reasons to think that this assimilation, and its effect on mortality, may not be the same in New York City and the balance of the United States. Simply residing in New York City may adversely influence mortality from certain causes, as the city has particularly high rates of crime and drug abuse relative to the country as a whole. Furthermore, Puerto Rican migrants inside and outside of New York City differ in levels of income and education. In 1980, among the Puerto Rican-born population 16 years and older, 31.0 percent of those in New York City had completed high school, versus 39.7 percent for those living in the balance of the mainland. Median household income was $8,750 for the New York City group, compared with $12,050 for those in the balance of the United States. Among the Puerto Rican-born population in New York City, 41.0 percent were in households that were below the poverty level, compared with 32.0 percent for those outside of New York City. In New York City, 43.3 percent of all households of the

Puerto Rican-born were female-headed, versus 28.2 percent for those outside of the city. (Data derived from U.S. Bureau of the Census, 1980 PUMS 5 percent A Sample.)

Nevertheless, it is important to note that both Puerto Rican groups have low levels of educational achievement and income compared to the U.S. average. A comparative study of recent and previous migrants from Puerto Rico concluded that recent migrants are not a more select group. Their higher educational level is largely the outcome of increased levels of education in general on the island. Improved education seems to have done little to improve their prospects on the mainland, as income and occupational statistics for recent and previous migrants were quite similar as of 1980 (Ortiz, 1986). That recent migrants are more likely to locate outside of New York City can only partially explain the socioeconomic differences between the Puerto Rican-born populations of New York City and the rest of the nation. Whether these differences are great enough to produce differences in mortality in the two populations should be of considerable interest.

MATERIALS AND METHODS

Death statistics used in this study for the mainland populations were derived from public-use mortality data tapes prepared by the National Center for Health Statistics (NCHS) for the period 1979–1981. Computerized mortality data for residents of Puerto Rico during the same years were made available by the Puerto Rican Health Department. Population data from the 1980 Census provided the denominators for all death rates. Population data on the Puerto Rican-born population in the United States by sex and by five-year age groups were from Summary Tape 5 (U.S. Bureau of the Census, 1983d). Data for residents of Puerto Rico come from published reports (U.S. Bureau of the Census, 1983b).

All age-specific rates were computed by dividing three-year averages of the NCHS death statistics by corresponding 1980 Census data and were expressed per 100,000 population. Causes of death were coded according to the Ninth Revision of the International Classification of Diseases (World Health Organization, 1977). The age-adjusted rates were computed by the direct standardization method using the age distribution of the total U.S. white population five years of age and over in 1980 as the standard. When relevant, standard confidence interval tests of statistical significance were performed to show where ratios of age-specific and age-adjusted death rates of the Puerto Rican groups to those of the standard population differed significantly from 1.0 (Kleinman, 1977).

In Puerto Rico there were 33,321 deaths of males over age five and 23,873 deaths of females over age five for the years 1979–1981. Comparable figures for the Puerto Rican-born population of New York City for the same period were 5,532 male and 3,949 female deaths. For the Puerto Rican-born pop-

Figure 6.1
Mortality Ratios According to Type of Puerto Rican Population and Age, Males,
1979–81

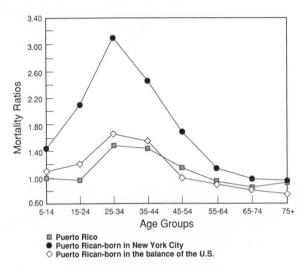

ulation outside of New York City there were 4,566 male deaths and 2,789
female deaths.

RESULTS

Figures 6.1 and 6.2 show the ratios of age-specific mortality rates for the
three Puerto Rican populations to rates for the U.S. white population, among
males and females, for the years 1979–1981. The ratios for males in Figure
6.1 show that the three Puerto Rican male populations have age patterns of
mortality which, relative to that of U.S. white males, are low-to-average at
both ends of the age range and high in the middle. Mortality ratios for all
three Puerto Rican populations peak at ages 25–34 years and then decline
to levels at or below those of the white population. Unlike the island population, the two mainland groups have death rates at ages 5–14 and 15–24
years that are higher than those of the standard population. Mortality is
highest relative to the standard among the Puerto Rican-born population in
New York City, particularly at ages 15–44 years.

The data indicate that this interesting "cross-over" pattern of age-specific
mortality rates is observed only among males. Among females in all three
Puerto Rican populations, the ratios of age-specific rates show no consistent
pattern by age, as seen in Figure 6.2. The relative mortality levels are
generally highest among the females resident in New York City, but they
do not come close to the levels reached by the males. This lack of a pattern
of major differentials among the female populations implies that the pattern

Immigrant Groups

Figure 6.2
Mortality Ratios According to Type of Puerto Rican Population and Age,
Females, 1979–81

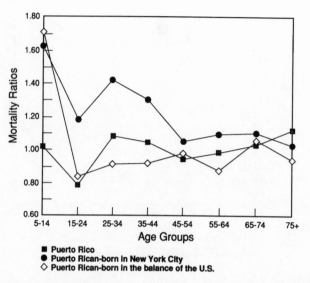

■ Puerto Rico
● Puerto Rican-born in New York City
◇ Puerto Rican-born in the balance of the U.S.

which distinguishes Puerto Rican mortality from that of U.S. whites is largely shaped by the mortality characteristics of males.

Ratios of the age-adjusted death rates for leading causes of death among the three Puerto Rican-born groups, relative to those of the standard population, are shown in Table 6.1. For all causes combined, the New York City group has the highest rate for both sexes, while the residual mainland group has the lowest. For heart disease, the leading cause of death in all populations, the Puerto Rican-born New York City population has an age-adjusted rate significantly higher than that of the standard population, while the other two Puerto Rican groups have rates which are significantly lower. For cancer, the second leading cause of death in all populations, all three Puerto Rican groups have death rates which are significantly lower than those of the standard. For cerebrovascular disease, the New York City group has rates which are lower than the other two populations and most divergent from the standard population. This may be due to diagnostic practices in New York City, where stroke is cited relatively infrequently as a cause of death (Goldberg, Lowenstein, and Habel, 1988).

For pneumonia and influenza, cirrhosis of the liver, and diabetes the mortality rates of the mainland Puerto Rican-born population outside of New York City are closer to those of the standard population than are those of the other two Puerto Rican groups. However, all three Puerto Rican populations have significantly excessive rates for diabetes and cirrhosis. For homicide, all three Puerto Rican populations also have significantly excessive

Table 6.1

Ratios of Age-Adjusted Death Rates for Major Causes of Death: Puerto Rico and Puerto Rican-born Residents of New York City and the Balance of the United States: 1979–81 (Rates per 100,000 population, ages 5 and over, U.S. whites as standard)

| Cause and Sex | Puerto Rican-Born to U.S. Whites | | | Age-Adjusted Death Rates, U.S. Whites |
	Puerto Rico	New York City	Balance of U.S.	
All Causes				
Total	0.99	*1.08	*0.90	885.1
Male	*0.93	*1.13	*0.84	1153.6
Female	*1.04	1.05	0.93	684.2
Heart Disease				
Total	*0.71	*1.08	*0.82	353.3
Male	*0.62	1.00	*0.50	468.1
Female	*0.82	*1.33	0.93	267.0
Malignant Neoplasms				
Total	*0.77	*0.82	*0.74	193.1
Male	*0.77	*0.85	*0.72	248.0
Female	*0.72	*0.82	*0.73	156.0
Cerebrovascular Diseases				
Total	*0.91	*0.64	*0.85	76.7
Male	*0.91	*0.67	0.81	80.1
Female	*0.90	*0.62	0.89	73.9
Accidents				
Total	*0.76	*0.71	0.92	46.8
Male	*0.85	0.83	1.00	70.0
Female	*0.54	*0.56	*0.72	25.2
Chronic Obst. Pulmonary Dis.				
Total	*0.87	0.88	0.88	27.6
Male	*0.59	*0.72	*0.62	46.2
Female	*1.44	1.35	1.46	14.4
Pneumonia and Influenza				
Total	*1.80	*1.79	0.77	23.3
Male	*1.68	*1.92	0.72	30.3
Female	*1.79	*1.73	0.79	18.9
Suicide				
Total	*0.84	0.89	0.99	13.7
Male	0.95	1.06	1.14	21.7
Female	*0.51	0.71	*0.46	6.5
Cirrhosis of the Liver				
Total	*2.67	*3.95	*1.85	13.2
Male	*3.07	*5.13	*2.11	18.9
Female	0.80	1.08	0.60	18.4
Homicide				
Total	*2.60	*7.80	*4.30	7.0
Male	*3.12	*10.48	*4.86	10.9
Female	1.23	*3.03	*2.48	3.1
All Other				
Total	*1.73	0.97	1.02	116.2
Male	*1.60	1.07	0.93	144.0
Female	*1.82	0.88	1.07	96.2

*Ratio is significantly different from 1.00 at the .01 level.

Table 6.2
Ratios of Age-Adjusted Death Rates, Selected Cancer Sites: Puerto Rico and
Puerto Rican-born Residents of New York City and the Balance of the United
States: 1979-81 (Rates per 100,000 population, ages 5 and over, U.S. whites as
standard)

| Cause and Sex | Puerto Rican-Born to U.S. Whites | | | Age-Adjusted Death Rates, U.S. Whites |
	Puerto Rico	New York City	Balance of U.S.	
All Sites				
Total	*0.77	*0.82	*0.74	193.1
Male	*0.77	*0.85	*0.72	248.0
Female	*0.72	*0.82	*0.73	156.0
Lung				
Total	*0.32	*0.41	*0.51	48.3
Male	*0.27	*0.40	*0.52	81.8
Female	*0.38	*0.47	*0.45	23.8
Colon				
Total	*0.35	0.76	*0.41	20.9
Male	*0.31	0.77	*0.36	24.4
Female	*0.39	0.78	*0.45	18.5
Pancreas				
Total	*0.59	0.79	0.83	9.9
Male	*0.57	1.02	0.88	12.3
Female	*0.59	0.66	0.77	8.2
Stomach				
Total	*2.35	*2.00	*1.95	6.3
Male	*2.35	*1.96	1.90	9.1
Female	*2.02	*2.18	*1.86	4.4
Esophagus				
Total	*3.45	*2.35	2.16	3.1
Male	*2.35	*2.47	1.92	5.3
Female	*2.02	2.47	2.60	1.5
Liver				
Total	*2.36	1.56	1.00	2.5
Male	*2.09	1.91	1.21	3.4
Female	*2.72	1.39	0.61	1.8
Breast				
Female	*0.39	*0.47	*0.56	30.4
Cervix uteri				
Female	0.92	*2.31	1.89	3.6
Prostate				
Male	0.97	0.72	0.73	25.9

*Ratio is significantly different from 1.00 at the .01 level.

rates, but the trend differs in that the island population's death rates are
closer to those of the standard than are those of the two mainland populations.

The homicide rate for the New York City Puerto Rican-born male population is ten times higher than the rate for U.S. white males. Among the
three Puerto Rican populations, the death rate due to accidents for the
mainland group residing outside of New York City is the highest (and closest
to that of the standard).

Table 6.2 breaks out the ratios of the age-adjusted death rates for the
three Puerto Rican groups to those of the standard population for the principal cancer sites. For some major sites (lung, esophagus, stomach, liver,
pancreas, female breast) the Puerto Rican-born group residing outside of
New York City has age-adjusted death rates which are closest to the standard
population and furthest from the island population. The New York City

population has intermediate rates. All three Puerto Rican-born populations have mortality rates for certain sites which are significantly higher (stomach) or lower (lung and female breast) than those of the standard population. For other sites, such as liver and pancreas, rates for the mainland populations do not significantly differ from the standard, while those of the island population do.

With regard to the Puerto Rican-born population of New York City, it is desirable to consider mortality data for the city's non-Puerto Rican-born white population, since the mortality distribution by cause differs in several important ways from that of the total U.S. white population. Table 6.3 shows ratios of age-adjusted death rates. The ratios of the age-adjusted death rates of the New York City Puerto Rican-born population to rates for U.S. whites are shown in the first column. The ratios of the age-adjusted death rates of the New York City Puerto Rican-born population to those of New York City whites (exclusive of the Puerto Rican-born) are shown in the second column. (The standard used to adjust the age-specific rates is the age distribution of the total U.S. white population.)

The data in Table 6.3 are useful in examining the mortality of the New York City Puerto Rican-born population in the context of that city's mortality profile. For example, the rates for heart disease and cerebrovascular diseases show that, relative to the national standard, the Puerto Rican-born New York City male and female populations have average or high rates for heart disease and low rates for stroke. On the other hand, when these rates are compared to the New York City standard, Puerto Rican-born males and females have average or above-average rates of stroke and average or below-average rates of heart disease. This implies that in New York City, mortality rates are lower for stroke and higher for heart disease relative to the standard population. This may well be an artifactual difference due to diagnostic practices in New York City rather than a reflection of true differences in rates of incidence. One recent study looking at death rates for leading causes in New York City characterized the low cerebrovascular disease rate as "unexpected" (Goldberg, Lowenstein, and Habel, 1988). (When stroke and heart disease are aggregated, the age-adjusted mortality rates of New York City non-Puerto Rican-born whites are close to those of the total U.S. white population: 1.12 for males and 1.09 for females.) We conclude that the Puerto Rican-born New York City population has mortality rates which are upwardly biased for heart disease and downwardly biased for stroke.

As shown in Table 6.3, the mainland population in New York City has low mortality rates for accidents relative to the U.S. standard population. Presumably, this largely reflects lower rates of motor vehicle accidents in New York City, where convenient public transportation is available (Shai and Rosenwaike, 1988). However, relative to the standard New York City population, the Puerto Rican-born have accident rates that are significantly

Table 6.3

Ratios of Age-Adjusted Death Rates from Selected Causes: Puerto Rican-born Residents of New York City with Two Different Standard Populations: 1979–81 (Rates per 100,000 population, ages 5 and over)

	Ratio of Rate for Puerto Rican–Born Residents of New York City to Rate for:	
Cause and Sex	U.S. Whites	New York City Whites
Males		
Total	*1.13	*1.11
Heart Disease	1.00	*0.83
Malignant Neoplasms	*0.85	*0.85
Cerebrovascular Diseases	*0.67	1.12
Accidents	0.83	*1.54
Pneumonia and Influenza	*1.92	1.29
Cirrhosis of Liver	*5.13	*3.06
Suicide	1.06	1.47
Homicide	*10.48	*4.39
Alcohol Dependence	*5.54	*4.16
Drug Dependence	*42.67	*2.21
Motor Vehicle Accidents	*0.61	1.32
Females		
Total	1.05	1.00
Heart Disease	*1.33	1.03
Malignant Neoplasms	*0.82	*0.74
Cerebrovascular Diseases	*0.62	1.01
Accidents	*0.56	0.95
Pneumonia and Influenza	*1.73	1.26
Cirrhosis of Liver	1.08	*1.90
Suicide	0.71	0.73
Homicide	*3.03	*1.96
Alcohol Dependence	1.83	1.38
Drug Dependence	*24.00	2.40
Motor Vehicle Accidents	*0.46	1.00

*Ratio is significantly different from 1.00 at the .01 level.

high for males and close to average for females. Puerto Rican-born males in New York City have excess mortality for motor vehicle accidents relative to the standard New York City population.

Clearly, a different perspective is gained on the mortality of the Puerto Rican-born in New York City when the mortality profile of the New York City population is considered. The mortality rates of Puerto Rican-born New Yorkers for such causes as pneumonia and influenza, cirrhosis, and homicide seem somewhat less excessive given the New York City mortality profile, although they are markedly higher than the levels for non-Puerto Rican whites. On the other hand, a large proportion of the Puerto Rican-born population outside of New York City lives in major cities such as Chicago and Philadelphia. Since the mortality profiles of such cities may not differ markedly from that of New York City, undue emphasis should not be placed on the uniqueness of the New York City environment when comparing the mortality experiences of the three Puerto Rican-born populations.

DISCUSSION

Comparability of Numerators and Denominators

In examining death rates using census data and numerators from NCHS a few points need to be kept in mind. Death statistics represent complete counts, whereas census data on place of birth are based on a sample of the population. Further, census counts may be incomplete. A recent study estimated that the net undercount of Puerto Ricans at the 1980 Census was approximately 6.5 percent, similar to the estimate for the U.S. black population. However, the study design did not permit separate estimates of coverage of the Puerto Rican-born population living on the island and on the U.S. mainland (Robinson, 1987). Due to this census undercount (as well as to a failure to include as Puerto Rican-born some Puerto Rican residents on the mainland who did not specify a place of birth), it is likely that death rates for Puerto Rican-born persons, particularly those residing on the mainland, are somewhat overstated relative to rates for non-Puerto Rican whites. However, when examining major differentials in rates, such as the excessive rates for homicide and cirrhosis, underenumeration is not really consequential.

Although death rates are not affected, it should be noted that the population of Puerto Rico does not consist solely of the Puerto Rican-born. At the time of the 1980 Census, approximately 8 percent of the population of the island were born elsewhere. Most of these were persons of Puerto Rican parentage born on the mainland United States In addition, a small component of the Puerto Rican population comes from Cuba, the Dominican Republic, Spain, and elsewhere (U.S. Bureau of the Census, 1984c).

Prevalence of the "Hispanic Mortality Pattern": Heart Disease and Cancer

This study of mortality among three Puerto Rican populations yields conclusions that agree closely with the results of previous studies of Hispanic mortality in general and Puerto Rican mortality in particular. Among the chronic diseases, the most notable characteristic of the "Hispanic mortality pattern" is a relative advantage in mortality from two major causes: heart disease and cancer (Rosenwaike, 1983, 1987). All three Puerto Rican-born populations had age-adjusted mortality rates from heart disease and cancer that were significantly lower than those of the standard population.

The single exception was heart disease in the Puerto Rican-born New York City population. However, this could be an artifact of reporting; the group had relatively low rates from heart disease when compared to the New York City standard.

Relatively low mortality from heart disease and cancer have been found in studies of Puerto Ricans in Puerto Rico. Garcia-Palmieri et al. (1965) checked death certificate listings of cause of death and concluded that, even after adjustments, rates of death from coronary heart disease were significantly lower in Puerto Rico than in the United States. Gordon et al. (1974) found the incidence of coronary heart disease among males in San Juan to be approximately half the level observed in the Framingham (Massachusetts) study. Regarding cancer, Martinez, Torres, and Frias (1975) compared incidence rates in Puerto Rico and the U.S. standard population, 1969–1971, and found that age-adjusted rates for all sites combined were one-third lower for males and females in Puerto Rico than for the U.S. population.

A number of earlier studies have shown that Puerto Rican-born residents of the mainland United States retain this mortality advantage from chronic diseases. Rosenwaike (1983), in a study of mortality among Puerto Rican-born residents of New York City in the years 1969–1971, found that the Puerto Rican-born had significantly lower rates of death from heart disease and cancer when compared to the New York City standard population. Although the present study finds that Puerto Rican-born residents of New York City have lower rates from these causes with respect to the New York City standard, their advantage may be diminishing. Ratios of age-specific mortality rates for heart disease and cancer among males and females are higher than those found for 1969–1971. This suggests that the gap between Puerto Ricans and non-Puerto Ricans is narrowing.

Regarding specific cancer sites, the conclusions of this study support much of the earlier research on Puerto Rican cancer mortality. Similar to previously reported New York City studies by Seidman (1970) and Rosenwaike (1984), all three Puerto Rican-born groups had low mortality rates for lung cancer relative to the standard population. Their rates were also low for cancers of the prostate, colon, and female breast. Mortality rates from cancers of the esophagus, stomach, cervix uteri, and liver were relatively high. It is important to note that differences were not statistically significant in all of these sites for all populations. The pattern of site-specific cancer mortality observed in Puerto Ricans has also been observed in other Hispanic populations, namely Mexican immigrants in Los Angeles County and Spanish populations in New Mexico (Thomas, 1979).

Behavioral Factors

With regard to cancers related to tobacco use, most notably lung cancer, lower prevalence of cigarette smoking among Hispanics has been thought to be an explanatory factor. Evidence that heavy smoking is relatively uncommon among Puerto Ricans came from a comparative study of males in San Juan and Framingham, which found that Puerto Ricans were less likely to be smokers and smoked fewer cigarettes per day than did Framingham residents (Gordon et al., 1974). However, the recently completed Hispanic

Health and Nutrition Survey (HHANES) found smoking levels among the approximately 3,000 Puerto Rican-origin residents of the New York regional area who were surveyed to be quite high. Over two-fifths of males and females at ages 20–44 years, and over three-tenths of those at ages 45–74 years reported that they were current smokers. Of these, over half of the males and more than a third of the females said they smoked a pack or more a day, with the number of cigarettes smoked per day showing little variation by age (National Center for Health Statistics, 1988). If this pattern persists, mortality rates from tobacco-related cancers may well rise for Puerto Rican populations in the United States.

The incidence of stomach cancer has often been linked to dietary practices. Some find support for this in the generally negative trend in rates over the past few decades, a decline which is attributed to changes in diet composition and food handling and storage practices (Devesa and Silverman, 1978; Graham and Mettlin, 1979; Weisburger, 1979). Differential rates of colorectal cancer have also been linked to diet. It is believed that characteristics of the Hispanic diet influence the high rates of stomach cancer and low rates of colorectal cancer which have been observed among Puerto Rican and other Hispanic populations.

Alcohol consumption has been implicated as a risk factor for esophageal cancer (Martinez, 1969). One study of alcohol consumption in Puerto Rico concluded that the island probably has the highest per capita consumption of hard liquor in the world (Fernandez, 1975). High levels of alcohol consumption among Puerto Ricans on the mainland are suggested by excessive mortality rates from cirrhosis.

SOCIAL PATHOLOGIES

Another important feature of the Hispanic mortality pattern is excessive rates of death resulting from behavior associated with "social pathologies." This term has been used to categorize deaths from drug and alcohol-related and violent causes (suicide, homicide, and accidents) (Rogers and Hackenberg, 1987). This tendency is particularly pronounced among males. All three Puerto Rican-born populations generally had excessive rates for cirrhosis of the liver and homicide.

Rates of death from "drug dependence" were very high for the Puerto Rican-born population resident in New York City. As seen in Table 6.3, the rate for Puerto Rican-born males in New York City was more than forty-two times as high as the U.S. white male level, but only about twice as high as that of New York City non-Puerto Rican white males. "Drug dependence," it should be noted, is not commonly assigned as a cause of death, even when death is related to drug abuse. Although Puerto Ricans in New York consider drug abuse to be the most important health problem faced by the community (Alers, 1978), the total number of deaths in 1979–1981 of Puerto Rican-born persons resident in New York City classified as drug dependence (ICD Code 304) was only 106, of which 84 were males. The death rates due to drug dependence shown in Table 6.3 are based on data categorized to ICD Code 304. Samkoff and Baker (1982) have pointed out that since the 1970s drug deaths that formerly were coded as unintentional ("accidental") or undetermined intent (E850–859) have been coded as due to drug dependence (304) if drug dependence is mentioned on the death certificate. Compared with other areas, drug deaths in New York City are much more likely to be classified as due to drug dependence than to alternative codes, in part because of the heightened awareness of drug dependency and its physical symptoms by the medical establishment.

Clearly, rates of death from drug abuse in general are far higher in New York City than in the rest of the United States. Although New York City is a major center of drug trafficking and use, this differential is believed to be due in part to the heightened awareness noted above. The high incidence of deaths from drug and alcohol-related causes accounts for a considerable amount of the excessive Puerto Rican mortality in early and middle adulthood in New York City, particularly among males.

Socioeconomic Characteristics and Assimilation

The different socioeconomic characteristics of the two mainland Puerto Rican-born populations discussed earlier may help explain the lower mortality rates of the mainland group outside of New York City from causes of death associated with substance abuse and/or violence. These causes include pneumonia and influenza, cirrhosis, and homicide. Yet this socioeconomic explanation does not work consistently. Mortality rates for lung cancer, for example, which in the general U.S. population vary inversely with social class, suggest that the Puerto Rican-born population outside of New York City has adopted the smoking practices of the U.S. white population to a greater extent than has the Puerto Rican-born group in New York City.

Assimilation is affected, in part, by the length of time spent in the host country. As mentioned above, the Puerto Rican-born population outside of New York City has been on the mainland a shorter time on average than has that in New York City. In 1980, only 30 percent of migrants who had come to the mainland between 1975 and 1980 lived in New York City compared with 65 percent of those who migrated between 1955 and 1960 (Ortiz, 1986). Thus, from the standpoint of length of time spent on the mainland alone, the Puerto Rican-born population outside of New York City should be relatively less assimilated than those residing in New York City. Although it is important to know more about the length of migrants' residence in the host country from the standpoint of both migration and public health research, such data are not available on death record tapes. Further, the decennial census does not query year of migration to the mainland of migrants from Puerto Rico (although the census includes a question on residence five years prior to the enumeration date).

The effects of acculturation and socioeconomic status are difficult to separate. For instance, the composition of the Puerto Rican diet is probably somewhat influenced by economic hardship, since income levels on the island of Puerto Rico are relatively low. Puerto Rican-born residents on the mainland, therefore, may change their diet because they have assimilated to the dietary practices of the host country and/or because increased income allows them to substitute new foods which reduce their risk of stomach cancer, yet increase their risk of colorectal cancer.

While it is difficult to separate the effects of assimilation and socioeconomic status on mortality, both factors have important effects on the relative mortality experience of a migrant group. In the present case, the Puerto Rican-born population outside of New York City has a mortality pattern which, of the three Puerto Rican-born groups studied here, is the closest to the U.S. white standard. It is known that the socioeconomic status of this group is somewhat higher than that of the New York City group, but its average length of residence on the mainland is shorter. Although the full consideration of socioeconomic and environmental variables is beyond the scope of this article, the results of this study suggest that both are important in explaining the different mortality profiles of these two Puerto Rican-born mainland populations.

CHAPTER 7

Mortality Patterns of Cubans in the United States

SERGIO DIAZ-BRIQUETS

THE CUBAN PRESENCE IN THE UNITED STATES

The Cuban presence in American society dates back well over a century. According to the 1870 U.S. Census, there were 5,300 persons of Cuban birth residing in the United States. By the turn of the century, the Cuban-born population had risen to 11,100, due in part to political problems in Cuba. Between 1900 and 1940, the Cuban-born population grew at a relatively slow pace and only 18,000 Cuban-born persons were enumerated in the 1940 U.S. Census. After 1940, a surge of Cuban immigration led to increased growth of this population. The 1950 U.S. Census showed almost 40,000 Cuban-born persons. By 1960, a year after Fidel Castro took power in Cuba, there were 124,500 persons of Cuban origin (79,200 foreign-born and 45,300 U.S.-born Cubans) (Boswell and Curtis, 1984).

Between 1960 and 1980 the growth of the Cuban-origin population has been phenomenal. At the 1970 Census, there were approximately 561,000 Cuban-Americans, an increase of 350 percent between 1960 and 1970. By 1980 the Cuban-origin population had increased to 803,000, excluding the more than 125,000 Mariel immigrants who arrived after the April 1 decennial census had been completed. For this reason, the following description of demographic and socioeconomic characteristics of the Cuban-American population in 1980 excludes the Mariel arrivals. While this is the only practical approach, it is not the ideal, since the Mariel immigrants differed significantly in several important characteristics from earlier waves of Cuban immigrants and their descendants in the United States.

Before this Cuban-American population is described, it is useful to review
the socioeconomic and demographic characteristics of the various waves of
Cuban immigration to the United States. The following brief summary is
culled from various sources (Bach, Bach, and Triplett, 1982; Boswell and
Curtis, 1984; Diaz-Briquets and Perez, 1981; Fagen, Brody, and O'Leary,
1968; Pedraza-Bailey, 1985; Portes, Clark, and Bach, 1977).

In what was largely a politically motivated emigration following the 1959
Cuban revolution, the first Cuban arrivals were mostly those from the upper
and middle classes whose material interest and political beliefs had been
threatened by the radical measures instituted by the Castro government.
Not all of these early post-revolutionary emigrants were exclusively or overwhelmingly drawn from the upper socioeconomic strata. According to survey
data (Fagen, Brody, and O'Leary, 1968), all social classes of Cuba were
represented but in declining proportions as one moved down the social strata.
By the 1970s, and during the peak years of the "Freedom Flights," the
original class selectivity of Cuban emigration had begun to weaken (Portes,
Clark, and Bach, 1977).

As the revolution continued, the impact of its radical measures began to
be felt more deeply within the fabric of Cuban society. The increasing
regimentation of social life and the almost total control of the national economy by the state helped drive out of Cuba increasing numbers of small
merchants, professionals, and skilled workers. During this period, family
networks were significant in the selection of the emigrants-to-be, since admission to the United States under the bilateral agreement was contingent
upon the principle of family reunification. While the selectivity of migration
diminished markedly, most emigrants were of socioeconomic status higher
than the national norm.

The cancellation of the organized emigration program of the 1960s and
1970s led to a period of relatively limited emigration. Most emigration was
by way of third countries, and family members already in the United States
continued to play an important role. As a result, the few Cubans arriving
in the latter part of the 1970s did not differ greatly from previous migrants.
This was to change with the 1980 Mariel sea lift.

Although it was first assumed that the vast majority of the Mariel migrants
came from the lowest social classes, careful analysis showed that this blanket
characterization was inaccurate. According to Bach, Bach, and Triplett
(1982), although migration selectivity had continued to decline, the new
arrivals did not differ greatly in some respects from those who had imme-
diately preceded them. They were, however, considerably different from
the earliest refugees. The Mariel arrivals were, moreover, far more characteristic of the Cuban population as a whole. There were far greater numbers
of blacks and mulattoes, and a wider cross section of Cuban localities was
represented. Most of the workers among the arrivals had been employed in
"urban manufacturing, construction, and service sectors, where they worked

in craft, laborer, and operative jobs." The authors concluded that "their economic origins are modest relative to the Cuban exiles of the 1960s, yet similar to the group arriving at the end of the aerial bridge, 1973–74" (pp. 46-47).

The above description suggests two important considerations for the purposes of this study. The most crucial one is that the earlier Cuban emigrants, originally from the upper and middle classes, likely had been drawn from the better-health and lower-mortality strata of the total Cuban population. This is a population that by developing country standards had reached a fairly advanced mortality profile by the 1950s. The second observation is that, concurrent with the decline in migrant selectivity, Cuban health and mortality standards continued to improve in the 1960s and 1970s. These factors suggest that the Mariel arrivals too had originated from a population with relatively high health standards and easy access to health services (see chapter 4 on Cuban mortality). As a result, if the mortality characteristics of Cuban-Americans are consistent with those of the Cuban population, the former should exhibit a comparable low mortality profile.

In summary, between 1960 and 1980, the Cuban-origin population of the United States increased by 678,500 people or 545 percent. At the time of the 1980 Census, Cuban-Americans represented 5.5 percent of the total Hispanic population of the United States. Of this total, about 75 percent were Cuban-born. Table 7.1 shows the distribution of the Cuban-born population at the 1980 Census by period of immigration. In the following discussion, "Cuban-born and U.S.-born" are used to describe the Cuban-origin population in the United States who were born in Cuba or the United States, respectively. The terms "Cuban-American" or "Cuban-origin population" consist of both Cuban-born and U.S.-born persons of Cuban parentage living in the United States.

AGE-SEX POPULATION STRUCTURE AND MEDIAN AGE

Due largely to heavy migration, the 1980 Cuban-origin population is characterized by an unusually high median age. Between 1960 and 1980 the median age of this population rose from 29.3 to 36.5 years. The median age increased from 32.6 to 43.1 years for the Cuban-born and declined from 16.0 to 11.4 years for the U.S.-born (Bean and Tienda, 1987). In contrast, the median age for the total 1980 population of the United States was 30.0 years (U.S. Bureau of the Census, 1983e). The effects of immigration on the Cuban-origin population are quite visible in the age-sex pyramid which, shows a severe indentation between age groups 25–29 years and 40–44 years, particularly for males (Bean and Tienda, 1987). This phenomenon is due in part to emigration restrictions which Cuban authorities imposed on the young, especially young males of military age, during the 1960s and 1970s, and in part to the large number of middle-age and elderly who emigrated

114   Immigrant Groups

Table 7.1

Sex and Age of Foreign-born Persons Born in Cuba, by Year of Immigration, United States: 1980 (Percent distribution)

		Year of Immigration				
Sex and Age	Total	1975 to 1980	1970 to 1974	1965 to 1969	1960 to 1964	1959 or earlier
Total	607,814	38,581	124,643	195,422	171,409	77,759
Male	284,800	19,171	57,179	87,478	83,339	37,633
Total	100.0	100.0	100.0	100.0	100.0	100.0
Under 15	4.5	19.5	9.9	4.0	–	–
15–24	19.3	14.7	26.7	26.9	14.6	3.2
25–44	29.7	34.3	21.1	22.7	42.1	28.7
45–64	34.7	20.5	30.7	34.8	33.1	51.6
65 and over	11.8	11.0	11.6	11.6	10.2	16.5
Median age	42.3	33.4	43.0	42.2	40.1	50.6
Female	323,014	19,410	67,464	107,944	88,070	40,126
Total	100.0	100.0	100.0	100.0	100.0	100.0
Under 15	3.7	19.0	7.5	3.1	–	–
15–24	16.2	13.6	21.3	21.0	13.2	2.6
25–44	31.1	25.6	29.9	30.5	36.4	26.0
45–64	33.3	23.5	26.1	30.2	36.3	51.8
65 and over	15.7	18.2	15.2	15.3	14.1	19.6
Median age	43.5	37.4	39.9	41.5	44.0	51.5

Source: U.S. Bureau of the Census, 1984f, Cuban-Born Immigrants in the U.S., Table 1, unpublished data.

during the first few years of the revolution (Diaz-Briquets and Perez, 1981). Another characteristic of the age-sex pyramid of the Cuban-origin population, highly atypical for a U.S. Hispanic population, is its very narrow base due to low fertility.

GEOGRAPHICAL DISTRIBUTION

Among all Hispanic groups, Cuban-Americans are the most geographically concentrated. In 1980, almost 60 percent of all Cuban-origin persons resided in one state: Florida. The New York-New Jersey metropolitan area accounted for an additional 19.6 percent: 10.1 percent in New Jersey and 9.5 percent in New York. California was a distant third with 7.6 percent, followed by Illinois (2.4 percent) and Texas (1.8 percent). Unlike other Hispanic groups, Cuban-Americans increased their geographical concentration between 1970 and 1980. Whereas in 1970 less than half (46 percent) of all Cuban-Americans lived in Florida, by 1980 this percentage, as indicated above, had risen to almost 60 percent. U.S.-born Cubans, however are not as concentrated in Florida as are the Cuban-born (Bean and Tienda, 1987).

Cuban-origin persons are overwhelmingly urban. Since 1960, only one of every twenty Cuban-born persons has resided in a nonmetropolitan area (Bean and Tienda, 1987). Better than one out of every two Cuban-born persons lives in the Miami (Dade County) metropolitan area despite considerable efforts by the federal authorities in the 1960s and 1970s to resettle refugees into other areas of the country (Boswell and Curtis, 1984). The percentage of Cuban-origin persons in central cities (39.5 percent) is considerably lower than that for all the Spanish-origin population combined (48.2 percent), but much higher than for the population of non-Hispanic origin (25.3 percent). These figures indicate that a very significant percentage of the Cuban-origin population resides in suburbs (57.2 percent), compared with the total Hispanic population (35.2 percent) and the total non-Hispanic population (40.6 percent) (Boswell and Curtis, 1984). This geographic distribution pattern is influenced by the extremely low percentage of Cuban-origin persons living in nonmetropolitan areas.

FERTILITY

Cuban-Americans are one of the ethnic groups in the United States with relatively low fertility. Estimates of the mean number of children ever-born, based on 1980 census data, indicate that fertility levels for ever-married Cuban American women, at all ages between 15 and 44, were not only significantly lower than those for all Spanish-origin women, but also lower than those of all U.S. women. Further, the Cuban-American rates are even more modest than those calculated for the non-Hispanic white population (Bean and Tienda, 1987). For example, ever-married Cuban-American women aged 35–44 had an average of 2.13 children compared with 2.60 for non-Hispanic women in the some age group. The low fertility of Cuban-origin women is consistent with the early trend of fertility decline in Cuba itself (Diaz-Briquets and Perez, 1982); with the social class origins and aspirations of an important segment of the Cuban emigrant population; and with the socioeconomic adjustments made by an upwardly mobile refugee population (Bean and Tienda, 1987; Diaz-Briquets and Perez, 1981; Perez, 1986). The educational and occupational characteristics of the Cuban-American population bear out these hypotheses.

EDUCATIONAL CHARACTERISTICS

According to the 1980 census, the Cuban-American population, aged 25 years and over, had 11.7 median years of schooling, slightly below the 12.0 years of the non-Hispanic white population (Bean and Tienda, 1987). In terms of educational attainment, the Cuban-origin population compares favorably with other Hispanic populations, as well as with blacks and non-Hispanic whites. As Table 7.2 shows, in 1980, a greater percentage of Cuban-

Table 7.2

Percentage of Cuban-born Males and Females Who Are High School and
College Graduates, by Year of Immigration, United States: 1980

Sex and Age	Total	Year of Immigration				
		1975 to 1980	1970 to 1974	1965 to 1969	1960 to 1964	1959 or earlier
High School Graduates						
Male						
25-34	80.3	55.5	64.8	71.0	88.7	87.9
35-44	63.6	49.7	49.3	55.1	78.3	70.4
45-54	51.6	41.1	35.7	46.8	67.7	56.3
55-64	39.7	39.4	32.1	39.4	68.3	50.8
65+	41.5	27.3	29.0	35.5	59.6	44.9
Female						
25-34	78.0	54.0	65.6	73.2	89.3	84.3
35-44	60.4	45.0	45.3	55.6	78.2	68.9
45-54	52.6	44.0	39.7	45.8	66.3	57.0
55-64	43.6	28.5	29.8	37.9	57.5	43.7
65+	31.4	21.7	25.0	25.8	43.7	36.4
College Graduates						
Male						
25-34	26.8	14.5	14.0	15.1	36.3	24.1
35-44	20.3	14.3	12.2	15.1	29.8	21.1
45-54	16.9	14.0	11.5	12.9	28.1	14.2
55-64	14.6	13.7	10.5	12.7	31.0	13.6
65+	16.5	9.9	9.9	13.7	28.1	14.3
Female						
25-34	17.6	11.4	8.7	11.5	26.8	19.8
35-44	13.4	10.0	10.3	11.7	19.5	11.7
45-54	14.7	11.4	11.2	13.3	21.0	11.3
55-64	12.7	8.9	9.9	10.9	18.8	8.7
65+	7.5	5.5	5.0	6.1	12.6	6.5

Source: U.S. Bureau of the Census, 1984f, Cuban-Born Immigrants in the U.S., Table 10,
unpublished data.

Americans were high school and college graduates than was the case for
Mexican-Americans, Puerto Ricans, or blacks. Likewise, Cuban-Americans
do comparatively well in school enrollment rates and have one of the lowest
drop-out rates reported by Bean and Tienda (1987) in their demographic
study of Hispanics. By these criteria, the Cuban-American population is well
educated and their educational attainment closely approximates that of the
non-Hispanic white population. This is particularly true with respect to the
U.S.-born Cuban-Americans. Table 7.2 shows the level of education of Cuban-born persons by period of immigration, age, and sex. In general, educational attainment among migrants in the 1970s was less than that of earlier
cohorts.

EMPLOYMENT/INDUSTRY/OCCUPATIONAL PATTERNS

Cuban-American labor force participation rates, for both men and women,
are among the highest for all major ethnic groups in the United States.

Table 7.3

Levels of Educational Attainment of Adults 25 Years of Age and Over, Selected Hispanic and Non-Hispanic Groups, United States: 1980

Educational Level and Sex	Hispanic-origin groups			Non-Hispanic groups	
	Mexican	Puerto Rican	Cuban	White	Black
Percent High School Graduates					
Male	38.9	41.3	57.7	70.3	50.8
Female	36.0	39.1	53.3	68.9	51.6
Percent College Graduates					
Male	6.1	6.5	19.7	21.7	8.4
Female	3.7	4.8	13.2	13.6	8.3

Source: U.S. Bureau of the Census, 1984c.

Table 7.4

Labor Force Participation Rates, Persons Age 16 and Over, Selected Hispanic and Non-Hispanic Groups, United States: 1980 (In percent)

Sex	Hispanic-origin groups			Non-Hispanic groups	
	Mexican	Puerto Rican	Cuban	White	Black
Male	79.7	71.4	78.0	76.0	66.7
Female	49.0	40.1	55.4	49.4	53.3

Source: U.S. Bureau of the Census, 1984c.

Cuban women, in particular, have labor force participation rates that are higher than those of other Hispanic women, as well as non-Hispanic white and black women as shown in Table 7.4. According to the 1980 Census, Cuban-American workers of both sexes not only have high labor force participation rates, but also low unemployment rates, with the lowest rates found among Cuban-born workers (Bean and Tienda, 1987).

The extraordinarily high Cuban female labor force participation rates are closely associated with low fertility rates. Their participation has a dramatic impact on the average household income. As Perez (1986) has shown, Cuban-American females are not only more likely to be employed but they are also more likely to be employed full time than are other women in the labor force. Data indicate that more married Cuban-American women with husband present and more Cuban-American women with children under the age of six are employed than other Hispanic women or all women in the U.S. population with similar family traits.

Consistent with their relatively high educational attainment and urban/ rural distribution, Cuban-American men and women are generally found in industries in which white-collar workers predominate. One notable feature of the occupational distribution of the Cuban-origin labor force is the low percentages in agriculture and mining, a result of the overwhelming urban concentration of the Cuban population. Cuban-American workers, however, tend to be disproportionately represented in the service sector, possibly a reflection of their geographical concentration in ethnic enclaves in Miami and certain regions of New Jersey where retail services and employment in Cuban-owned enterprises predominate (Wilson and Portes, 1980).

In terms of occupational distribution, Cuban-Americans occupy a privileged position when compared with Mexican-Americans and mainland Puerto Ricans. According to the classification scheme used by Tienda (Bean and Tienda, 1987), 44.9 percent of Cuban-origin males and 57.5 percent of females worked in white-collar occupations. The comparable statistics for Mexican-Americans were 21.0 and 45.0 percent, respectively, and for mainland Puerto Ricans 28.7 and 53.1 percent, in that same order. An assessment of the occupational distribution of Cuban-American workers is presented in Table 7.5. These data show the 1980 occupational distribution of Cuban workers based on census classifications. Particularly remarkable is the percentage of Cuban-origin males in upper white-collar occupations (managerial and professional): it is twice as high as those for the other two Hispanic origin groups. Cuban-origin women, in turn, do considerably better than Mexican-American women, but only slightly better than Puerto Rican women. As expected, the percent of Cuban workers in farm occupations is extremely low. Cuban females are underrepresented in the service sector, although men are not. An interesting feature of the table is that the percentage of Cuban males in managerial and professional categories is nearly identical to that among non-Hispanic whites. Among Cuban men the percentages are higher in the sales and service occupations, but significantly lower in the skilled crafts. Although the percentage of Cuban-origin females classified in labor and transportation far exceeds that of non-Hispanic whites or blacks, the reverse is true for service occupations.

INCOME

Income levels among Cuban-origin persons are relatively high in comparison to those of other Hispanic groups. Such an outcome is not unexpected due to the Cuban-Americans' high levels of educational and occupational attainment. In 1980, the median income of Cuban-American families was just 12 percent below that of non-Hispanic white families (Table 7.6). The median income for Cuban-origin families was 24 percent higher than the median for Mexican families, and well above the median incomes of Puerto

Table 7.5
Occupational Distribution of Employed Persons Age 16 and Over, Selected Hispanic and Non-Hispanic Groups, United States: 1980 (Percent Distribution)

Occupational Categories	Hispanic-origin groups			Non-Hispanic groups	
	Mexican	Puerto Rican	Cuban	White	Black
Males					
Total Labor Force (number)	1,985,318	365,241	227,535	46,916,660	4,608,195
Total	100.0	100.0	100.0	100.0	100.0
Managerial and Professional	9.0	11.4	22.3	25.4	11.7
Sales and Administrative	12.2	18.6	23.1	19.6	15.2
Service Occupations	12.2	17.4	12.4	8.1	16.9
Farming, Forestry and Fishing	9.2	2.2	1.4	4.2	3.4
Production, Craft and Repair	21.9	16.1	18.7	21.4	15.5
Labor and Transportation	35.4	34.3	22.1	21.3	37.3
Females					
Total Labor Force (number)	1,189,458	235,025	180,987	33,875,824	4,598,792
Total	100.0	100.0	100.0	100.0	100.0
Managerial and Professional	10.8	13.4	15.7	22.7	16.6
Sales and Administrative	37.5	42.0	42.8	47.6	35.2
Service Occupations	22.8	15.2	12.4	16.1	29.2
Farming, Forestry and Fishing	2.9	0.4	0.3	1.0	0.5
Production, Craft and Repair	4.0	3.5	4.4	2.2	2.3
Labor and Transportation	22.0	25.5	24.4	10.4	16.1

Source: U.S. Bureau of the Census, 1984c.

Table 7.6

Median Family Income, Income Distribution, and Poverty Rates for Families and Individuals, Selected Hispanic and Non-Hispanic Groups, United States: 1980

Educational Level and Sex	Hispanic-origin groups			Non-Hispanic groups	
	Mexican	Puerto Rican	Cuban	White	Black
Median family income	$14,765	$10,734	$18,245	$21,014	$12,627
Family income distribution (percent)					
Total	100.0	100.0	100.0	100.0	100.0
Less than $5,000	12.5	24.7	9.8	5.4	19.3
$5,000 to $9,999	19.2	22.4	13.9	11.7	20.9
$10,000 to $19,999	35.4	30.1	31.5	29.6	30.3
$20,000 to $34,999	25.8	18.3	30.9	35.4	22.1
$35,000 or more	7.2	4.4	14.0	17.9	7.5
Poverty Rate (percent)					
Families	20.6	34.9	11.7	6.6	26.4
Individuals	23.3	36.3	13.2	8.9	29.8

Source: U.S. Bureau of the Census, 1984c.

Rican and black families. The Cuban income distribution was closer to that of non-Hispanic whites than to those for Mexicans, Puerto Ricans, and blacks.

In 1980, poverty rates of Cuban-Americans were one-third to one-half as high as those of Mexicans, Puerto Ricans, and blacks, but approximately half again as high as those of non-Hispanic whites (Table 7.6). The differences between the poverty rates of Cuban-Americans and non-Hispanic whites can largely be explained by the high prevalence of poverty among the elderly Cuban-American population. Among Cuban-Americans aged 60 years and over, poverty rates were nearly three times as high as those of non-Hispanic whites in the same age group. In younger age groups, the rates were comparable (Bean and Tienda, 1987). This major contrast is not surprising, given the very high average age of the Cuban-origin population and the fact that many Cubans arrived in the United States at an advanced age, with virtually no assets and lacking language skills, or were too old to work.

RACE

Whereas nearly 34 percent of the population of Cuba in the 1981 census was classified as black or mulatto, relatively few black Cubans emigrated to the United States after the revolution. This changed with the 1980 Mariel boatlift. According to census data reported by Boswell and Curtis (1984), 96.0 percent of all Cuban-Americans in 1970 were white and 3.1 percent black. The marked race selectivity of Cuban emigration to the United States can be explained by the social class origins of many of these emigrants. Few blacks were found among the Cuban upper and middle classes. In addition, lower-class Cuban emigrants were overwhelmingly drawn from among the white population. Many blacks perceived the social and economic changes introduced by the revolution as beneficial to them, while others feared U.S. racial intolerance, a political message constantly reiterated by the state-controlled Cuban media.

CORRELATES OF THE CUBAN-AMERICAN MORTALITY PROFILE

In summary of statements given above, Cuban-Americans are in an advantageous position in terms of income, occupation, and educational attainment, relative to other Hispanic ethnic groups and blacks in the United States. Although socioeconomic status is not the only determinant of mortality, it has been shown to be a significant predictor of both levels and cause-specific components of mortality (Kitagawa and Hauser, 1973). The combination of relatively high rankings on indicators of socioeconomic status and fairly advanced health facilities in Cuba would lead one to expect that the mortality profile of Cuban-Americans would be quite favorable, at least relative to that of other Hispanic-origin groups in the United States.

Our data indicate Cuban-Americans do have a favorable health and mortality profile. There is no simple explanation, but a number of factors discussed above appear to be involved. In addition to relatively high levels of socioeconomic status in the United States, Cuban-Americans, a recent immigrant group, originate from a society that historically enjoyed relatively low mortality and fairly adequate health services. This society has now attained mortality levels similar to those found in countries far more economically advanced (see discussion of mortality conditions in Cuba in Chapter 4).

Also, as Scott (1981) indicates, Cubans in Miami (and to some extent in other areas of high Cuban concentration) have duplicated the traditional health care system to which they were accustomed in Cuba, including the

U.S. manufacture of some medications. This has been facilitated by the significant number of Cuban health professionals who have joined the U.S. health care system, and by the emergence of Cuban ethnic enclaves. These two factors have permitted the Cuban population to take advantage of the high concentration of ethnic health workers. Scott (1981) notes, for example, that "when a Cuban goes to the public health clinics or to Jackson Memorial Hospital, he is often cared for by Cuban nurses, physicians, technicians or social workers." Limited evidence suggests, however, that for many low-income Cuban Americans health care utilization, particularly immunization programs, is below the recommended norms in Miami and northern New Jersey (Diaz, 1980).

Further evidence of the favorable health and mortality profile of the Cuban-American population may also be found in the Hispanic Health and Nutrition Examination Survey (HHANES) of 1982–1984. This survey included 2,000 Cuban-Americans, aged 6 months to 74 years, residing in the Miami (Dade County) metropolitan area. This survey, as others in the HANES series, collected data on smoking, drinking and dietary patterns. In addition, questions on chronic conditions, obesity, acculturation and other health determinants were included. HHANES statistics for Cuban-Americans, Mexican-Americans, and Puerto Ricans are reviewed below to assess the potential significance of selected mortality correlates on the Cuban-American mortality profile.

Smoking

Younger Cuban-American males (20–44 years of age) were more likely to be current smokers than were young Mexican-Americans or Puerto Ricans, but the differences were minimal (Table 9.1). At these ages, 46 out of every 100 Cuban-Americans were smokers at the time of the survey, a proportion similar to the national average. After age 45, Cuban-American males report a lower incidence of smoking than the two other Hispanic groups. Older Cuban-American women have a lower tendency to smoke than younger women. At the older ages, a lower percentage of Cuban-American than Mexican-American or Puerto Rican females smoke, although the differentials are not substantial.

Young Cuban-Americans, regardless of sex, are more prone to be heavy smokers than are other Hispanics (Table 9.2). Sixty-one percent of male Cuban-American smokers under age 45 smoke 20 or more cigarettes a day, as compared to 30 and 55 percent respectively for Mexican-Americans and Puerto Ricans. The figures for women, in the same order, were 55, 24, and 41 percent. Not surprisingly, Cuban-Americans, for well-known cultural preferences, are more likely to be cigar smokers than are other Hispanic groups queried in the HHANES.

It should be noted, however, that the HHANES smoking data for Cuban-Americans should be interpreted cautiously. A much larger localized study of 10th graders in the Dade County School System in 1979 found among Cuban-Americans a low incidence of smoking relative to whites or blacks (Diaz, 1980). The difference may be associated with greater parental discipline in more traditional Cuban-origin households. Young Cuban-Americans, however, may begin to smoke at a more rapid rate once they leave high school.

Alcohol Intake

The HHANES data suggest that Cuban-Americans are relatively moderate consumers of alcoholic drinks in comparison to Mexican-Americans and Puerto Ricans. The percentage of respondents reporting having had a drink during the referent period differs only slightly across ethnic groups (Table 9.3). A higher percentage of younger Cuban-American men answered in the affirmative than did respondents from the other groups. Fewer Cuban-American women of all ages reported drinking than did Puerto Rican women or Mexican-American women.

Having a drink more frequently does not necessarily translate into a health problem. Only nine percent of younger male Cuban-origin respondents who drink reported six drinks or more a day during the referent period, a figure much lower than that shown for Mexican-Americans and Puerto Ricans (Table 9.6). The same appears to be true among women, but the results appear to be erratic given small sample sizes. The data presented in Table 9.6 appears to confirm that drinking is less of a public health problem among Cuban-Americans than it is among Mexican-Americans and Puerto Ricans. Among Cuban-Americans, aged 20–44 and 45–74 years, 13 and 17 percent respectively are classified as heavy drinkers according to an objective drinker classification (based on the number of alcoholic beverages consumed per day). The percentages for Mexican-Americans and Puerto Ricans classified as heavy drinkers tend to be much higher. Cuban-American drinkers, in general, tend to be light or moderate consumers of alcohol.

On the other hand, there are data which suggest that Cuban-Americans suffer from a higher than average incidence of nonalcoholic cirrhosis. A small study of hospital records conducted in 1971–1972 found that among Cuban-Americans 54 percent of cirrhosis cases at Jackson Memorial Hospital in Miami were nonalcoholic related. Among non-Cuban-Americans, only five percent of cirrhosis patients were suffering from the nonalcoholic variety. Viral hepatitis was suspected as the cause of the high incidence of nonalcoholic cirrhosis among the Cuban-American patients, but this hypothesis was not supported by the data (Diaz, 1980).

Weight Status and Diet

According to the HHANES data, Cuban-Americans of both sexes and at all ages are somewhat less likely to be obese than are Mexican-Americans or Puerto Ricans (Table 9.7). Cuban females in general are more likely to be overweight (and obese) than are their male counterparts. As Boswell and Curtis (1984) have noted, "the Cuban-American diet is still dominated by traditional Cuban foods," although it is evident that food preferences are changing among some groups. Traditional Cuban food is heavy on starches, fats, sugars, and proteins, with fewer salads and vegetables than are found in the typical American diet. Rice and beans are important staples, and most Cubans like to eat beef, chicken, or pork, although fish and other seafood is often consumed. This diet is conducive to obesity and may be associated with heart disease because of its heavy cholesterol content.

Other Health Indicators

The prevalence of high blood pressure among older Cuban-Americans appears to be somewhat higher than that for Mexican-Americans but lower than that for Puerto Ricans (Table 9.8). High blood pressure is found among 20 percent of older Cuban-American males. The HHANES results are consistent with the findings of a study conducted by the American Heart Association (AHA) in the Dade County School System in 1979. The AHA study found that Hispanic male youths (10th graders), an estimated 80 percent of whom were Cuban-Americans, suffered from hypertension more frequently than did non-Hispanic whites or blacks (Diaz, 1980). Concern about the high hypertension rate among Cuban-Americans has also been expressed by health authorities interviewed in the area.

In comparison to other Hispanic groups, Cuban-Americans have a markedly lower prevalence of diabetes at ages 45–74 years (Table 9.9). At these ages, the Cuban rates are one-half to two-thirds lower than those of other Hispanic groups.

MORTALITY PATTERNS

We can only examine mortality patterns among the Cuban-born with data for 1979–1981 for reasons stated earlier. Average annual age-adjusted cause-specific mortality rates for the Cuban-born populations aged 5 years and over are available for 1979–1981, and separately for 1979 and 1981, so as to take into account the arrivals in the 1980 Mariel boatlift who reached the United States after the April 1, 1980 Census enumeration, as computed by Rosenwaike and Shai (1989) for this and earlier studies. These rates, along with similar statistics for Mexico-born, Puerto Rico-born, and U.S. whites and blacks are shown in Table 7.7. Table 7.8 provides the rates for the Cuban-born only in 1979 and 1981.

The most striking feature of Table 7.7 is that the Cuban-born population had the lowest age-adjusted death rate, and nearly half the rate for blacks. Even more remarkable is that mortality rates for Cuban-born males and females are over 20 percent lower than the rates for whites. This pattern is replicated for nearly all causes of death.

The Cuban-born, for example, have the lowest death rates for diseases of the heart and are closest to those of the Mexican-born. Mortality rates for malignant neoplasms among the Cuban-born, however, resemble those of Mexican- and Puerto Rican-born persons, which are much lower than those for whites and significantly lower than those for blacks. Lung cancer death rates among Cuban-born males are higher than those for Mexican- and Puerto Rican-born, but considerably lower than those for U.S. white and black males. As in all other ethnic groups, death rates for cancer of the lung are much lower for females than for males. Mortality from breast cancer among Cuban-born females is similar to that for U.S. white and black females. Death rates from cerebrovascular disease, accidents, chronic obstructive pulmonary diseases, and pneumonia and influenza are generally lower among the Cuban-born than those among all other groups.

Chronic liver disease death rates are also lower for the Cuban-born population. The incidence of deaths attributed to cirrhosis is lower for Cuban males than for whites despite concern about a high incidence of nonalcoholic cirrhosis in the Miami area. This is consistent with the relatively low incidence of alcoholism among Cuban-Americans detected in the HHANES. The high death rate among the Puerto Rican-born from cirrhosis is also in agreement with the survey findings. Death rates from diabetes mellitus among the Cuban-born are quite low and are almost identical to those for whites.

For only one cause—suicide—are rates highest among the Cuban-born. Suicide rates are substantially higher for Cuban-born males than for females, a sex pattern found across all ethnic groups. The higher-than-average suicide rate among Cubans is consistent with the trauma of political emigration implicit in the forced, and in most cases, permanent separation from a familiar environment and loved ones. In many instances, emigration has involved downward social mobility and loss of status, conditions often associated with despondency and despair. The high suicide rate among Cuban-born persons is also consistent with the rate in Cuba, one of the highest in the Western Hemisphere. The drastic changes induced in Cuban society by the revolution and a never-ending state of social and political tension may account for high suicide rates.

The high homicide rate among the Cuban-born is a special case that deserves separate treatment. Rosenwaike and Shai (1989), who have studied the problem in some detail, found that the high homicide rate can be traced

Table 7.7

Age-Adjusted Death Rates[a] for Selected Causes of Death of Cuban-born, Mexican-born, and Puerto Rican-born, and of All Whites and Blacks, by Sex, United States: 1979–81 (Average annual rates per 100,000 population)

Cause of Death (ICD code) and Sex	Cuba Born	Mexico Born	Puerto Rico Born	White	Black
All causes, Total	689.4	819.3	872.8	885.1	1,154.5
Male	900.7	1,012.0	1,121.1	1,153.6	1,505.3
Female	526.8	637.9	680.5	684.2	890.6
Diseases of heart (390-398, 402, 404-429), Total	252.8	272.4	338.8	353.3	400.2
Male	320.8	328.8	400.7	468.1	496.3
Female	200.4	224.2	292.8	267.0	329.0
Malignant neoplasms (140-208), Total	155.1	146.9	150.5	193.1	243.5
Male	198.0	173.1	193.8	248.0	336.0
Female	126.8	126.7	122.1	156.0	178.0
Lung (162), Total	32.4	28.6	22.9	48.3	58.7
Male	58.7	45.2	39.2	81.8	106.4
Female	13.5	15.0	11.5	23.8	23.6
Breast (174) Female	24.1	17.7	16.1	30.4	29.8
Cerebrovascular disease (430-438) Total	47.7	72.3	56.7	76.7	112.8
Male	48.6	75.5	59.5	80.1	124.3
Female	46.5	69.4	54.3	73.9	104.3
Accidents and adverse effects (E800-E949), Total	36.1	67.4	38.7	46.8	54.2
Male	58.2	107.8	64.6	70.0	87.8
Female	16.8	23.1	16.5	25.2	26.4
Chronic obstructive pulmonary diseases (490-496), Total	14.6	15.4	24.1	27.0	17.9
Male	23.4	22.8	30.5	46.2	31.7
Female	9.0	9.6	20.0	14.4	8.4
Pneumonia, influenza (480-487), Total	16.0	25.1	30.7	23.3	26.8
Male	21.7	31.4	39.2	30.3	39.0
Female	12.3	20.0	25.1	18.9	18.0
Chronic liver disease, cirrhosis (571), Total	13.4	18.3	38.1	13.2	22.3
Male	17.1	27.4	66.0	18.9	31.9
Female	10.5	9.8	15.7	8.4	14.7
Suicide (E950-E959) Total	14.6	7.2	12.9	13.7	7.3
Male	26.3	11.7	24.2	21.7	12.7
Female	4.8	2.4	3.5	6.5	2.8
Homicide (E960-E978), Total	33.6	34.8	39.9	7.0	41.4
Male	63.1	60.4	75.6	10.9	73.7
Female	7.9	5.0	8.4	3.1	13.8
Diabetes mellitus (250), Total	14.7	28.8	29.6	14.9	30.0
Male	15.7	24.7	26.7	15.4	25.5
Female	13.9	32.2	31.0	14.5	33.1
All other causes Total	90.7	130.5	112.9	116.2	198.0
Male	107.9	148.4	140.3	144.0	246.4
Female	78.0	115.4	91.1	96.2	162.2

Source: Rosenwaike, 1987: Table 3.

[a]Persons 5 years of age and over.

Table 7.8
Age-Adjusted Death Rates for Selected Causes of Death of Cuban-born
Population, United States: 1979 and 1981 (Rates per 100,000 population)

Sex and Cause of Death	1979	1981	% Change
Total causes			
Total	579.0	611.6	+5.6
Male	738.2	785.7	+6.4
Female	459.3	461.1	+0.4
Diseases of heart			
Total	223.5	213.3	-4.6
Male	281.7	264.3	-6.2
Female	178.9	171.0	-4.4
Malignant neoplasms			
Total	137.9	136.2	-1.2
Male	172.4	175.9	+2.0
Female	114.4	108.9	-4.8
Cerebrovascular diseases			
Total	41.4	40.7	-1.7
Male	43.8	40.6	-7.3
Female	39.2	40.9	+4.3
Accidents and adverse effects			
Total	24.0	34.5	+43.8
Male	37.4	51.5	+37.7
Female	12.5	16.0	+28.0
Chronic obstructive pulmonary disease			
Total	12.0	14.3	+19.2
Male	20.9	21.6	+3.3
Female	6.4	9.4	+46.9
Pneumonia and influenza			
Total	14.2	12.7	-10.6
Male	19.8	16.9	-14.6
Female	10.6	9.9	-6.6
Chronic liver disease and cirrhosis			
Total	10.0	13.3	+33.0
Male	13.8	16.7	+21.0
Female	7.2	10.7	+48.6
Suicide			
Total	11.0	12.3	+11.8
Male	19.2	20.8	+8.3
Female	4.5	3.5	-22.2
Homicide			
Total	15.3	38.4	+151.0
Male	27.7	63.3	+128.5
Female	4.3	10.0	+132.6
Diabetes mellitus			
Total	13.4	13.2	-1.5
Male	13.1	15.3	+16.8
Female	13.2	11.6	-12.1
All other causes			
Total	76.2	82.6	+8.4
Male	88.4	98.6	+11.5
Female	68.1	69.2	+1.6

Source: Rosenwaike and Shai, 1989: Table 1.

to many of the immigrants who arrived during the Mariel boatlift. Table 7.7
shows the annual average homicide rate for the Cuban-born in the three
year period, 1979–1981. Table 7.8 presents rates for individual years, 1979
and 1981. In 1979 the homicide rates for the Cuban-born, while higher than
the 1979–1981 rates for whites, were at least 50 percent lower than the rates
among the Mexican-born, the Puerto Rican-born, and blacks. Yet by 1981,
the homicide rate among the Cuban-born was similar to that of the Puerto

Rican-born in 1979–1981 and was only exceeded by the rate among blacks. Rosenwaike and Shai (1989) concluded:

The dramatic increases in homicide mortality between 1979 and 1981 have been associated with the Mariel migration. Many of the immigrants came from the same socioeconomic groups as Cubans who migrated to the US prior to 1980. However, a sizable portion, approximately 26,000, had criminal records. Many of these had been jailed for political reasons or minor crimes, such as trading on the black market. Some 5,000 persons, however, were considered to be hard-core criminals. The boatlift, therefore, included not only those who left but those who were sent.

This criminal element among the Mariel emigrants is an important factor in explaining the high homicide rate in the Cuban-American population and the dramatic upsurge in murders. As Table 7.7 indicates, the upsurge in the homicide rate, although not unique, was replicated to a lesser extent in other lifestyle-related causes of death, that is, cirrhosis of the liver, possibly alcohol related, and accidents. Increased mortality from these causes may be associated with the high concentration of criminal elements among the Mariel arrivals. For example, although the age-adjusted death rate from all causes increased only 5.6 percent, the rate for homicide increased by 151 percent, accidents by 44 percent, and cirrhosis by 33 percent. The rates for other causes of death showed only relatively minor changes. The magnitude of these changes may be somewhat influenced by the small number of observations in some categories, but the overall direction of the changes is not a statistical artifact.

COMPARISON OF CUBAN-AMERICAN AND CUBAN MORTALITY PATTERNS

It can be concluded, by and large, that the Cuban-American and Cuban populations have similar mortality profiles, although precise distinctions cannot be determined. An interesting finding is that the high prevalence of certain causes of death in the parent and daughter populations appears less significant when mortality rates for Cuban-Americans are contrasted with those of other subgroups of the U.S. population. Death rates for lung cancer and cardiovascular disease are cases in point.

It should be noted that the Cuban-American and Cuban populations share disproportionately high rates for suicide. It may be postulated that this correspondence is due to a similar set of determinants that manifest themselves differently in the two nations, that is, the major changes in Cuban society both domestically and abroad, brought about by the Cuban Revolution.

Of particular interest are the differences in rates for homicide. In Cuba, mortality rates for homicide are quite low in relation to those in the United

States. The difference is even more striking when considering the post–1980 data which reflect the dramatic increase in violent deaths as a result of the Mariel boatlift. Far less stringent social controls in the receiving society, and a disproportionate number of violence-prone individuals in a (Cuban-American) population base about one-tenth the size of that of the mother country help explain the dramatic difference between the post-Mariel U.S. homicide rate and that of Cuba.

That the mortality of Cuban-Americans is lower than that of the total U.S. population, and even that of whites, suggests that the Cuban-American population is a transitional population. It has preserved the advantage of a low-mortality developing nation as exhibited by low death rates from de-generative causes such as cardiovascular disease and malignant neoplasms. As the immigrant population matures, and begins to acquire the lifestyles typical of the host society, we may expect a convergence of mortality patterns. Over time, the immigrant population should lose the relative advantages it enjoys by virtue of its transitional standing. This hypothesis merits more attention and should be pursued once the required detailed mortality data become available. The high selectivity of much of the pre-Mariel emigration and the favorable mortality indices attained by Cuba in the 1980s, largely as a result of the universal availability of health services, are important factors in the low mortality profile of the Cuban-American population.

PART FOUR

Determinants of Mortality: Socioeconomic Status, Health, and Risk Factors

CHAPTER 8

Socioeconomic Differences in Mortality: Puerto Rico, 1979–1981

DONNA SHAI AND IRA ROSENWAIKE

INTRODUCTION

The differences in causes of death among the world's populations reflect both the natural hazards of the environment and man's ability to control them. For example, leading causes of death in developing countries include infectious diseases, malnutrition, and intestinal parasites. In developed countries these causes have been largely controlled, and mortality is primarily affected by diseases of a chronic nature (Howe, 1976). However, even within developed countries, there are still marked differences in mortality among various socioeconomic strata of the population. Data from the 1960 Matched Records Study for the United States were extensively examined by Kitagawa and Hauser (1973). Their findings showed mortality was inversely related to educational attainment among males and females. These differences in life-chances have also been found in more recent studies in the United States (Lerner and Stutz, 1977; Yeracaris and Kim, 1978; Stockwell, Wicks, and Adamchak, 1978; Frey, 1982; Nangle, Brokert, and Levy 1985), and in other industrialized nations (Kristofersen, 1979; McMichael and Hartshorne, 1982; Pamuk, 1985; Pearce et al., 1985). Indeed, recent research suggests that the gap in differential mortality between the poorest sectors and the rest of the population in various countries seems to be widening (Antonovsky, 1981).

One approach in studying the relation between socioeconomic status and mortality is to examine data for countries which have experienced rapid improvements in living conditions. By comparing data for a number of co-horts within such a population, we can identify changes that might be occurring more slowly elsewhere. A case in point is Puerto Rico. Until recently Puerto Rico has been considered a "developing" population (Yang and Pendleton, 1980) with mortality similar to other tropical Latin American countries (Preston, 1976). However, remarkable improvement in health care in Puerto Rico has profoundly reduced mortality levels, particularly among the younger segments of the population. The present life expectancy of 74 years is one of the highest in the world. In addition, unlike other developing countries, Puerto Rico has an unusually complete vital registration system and has for a decade recorded educational attainment on death certificates. For these reasons, Puerto Rico provides an unusual opportunity to examine differential mortality by socioeconomic status.

MATERIALS AND METHODS

Socioeconomic status (SES) is usually measured by occupation, income, education, or an index incorporating all three. The use of these indicators in the study of differential mortality has been fraught with difficulties. Death certificates in most countries, and in nearly all states of the United States (prior to 1988), list occupation as the only indicator of SES. The validity of occupation as an indicator of SES is questionable, since it may be deliberately inflated by next-of-kin (Pamuk, 1985). Income, even if available, would have serious deficiencies since income may fluctuate over a person's lifetime and be especially low at the end of life. Education, on the other hand, has the advantage of being virtually fixed after young adulthood, more easily defined than occupation (National Center for Health Statistics, 1986), and easy to report and code. Educational denominator data are also readily available on a national basis, at least for census periods. For these reasons education is generally considered the best indicator of SES (Kitagawa and Hauser, 1973).

The mortality data for Puerto Rico used in this study were obtained from a death record computer tape provided by the Demographic Registry of the Commonwealth of Puerto Rico. This tape contains all deaths for 1979–1981 and permits tabulations of deaths by age, sex, cause of death, and level of education. All deaths of nonresidents were omitted. Population figures used for the denominators are the published statistics of the U.S. Bureau of the Census (1984a) for the 1980 Census. Death rates were computed by sex, age, and educational attainment and expressed per 100,000 population. For purposes of this study, only deaths of persons aged 20 and over were considered. For specific causes, analysis was limited to ages 20–64. The number of deaths within this age range (exclusive of records without information on education) was 16,367 (11,135 males and 5,232 females). Table 8.1 shows frequencies for various causes of death.

A total of 2,051 records for decedents 20–64 years of age, or 11.1 percent, had no response to the educational attainment query. The analysis is based on those cases for which education was reported. Therefore all rates are

Table 8.1
Frequencies of Death by Cause and Sex, Residents Aged 20–64 Years, Puerto
Rico: 1979–81

Cause of Death	Males	Females
All Causes	11,135	5,232
Heart disease	2,043	1,076
Malignant neoplasms	1,683	1,743
Lung cancer	209	90
Breast cancer	–	235
Esophageal cancer	166	27
Stomach cancer	136	73
Colon cancer	83	81
Accidents and adverse effects	1,349	214
Motor vehicle accidents	810	156
Liver disease and cirrhosis	1,142	248
Homicide	956	109
Suicide	488	91
Cerebrovascular diseases	354	278
Pneumonia and influenza	331	145
Diabetes mellitus	305	289
Infectious/parasitic diseases	179	97
Chronic obstructive pulmonary diseases	169	128

understated, since those records lacking educational attainment are excluded
from the numerator. Causes of death presented here are classified according
to the Ninth Revision of the International Classification of Diseases (World
Health Organization, 1977).

Age-standardized rates were computed by the direct method of standardization, using the Puerto Rican 1980 population aged 20–64 years as the
standard, based on nine five-year age groups. All mortality rates are based
on three-year averages of deaths and expressed per 100,000 population.

RESULTS

There is a clear inverse relationship between all causes of death and
education (Table 8.2) except at the older ages (over 65 years), where there
is likely to be more inaccurate reporting of age. For males the pattern is
most marked for those aged 20–64 years. However, for males aged 20–44
years, there is very little difference in death rates between those with 8–11
years of education and high school graduates. For males over 44, mortality
is higher for high school graduates. For women between ages 20 and 64
years, there is an equally strong inverse relationship. However, for women
over age 65 there is little consistency to the pattern of the rates by education.

Table 8.2
Death Rates for Persons 20 Years and Over by Age, Sex, and Years of
Education, Puerto Rico: 1979–81 (Rates per 100,000 population)

Sex and Age	Years of School Completed			
	7 or less	8-11	12	13 or more
Males				
20-44	403.2[a]	250.3	248.8	119.8[a]
45-54	879.0[a]	604.2[a]	693.6	366.4[a]
55-64	1542.7[a]	1203.3[a]	1477.4	919.2[a]
65-74	2740.0	3028.6	3381.9[a]	2985.2
75+	7890.6	9042.0[a]	8080.8	8671.0
Females				
20-44	145.3	82.4	69.8[a]	38.1[a]
45-54	352.6[a]	296.2	263.6[a]	227.3[a]
55-64	783.0[a]	664.8	543.9[a]	487.0[a]
65-74	1798.5	1739.7	1875.0	1252.0[a]
75+	7093.3	6528.8[a]	6899.2	7072.3

[a]Rate is significantly different from the standard population (all education groups combined) at the 5 percent level.

This is likely due to misreporting of education for older men and women. Since the data for older persons may be biased, the mortality data presented in the remainder of this chapter are limited to rates for persons aged 20–64 years of age.

The patterns of education level for mortality by cause of death among males are shown in Table 8.3. For all ten leading causes of death as well as for all causes combined, the group with the highest education level has the lowest level of mortality. Rates among those with some college education are especially low for the "preventable" causes such as pneumonia and influenza, liver cirrhosis and, the violent causes of death. While rates for these causes are all relatively high among those with the least schooling, there is a clear gradient with education only for liver disease and cirrhosis and infectious and parasitic diseases. This is due to the apparent presence of a secondary peak in mortality at the high school level (12 years of education) for all other leading causes.

Examination of the age-adjusted rates among males for some selected causes of death shows that males with the highest education also have an advantage in infectious/parasitic diseases, esophageal cancer, stomach cancer, and motor vehicle accidents. There is a clear gradient with education

Table 8.3

Standardized Mortality Ratios for Selected Causes of Death by Years of School Completed, Males Aged 20–64, Puerto Rico: 1979–81

Cause of Death	Years of School Completed			
	0-7	8-11	12	13+
All Causes	1.29[a]	0.94	1.05	0.58[a]
Heart disease	1.10	0.93	1.18	0.79[a]
Malignant neoplasms	1.11	1.01	1.09	0.67[a]
Lung cancer	0.86	1.21	1.14	1.10
Breast cancer	-	-	-	-
Esophageal cancer	1.41	0.74	0.90	0.15[b]
Stomach cancer	1.32	0.63	1.12	0.38[a]
Colon cancer	0.81	1.08	1.33	1.39
Accidents and adverse effects	1.28[a]	0.93	1.10[a]	0.57[a]
Motor vehicle accidents	1.26	0.93	1.11	0.61[a]
Liver disease and cirrhosis	1.38[a]	1.02	0.87	0.41[a]
Homicide	1.38[a]	1.09	1.17	0.46[a]
Suicide	1.40[a]	0.92	1.09	0.46[a]
Cerebrovascular disease	1.14	0.83	1.08	0.82
Pneumonia and influenza	1.68[a]	0.68	0.72	0.32[a]
Diabetes mellitus	1.13	0.90	1.29	0.69
Infectious/parasitic diseases	1.75[a]	0.61	0.59	0.44[a]
Chronic obstructive pul. dis.	1.24	0.84	1.26	0.49[a]

[a]Rate is significantly different from the standard population (all education groups combined) at the 5 percent level.

[b]Based on less than 10 cases.

only for infectious/parasitic diseases. On the other hand, highly educated males have higher rates of death for colon cancer, with a clear gradient of ascending mortality with increased education.

The age-adjusted mortality rates among females for the ten leading causes show favorable ratios for the highest educated women for all causes with one exception, malignant neoplasms (Table 8.4). College educated women show particularly low ratios for heart disease (0.45), liver cirrhosis (0.20), and diabetes (0.38). For these three causes and for all causes there is a clear gradient of diminishing mortality with higher education. While in general, women with the least education have the highest mortality rates for all the leading causes of death, their ratio is below 1.00 for suicide, which peaks at the high school level.

For selected sites of cancer deaths among females, the age-standardized figures (Table 8.4) show a clear gradient with education only for breast cancer, where mortality increases with increased education. For lung cancer and

Table 8.4
Standardized Mortality Ratios for Selected Causes of Death by Years of School
Completed, Females Aged 20–64, Puerto Rico: 1979–81

| | Years of School Completed | | | |
Cause of Death	0-7	8-11	12	13+
All Causes	1.25[a]	0.98	0.85[a]	0.67[a]
Heart disease	1.23[a]	0.96	0.88	0.45[a]
Malignant neoplasms	1.00	1.08	0.95	1.09
Lung cancer	1.03	0.78	0.89	0.97
Breast cancer	0.72	1.14	1.24	1.75
Esophageal cancer	1.45	0.36[b]	_[b]	_[b]
Stomach cancer	1.31	1.10	0.31[a]	0.62
Colon cancer	0.91	0.78	0.91	1.81
Accidents and adverse effects	1.20	0.71	1.15	0.89
Motor vehicle accidents	1.08	0.74	1.11	1.10
Liver disease and cirrhosis	1.40	0.88	0.78	0.40[a]
Homicide	1.56	0.93	1.12	0.63
Suicide	0.94	1.00	1.67	0.56
Cerebrovascular disease	1.08	1.13	0.79	0.64
Pneumonia and influenza	1.91[a]	0.91	0.45[a]	0.29[a]
Diabetes mellitus	1.34	0.83	0.63	0.38[a]
Infectious/parasitic diseases	1.59	0.79	0.97	0.64
Chronic obstructive pul. dis.	1.27	0.90	0.49	0.57

[a]Rate is significantly different from the standard population (all education groups combined) at the 5 percent level.

[b]Based on less than 10 cases.

colon cancer, women with a high school or college education show higher mortality than those with 8–11 years of school; for stomach cancer the opposite is true.

AGE-SPECIFIC DEATH RATES

Age-specific death rates are shown by sex and educational attainment for the major chronic diseases in Table 8.5 and for the major causes of violent deaths in Table 8.6. The findings for each cause are briefly summarized in the following sections.

Heart Disease

Among males a clear inverse relationship with education only holds for those aged 45–54 (see Table 8.5), although college educated males have the lowest mortality for heart disease at every age. At age 55–64 years, the

Table 8.5
Death Rates for Selected Chronic Diseases by Age, Sex, and Years of Education, Puerto Rico: 1979–81 (Rates per 100,000 population)

Sex, Age, and Cause of Death	Years of School Completed			
	7 or less	8-11	12	13 or more
Heart Disease				
Males				
20-44	32.2[a]	15.2	18.5	12.1[a]
45-54	157.2	132.3	126.9	89.0[a]
55-64	383.4	353.5	458.7[a]	303.9[a]
Females				
20-44	20.2[a]	11.8	9.1	3.2[a]
45-54	71.4[a]	40.3	53.5	19.7[a]
55-64	210.2	177.2	143.1[a]	85.9[a]
Malignant Neoplams				
Males				
20-44	24.5[a]	16.3	17.6	9.8[a]
45-54	139.3	142.9	105.1	68.0[a]
55-64	316.4	269.5	331.7	203.4[a]
Females				
20-44	24.3[a]	18.7	14.6	10.3[a]
45-54	88.8[a]	99.5	82.9	98.5[a]
55-64	180.4	189.0	171.0	226.0
Diabetes Mellitus				
Males				
20-44	5.1	2.2[b]	1.8[b]	1.3[b]
45-54	20.6	23.8	20.5	9.2[b]
55-64	61.9	44.4	81.8	44.1
Females				
20-44	4.3	1.7[b]	0.8[b]	0.4[b]
45-54	21.7	14.2	6.7[b]	3.0[b]
55-64	67.2	40.5	37.2	22.3[b]

[a]Rate is significantly different from the standard population (all education groups combined) at the 5 percent level.

[b]Based on less than 10 cases.

highest mortality occurs among males with 12 years of education. Among females there is a clear inverse relationship at all ages, with a single (not statistically significant) exception. As among the men, the differences in mortality between the college-educated and the grade school-educated groups are very large.

Malignant Neoplasms

Among males there is no clear relationship with education for malignant neoplasms, although men with the highest education have relatively low rates of death at every age. Among males aged 55–64 years, mortality is highest among those with 12 years of schooling. Among females, however,

Table 8.6
Death Rates for Violent Causes of Death by Age, Sex, and Years of Education,
Puerto Rico: 1979–81 (Rates per 100,000 population)

Sex, Age, and Cause of Death	Years of School Completed			
	7 or less	8-11	12	13 or more
Accidents and Adverse Effects				
Males				
20-44	76.1[a]	56.5	66.3	34.6[a]
45-54	82.3[a]	58.2	64.0	32.7[a]
55-64	71.0	47.6	66.8	31.9[a]
Females				
20-44	10.0	6.6	7.5	7.1[b]
45-54	6.8	5.9[b]	12.0[b]	12.1[b]
55-64	14.5	3.4[b]	17.2[b]	6.4[b]
Homicide				
Males				
20-44	67.3[a]	55.4	58.3	20.5[a]
45-54	29.9	31.8	39.9	22.2
55-64	18.7	19.0	23.7	7.4[b]
Females				
20-44	7.0	5.5	6.1	2.6[a]
45-54	4.3[b]	1.2[b]	2.7[b]	4.5[b]
55-64	1.8[b]	0.0[b]	0.0[b]	0.0[b]
Suicide				
Males				
20-44	31.4[a]	21.2	21.2	9.2[a]
45-54	31.8	19.8	31.4	15.7[a]
55-64	27.3	12.7[b]	23.7	4.9[b]
Females				
20-44	3.8	2.8	4.7	1.4[b]
45-54	2.9[b]	5.9[b]	8.0[b]	1.5[b]
55-64	4.8	5.1[b]	8.6[b]	3.2[b]

[a]Rate is significantly different from the standard population (all education groups combined) at
the 5 percent level.

[b]Based on less than 10 cases.

there is a clear inverse relationship only at the younger ages (20–44). Women
with the highest level of education among those aged 55–64 years show
elevated rates.

Diabetes

The small numbers of deaths, especially among those at the higher levels
of education, make it difficult to generalize concerning diabetes. Among
males there seems to be an inverse relationship between education and
mortality at the younger ages (20–44). Among females there is a definite
pattern of an inverse relationship at all ages examined, but the numbers are
too small to permit valid conclusions.

Violent Causes of Death

Among males there is no clear inverse relationship with education for deaths due to violence except for suicide among the younger men (20–44). However, those with college education have the lowest rates in all instances (see Table 8.6). Death rates for accidents among college-educated males are about half those of grade school-educated men. Among females, the numbers of deaths are very small, and no clear relationship is discernible.

DISCUSSION

The results of this analysis of mortality by educational level for Puerto Rico in 1979–1981 correspond with those of numerous other studies that show a general tendency for mortality to decrease with increased social status. Among Puerto Rican males and females in age groups from 20 to 64 years, mortality among the least educated was between 1.6 and 3.8 times greater than that of the highest educated. Nevertheless, unlike other studies, our study found that at ages 45–64 years males with 12 years of school had higher mortality than those with 8–11 years. These results suggest strong heaping in reporting at 12 years of schooling as well as overstatement of educational attainment of decedents by next of kin, especially for the older ages. It must be determined whether these biases are characteristic of Puerto Rico only or characterize other populations as well.

One way to determine this is by comparing the Puerto Rican rates with those for Utah, one of two states that historically has coded education on death certificates. In comparing mortality statistics by education in Puerto Rico and Utah, the very different educational and population profiles of the two areas must be kept in mind. In Puerto Rico 39.5 percent of the population aged 25 and over have completed high school (U.S. Bureau of the Census, 1984a), whereas in Utah 80 percent have completed high school, the second highest percentage of high school completion in the nation after Alaska (U.S. Bureau of the Census, 1984c).

Nangle, Brockert, and Levy (1985) found two prevailing patterns in the Utah data. Among younger persons, mortality rates are clearly inversely related to educational achievement. However, with increasing age, mortality sharply peaks among high school graduates (12 years of school) and then declines in the college group, with only accidents and suicide varying from these two patterns. In our comparison, the first pattern held for younger Puerto Rican women, but younger Puerto Rican men followed the second pattern of a peak among high school graduates. The second pattern specified by Nangle, Brockert, and Levy is found among Puerto Ricans aged 65–74, but among the oldest, mortality is higher among those with some college education than among high school graduates. The reason for this is likely to be age overstatement among the poorly educated.

Table 8.7
Percentage of Records of Decedents 20 Years and Older Missing Information on
Years of Education, by Age and Sex, Puerto Rico: 1979–81

		Age Groups			
Sex	20-44	45-54	55-64	65-74	75+
Males	8.7	11.3	12.5	13.1	15.8
Females	9.3	10.8	13.2	13.8	15.1

Although reporting biases probably are of paramount importance, another possible factor contributing to the differences in the two areas may be the treatment of missing information. Nangle, Brockert and Levy's study found that 15 percent of records for some age groups had no information on education level. In Puerto Rico, the missing information ranged between 8.7 percent and 15.8 percent of the records (Table 8.7). However, the missing cases were distributed in the Utah study but not in the Puerto Rican data. In the Utah data, the distribution of the missing cases may have raised the rates in some educational groups, particularly if the missing cases were disproportionately of low education level. In the Puerto Rican data the exclusion of the missing-information cases likely decreased the education-specific rates. It may be possible that in Utah inflation of a next-of-kin's education is mainly at an intermediate level, thus creating a peak at the high school graduate level, while in Puerto Rico this inflation takes place both at this level and, particularly among the most elderly (for whom detailed data were not presented in this study), at the higher levels of education.

To assess, insofar as possible, the direction of bias due to the fact that educational attainment was unknown for a considerable number of decedents, we cross-classified the item on education with that on occupation, which is also coded in Puerto Rico. Among records that had no information on education, occupation was reported for more than 95 percent of adult males, but for fewer than 20 percent of adult females. Since information for female decedents is relatively sparse, our analysis in Table 8.8 has been limited to males. The data indicate that information on education is more likely to be missing among blue-collar workers and farmers than among white-collar workers. Professional and technical workers, presumably with more education than those in other occupational groups, are most likely to have years of school reported. Apparently, educational information is more likely to be missing on records for persons in occupations of lower socioeconomic status. However, the relationship is not especially marked. Table 8.8 indicates that for seven of the nine occupational groups the proportion with missing data ranged only from 8.4 percent to 13.7 percent. Thus it

Table 8.8
Percentage of Records of Male Decedents 20 Years and Older Missing
Information on Years of Education, by Occupation, Puerto Rico: 1979–81

Occupation	Percent
Total	13.3
White collar:	
Professional and technical	6.0
Managers and administrators	10.2
Sales	12.0
Clerical	8.4
Blue collar:	
Craft and kindred	11.6
Operatives	12.7
Nonfarm labor	15.4
Service	11.4
Farm	13.7

seems doubtful that bias due to missing data can explain the observed socioeconomic differentials in mortality.

The finding of a more limited relationship between education and heart
disease among Puerto Rican males at each age group than for all causes in
general is not unexpected since no urban-rural differences in heart disease
have been found among Puerto Rican males examined, even though the two
groups could be expected to differ in education and lifestyle (Garcia-Palmieri
et al., 1970). For Puerto Rican females the relationship between education
and heart disease appears stronger than for males. Research in the United
States based on matched census and death records for 1960 showed that for
coronary heart disease the age-adjusted rates for women had an inverse
relationship to number of years of education completed, with high death
rates among women with low education and low rates among those with high
attainment. For men, no relationship appeared except for lower rates among
those with some high school education (Moriyama, Krueger, and Stamler,
1971). Research from the United Kingdom also supports an inverse socioeconomic class gradient, although not as strong as that for traditional diseases
of poverty (McMichael and Hartshorne, 1982; Pearce et al., 1985).

The lack of a clear gradient in respect to malignant neoplasms is not
unexpected since cancers comprise a group of causes, many of which vary
in their relation to education. For example, cancer of the stomach is usually

observed to be more prevalent in the lower socioeconomic groups of a population, and breast cancer incidence is highest among upper-income women (Howson, Hiyama, and Wynder, 1986; Devesa and Diamond, 1980). Therefore it is likely that a number of important causes within the broader category of malignant neoplasms are working in opposite directions.

Studies of diabetics have shown that they have less formal education than the general population 20 and older and have lower income (Drury, Danchik, and Harris, 1984). It was not surprising that we found an inverse relationship with education, although the numbers of deaths are very small.

Studies of the relationship between violence and SES have generally found a substantial inverse relationship (Frey, 1982), although for women the small numbers of deaths involved make generalizations difficult.

Our research showed a strong relationship between education and mortality for all causes of death except at the older ages, and for many major causes of death. These relationships whether inverse, as in the case of liver cirrhosis for men, or direct, as in the case of breast cancer among women, confirm other studies of the importance of socioeconomic status, which strongly influences lifestyle, diet, and standards of living, in determining the risk of death. Our findings for Puerto Rico may be predictive of the changing mortality patterns of rapidly developing nations and the importance of education in determining life-chances.

CHAPTER 9

Health-related Lifestyles Among Mexican-Americans, Puerto Ricans, and Cubans in the United States

RICHARD G. ROGERS

Associating lifestyles and health behavior to risk of morbidity and mortality among ethnic subpopulations is important for three reasons. Such associations can (1) clarify the interactions among lifestyle, ethnicity, and death; (2) determine which subpopulations are at risk of sickness or death; and (3) target "at risk" populations characterized by lifestyle. Most insults to health now result from harmful personal behaviors such as excessive drinking and smoking, reckless driving, and poor dietary habits, all of which are related to socioeconomic status and individual lifestyles (Rogers and Hackenberg, 1987). Since mortality and morbidity rates differ among Mexican-Americans, Puerto Ricans, and Cubans, it is important to determine which lifestyle factors contribute to these differences.

Hispanic subpopulations are heterogeneous in their culture, socioeconomic and demographic characteristics, lifestyle, and geographic location. Among all 20 million Hispanics in the United States in 1988, Mexican-Americans accounted for 62 percent, Puerto Ricans for 13 percent, and Cubans for 5 percent. Mexican-Americans are concentrated in the Southwest, Puerto Ricans in New York and New Jersey, and Cubans in Florida. Cubans, the smallest of the three groups, increased their migration to the United States after the 1959 Cuban Revolution. Many Cuban immigrants have been advantaged in their socioeconomic background and their reception by the United States. This selective migration affected other demographic variables, such as income and education, which are substantially higher among Cubans than the other two Hispanic subgroups. Also affected is the median age, which in 1980 ranged from a high of 41 years among Cubans to a low of 22 years among Mexican-Americans; and fertility, which is low for Cubans, high for Mexican-Americans, and intermediate for Puerto Ricans (Davis, Haub, and Willette, 1983; Bean and Tienda, 1987; Valdivieso and Davis, 1988). It is our assertion that such differences in migration patterns, age structure, and socioeconomic status will interact with past and current lifestyles to affect future health and survival.

Rosenwaike (1987) has contrasted the health and longevity of Hispanic foreign-born subpopulations. Although not available for Hispanics of all generations, mortality rates have been reported for immigrant Cubans, Mexicans, and Puerto Ricans who were residing in the United States. Such rates can be compared with white and black mortality. For all causes of death in the United States, Cuba-born individuals have the lowest rates, followed by Mexico-born, Puerto Rico-born, whites, and blacks. This ordering reinforces the notion that migration is selective. By cause, Cuba-born people exhibit low rates of mortality due to diseases of the heart, cerebrovascular disease, accidents, chronic obstructive pulmonary diseases, and diabetes. Mexico-born individuals exhibit lower mortality due to malignant neoplasms and suicide. Puerto Rico-born individuals have low rates of mortality due to lung cancer (Rosenwaike, 1987). Therefore, we see large variations in cause-specific mortality by Hispanic subpopulation.

As few studies have examined lifestyle factors and morbidity among Hispanic subpopulations, an examination of recent trends in health-related lifestyles provides some useful insights. Cigarette smoking, the single most important preventable cause of morbidity and mortality in the United States, is the primary cause for 25% of all deaths and is the major reason for the difference in life expectancies of males and females (Shopland and Brown, 1987; McKeown, 1979; Miller and Gerstein, 1983). Moreover, the U.S. Surgeon General recently underscored the importance of examining cigarette smoking within the total context of minority health (Centers for Disease Control, 1987).

Smoking patterns are strong indicators of increased morbidity risks. The decrease in cigarette smoking among white males has been associated with recent declines in lung cancer mortality rates. On the other hand, as smoking increased among successive cohorts of women since the 1940s, lung cancer among women has surpassed stomach and breast cancers to become the leading cause of cancer deaths in women (Cockerham, 1988). Cigarette smoking not only increases the risk of lung cancer, but also of cancers of the larynx, esophagus, kidney, and uterine cervix. Further, it increases the risk of coronary heart disease, hypertension, bronchitis, emphysema, and diabetes (Susser, Watson, and Hopper, 1985). Moreover, smoking is linked to other unhealthy behaviors, such as excessive drinking and physical inactivity (Remington et al., 1985; Schoenborn and Benson, 1988) and can act synergistically with other unhealthy behaviors to increase the risk of mortality.

It might therefore be possible to reduce other risks by reducing cigarette smoking.

Should smoking become more widespread, especially among minorities, subsequent changes in disease and mortality patterns can be expected. Studies which have examined smoking among Mexican Americans have demonstrated the importance of age and sex for identifying differences in smoking patterns, and have associated differential patterns of cigarette smoking with lung cancer. Mexican-Americans are more likely than non-Hispanics to have never smoked. If they do smoke, they smoke fewer cigarettes than non-Hispanics (Holck et al., 1982; Humble et al., 1985; Marcus and Crane, 1984, 1985; Markides, Coreil, and Ray, 1987; Rogers and Crank, 1988). Fewer studies, however, have examined smoking among other Hispanic subpopulations. Escobedo and Remington (1989) employed the Hispanic Health and Nutrition Examination Survey to examine cohort differences in the prevalence of cigarette smoking among Mexican-Americans, Cubans, and Puerto Ricans. They concluded that over time smoking patterns between men and women were converging. Specifically, smoking prevalence for men was declining while smoking for women was increasing. One study that examined Puerto Ricans found that Puerto Ricans smoked less than their Anglo counterparts (Sorlie et al., 1982). Such findings coincide with the low lung cancer mortality among Puerto Rico-born individuals in the United States. Generally, Puerto Rico-born persons have the lowest rates of lung cancer, followed by Mexico- and Cuba-born persons, whites, and blacks (Rosenwaike, 1987).

Coronary heart disease is a major cause of death in the United States. Recent declines in coronary heart disease mortality for the general population have been associated with changes in health behavior such as reduced cigarette smoking, increased physical activity, and reduced intake of saturated fats, and with medical and public health advances such as the development of the treadmill electrocardiogram, drug and surgical treatments, and screening programs (Crimmons, 1981). Among Hispanic subgroups, coronary heart disease mortality rates vary, as do their risk factors (Castro, Baezconde-Garbanati, and Beltran, 1985). Nevertheless, heart disease mortality is lowest for Cuba-born individuals, followed closely by Mexico-born persons, and then by Puerto Rico-born persons, whites, and blacks (Markides and Coreil, 1986; Rosenwaike, 1987).

Alcohol consumption is considered to be a major risk factor in cirrhosis of the liver as well as homicide and motor vehicle accidents. Although Hispanics usually drink smaller quantities of alcohol than Anglos, there are proportionately more heavy drinkers among Hispanic than Anglo men (Markides and Coreil, 1986). Although Puerto Ricans (on the island) have moderate rates of beer and wine consumption, they are reputed to have one of the largest levels of hard liquor consumption per capita in the world (Fernandez, 1975). Indeed, the Puerto Rican death rate of cirrhosis of the liver almost doubled between 1964 and 1973 (Fernandez, 1975). Not surprisingly, Puerto Rico-born people, compared to Cuba- and Mexico-born people, have over twice the rates of mortality due to chronic liver disease and cirrhosis of the liver. They also have higher mortality rates due to homicide (Rosenwaike, 1987).

Mexican-Americans have especially high rates of diabetes. For instance, the prevalence rates for type II diabetes mellitus are two to five times greater for Mexican-Americans than for the general population (Markides and Coreil, 1986). Factors associated with diabetes include obesity and dietary intake. In comparison to Anglos, Hispanics as a group have a greater tendency to be obese and less physically active (Hazuda et al., 1988). Generally, mortality due to diabetes is highest for Mexico- and Puerto Rico-born individuals and blacks. Mortality due to diabetes is half as high for Cubans and whites (Rosenwaike, 1987). Further research is warranted to determine why some Hispanic groups have high, and others low, rates of diabetes.

This study aims to expand current knowledge about healthy lifestyle patterns, such as refraining from cigarette smoking, low alcohol consumption, and proper diet, among Mexican-Americans, Puerto Ricans, and Cubans. Further, we relate lifestyles with their potential fatal consequences. This line of research is facilitated through the release of a new data set that focuses on Hispanic subgroups.

METHODS

To study patterns of health lifestyle factors among Hispanic subpopulations, we used the Hispanic Health and Nutrition Examination Survey (HHANES), which was conducted 1982–1984 (NCHS, 1988). The purpose of the HHANES survey was to produce estimates of health and nutritional status for the three major Hispanic subpopulations, estimates that would compare to those developed for the general population through the Health and Nutrition Examination Survey (HANES).

HHANES is a probability sample of Mexican-Americans who live in the five southwestern states; of Cuban-Americans who live in Dade County, Florida (Miami); and of Puerto Ricans who live in the New York City area, including parts of New Jersey and Connecticut. Although the sample includes individuals aged 6 months to 74 years, the results reported here, which are concerned with health behavior and morbidity, are limited to adults, those aged 20–74 years. HHANES interviewed approximately 7,100 adults; 4,200 Mexican-Americans; 1,700 Puerto Ricans; and 1,200 Cuban-Americans. The HHANES data include information on factors such as the respondent's diet, cigarette smoking, alcohol consumption, and obesity (NCHS, 1985b). HHANES relied on physical examinations, diagnostic testing, and laboratory analyses as well as personal interviews. The personal interviews of the adult respondents were conducted in English or in Spanish by trained bilingual interviewers.

For purposes of this study, we identified current cigarette smokers as those respondents who had ever smoked at least 100 cigarettes and who still smoked; former cigarette smokers were those respondents who had ever smoked 100 cigarettes and who no longer smoke; respondents were classified as having never smoked if they had never smoked or had never smoked 100 or more cigarettes. Alcohol consumption was based on the number of drinks respondents had consumed in the last four weeks and was subdivided into beer, wine, and liquor consumption. Weight status was completed by the physician during the physical examination and was one of three categories— normal, obese, or underweight. Blood pressure was coded as high if the respondents' diastolic blood pressure was over 95 or if their systolic was 150 or over. Diabetes was coded "yes" if the respondents answered that they had diabetes or sugar diabetes (NCHS, 1988).

Because this data set was created through a probability sample, with oversampling of certain groups, we have weighted the data observations by the sample weight. This provides a more accurate picture of each group and allows us to generalize our results to the U.S. population of Mexican-American, Puerto Rican, and Cuban adult men and women. Nevertheless, we include the actual sample numbers in each table to provide an accurate reflection of the sample size.

Results from previous Hispanic mortality and morbidity studies have been limited by their aggregation of Hispanic subpopulations. Hispanics are a heterogeneous group, and examining them as a single ethnic group can result in misleading findings (see Hayes-Bautista, 1980, 1983; Sullivan et al., 1984; and Trevino, 1982). Therefore, we separately analyze health status among Cubans, Mexican-Americans, and Puerto Ricans.

RESULTS

Table 9.1 shows the cigarette smoking status of the three Hispanic subpopulations. These findings are similar to those presented by Escobedo and Remington (1989), but are also desegregated by age. Within each ethnic group, females are more likely than males to have never smoked. Generally, compared to older age groups (45–74), the younger age groups (20–44) are more likely to have never smoked. The two exceptions are Cuban and Puerto Rican females, where older women display a high propensity to have never smoked. Compared to the older age group, the younger group is usually more likely to smoke currently. The latter finding may be due to the fact that the younger groups have a higher smoking rate, a lower quit rate, or lower mortality than older smokers. Compared to other Hispanic men, Puerto Rican men are more likely to have never smoked. Conversely, com-

Table 9.1

Cigarette Smoking Status Among Hispanics, by Age and Sex, United States
(In percentages)

Smoking	Male		Female	
Status	20-44	45-74	20-44	45-74
A. Mexican				
Never Smoked	37	21	62	60
Present Smoker	43	44	26	24
Former Smoker	20	34	12	15
(Sample N)	(1208)	(722)	(1415)	(873)
B. Cuban				
Never Smoked	35	31	57	69
Present Smoker	46	35	27	17
Former Smoker	19	33	15	14
(Sample N)	(214)	(311)	(293)	(375)
C. Puerto Rican				
Never Smoked	41	33	51	58
Present Smoker	43	36	38	23
Former Smoker	16	31	11	19
(Sample N)	(354)	(299)	(578)	(457)

Source: *Hispanic Health and Nutrition Examination Survey, 1982–1984.*

Note: Some percentages may not total 100 due to rounding.

pared to other Hispanic women, Puerto Rican women are least likely to
have never smoked.

The number of cigarettes smoked is an important measure, since it is
directly associated with higher rates of morbidity and mortality. Of those
Hispanics who smoke, Mexican-American males and females are most likely
to smoke occasionally or smoke few cigarettes (Table 9.2). For instance,
about 50 percent of Mexican-American females smoke less than half a pack
of cigarettes per day. Cuban and Puerto Rican smoking patterns are similarly
distributed but with higher consumption levels among Cubans. Cuban females smoke about three-quarters of a pack of cigarettes per day, while
Cuban males smoke an average of over a pack of cigarettes per day. It is
interesting to note that among older Cuban males who smoke, almost three-
quarters consume over a pack of cigarettes per day. Our finding, that Mexican-Americans smoke smaller quantities than Cubans, coincides with lower
rates of lung cancer mortality for Mexican-Americans and high lung cancer
mortality for Cubans (Rosenwaike, 1987). The association of smoking patterns
and lung cancer rates among Puerto Ricans and Mexican-Americans, however, is more complex. Rosenwaike (1987) has reported that Puerto Ricans

Table 9.2

Cigarette Consumption Among Hispanics Who Smoke, by Age and Sex, United States (In percentages)

Cigarette Consumption Per Day	Male		Female	
	20-44	45-74	20-44	45-74
A. Mexican				
0-9	46	33	49	47
10-19	24	22	28	27
20-39	24	37	21	21
40+	6	9	3	5
Mean Number of Cigarettes	12	16	10	11
(Sample N)	(518)	(322)	(365)	(211)
B. Cuban				
0-9	18	16	28	37
10-19	22	12	17	22
20-39	48	47	47	35
40+	13	25	8	6
Mean Number of Cigarettes	20	23	17	15
(Sample N)	(98)	(111)	(79)	(63)
C. Puerto Rican				
0-9	21	25	24	37
10-19	24	22	34	24
20-39	39	43	32	30
40+	16	10	9	9
Mean Number of Cigarettes	20	18	16	15
(Sample N)	(153)	(114)	(221)	(103)

Source: See Table 9.1.

Note: Some percentages may not total 100 due to rounding.

have the lowest lung cancer mortality of the three Hispanic groups. Although Puerto Ricans who smoke cigarettes smoke more than Mexican-Americans, Puerto Ricans are more likely than Mexican-Americans to have never smoked. Therefore, we must balance smoking prevalence with cigarettes consumed. Moreover, the mortality rates are based on first-generation individuals, while our cigarette consumption data are based on a sample of all generations within the United States. Clearly, further research is required to disentangle these interactions.

Tables 9.3 through 9.6 show alcohol consumption among Hispanic males and females. Overall, males rather than females, and younger rather than older persons are more likely to drink alcoholic beverages (Table 9.3). Among

Table 9.3

Prevalence of Alcohol Consumption[a] Among Hispanics, by Age and Sex, United States (In percentages)

Drinking	Male		Female	
Status	20-44	45-74	20-44	45-74
A. Mexican				
Current Drinkers	73	62	36	21
Current Drinkers Who Drink:[b]				
Beer	94	91	58	57
Wine	20	22	32	36
Liquor	38	38	54	53
(Sample N)	(969)	(603)	(1252)	(731)
B. Cuban				
Current Drinkers	75	52	29	8
Current Drinkers Who Drink:				
Beer	76	67	37	33
Wine	48	41	59	65
Liquor	58	58	65	54
(Sample N)	(153)	(240)	(226)	(288)
C. Puerto Rican				
Current Drinkers	67	57	32	15
Current Drinkers Who Drink:				
Beer	87	80	59	54
Wine	28	17	39	31
Liquor	50	64	49	52
(Sample N)	(269)	(228)	(495)	(360)

Source: See Table 9.1.

[a]Percentages based on those individuals who have had one or more alcoholic drinks during the last four weeks, the reference period.

[b]Because these are not mutually exclusive categories, the percentages do not sum to 100.

the Hispanic subgroups, Mexican-American males and females are generally more likely to drink. Except for young males, who have a high prevalence of drinking, Cubans are the least likely to drink alcoholic beverages.

The alcoholic beverages which Mexican-Americans, Puerto Ricans, and Cuban men drink are primarily beer, then liquor, and finally wine. Cuban females are exceptional in that they are more likely to drink wine and liquor and least likely to drink beer. Over 90 percent of those Mexican-American men who consume alcoholic beverages drink beer. Although Mexican-American males are more likely than other Hispanic males to drink beer, they are less likely to drink other alcoholic beverages. For instance, only 20

Table 9.4
Beer Consumption Among Hispanics Who Drink, by Age and Sex, United States
(In percentages)

Number of Beers Consumed Per Day	Male		Female	
	20-44	45-74	20-44	45-74
A. Mexican				
1-2 Beers	34	40	51	61
3-5 Beers	32	34	30	31
6 or more Beers	33	26	19	8
Mean Number of Beers	4.9	4.1	3.3	2.4
(Sample N)	(671)	(345)	(252)	(93)
B. Cuban				
1-2 Beers	52	73	91	89
3-5 Beers	29	20	9	11
6 or more Beers	20	7	0	0
Mean Number of Beers	3.1	2.4	1.4	1.5
(Sample N)	(88)	(83)	(24)	(8)
C. Puerto Rican				
1-2 Beers	40	53	57	65
3-5 Beers	31	26	25	32
6 or more Beers	29	20	18	3
Mean Number of Beers	4.4	3.7	3.1	2.4
(Sample N)	(157)	(102)	(95)	(31)

Source: See Table 9.1.

Note: Some percentages may not total 100 due to rounding.

percent of Mexican-American men who use alcoholic beverages drink wine, yet over twice that percentage of Cuban males drink wine. Less than 40 percent of Mexican-American males who use alcohol drink liquor, but over 50 percent of Cuban and Puerto Rican males drink liquor. Within Hispanic subpopulations who drink, females are more likely than males to drink wine and liquor. For example, among Mexican-Americans who drink, only one-fifth of the males drink wine, yet one-third of the females drink wine. Therefore, more males than females drink, more males than females drink beer, and females who drink are more likely than males to consume wine and liquor.

Table 9.4 shows beer consumption by those in the Hispanic subgroups who drink. Those in the older age groups are less likely to drink moderate or large amounts of beer. Among males and females who drink beer, females are much more likely to drink small quantities. For example, Cuban females

Table 9.5

Wine Consumption Among Hispanics Who Drink, by Age and Sex, United States (In percentages)

Glasses of Wine Consumed Per Day	Male 20-44	Male 45-74	Female 20-44	Female 45-74
A. Mexican				
1 Glass	35	55	49	58
2 Glasses	33	32	28	34
3 or more Glasses	32	14	23	8
Mean Glasses of Wine	2.2	1.9	2.0	1.6
(Sample N)	(141)	(85)	(138)	(55)
B. Cuban				
1 Glass	44	65	42	66
2 Glasses	29	19	26	20
3 or more Glasses	27	16	33	14
Mean Glasses of Wine	1.9	1.6	2.0	1.5
(Sample N)	(54)	(50)	(38)	(15)
C. Puerto Rican				
1 Glass	24	45	33	66
2 Glasses	26	15	42	34
3 or more Glasses	49	40	25	0
Mean Glasses of Wine	2.9	3.3	2.1	1.3
(Sample N)	(48)	(18)	(58)	(13)

Source: See Table 9.1.

Note: Some percentages may not total 100 due to rounding.

who drink beer drink about a beer-and-a-half per day. Mexican-American and Puerto Rican males are more likely than Cuban males to drink moderate to large amounts of beer. And young Mexican-American males can expect to drink the most beer, about five beers per day.

Table 9.5 shows wine consumption by those in the Hispanic subgroups who drink. By far, Puerto Rican males drink more wine than any other group. They are also the only group in which the older men drink more than the younger men. For example, older Puerto Rican males who drink wine consume over three glasses of wine a day. Even though women are more likely than men to drink wine (Table 9.3), they generally drink less wine per day.

Table 9.6 illustrates liquor consumption among Hispanics. Once again, those Hispanics who generally consume more liquor are younger rather than older, and male rather than female. Puerto Ricans are more likely than

Table 9.6
Liquor Consumption Among Hispanics Who Drink, by Age and Sex, United
States (In percentages)

Drinks of Liquor Consumed Per Day	Male 20-44	Male 45-74	Female 20-44	Female 45-74
A. Mexican				
1-2 Drinks	42	59	56	76
3-5 Drinks	36	28	35	17
6 or more Drinks	23	13	9	6
Mean Drinks of Liquor	4.0	3.1	2.8	2.0
(Sample N)	(263)	(146)	(232)	(81)
B. Cuban				
1-2 Drinks	49	65	65	72
3-5 Drinks	42	24	24	21
6 or more Drinks	9	11	11	7
Mean Drinks of Liquor	3.4	2.3	2.1	2.1
(Sample N)	(67)	(70)	(41)	(13)
C. Puerto Rican				
1-2 Drinks	24	32	43	41
3-5 Drinks	47	44	41	38
6 or more Drinks	30	24	16	21
Mean Drinks of Liquor	5.7	4.5	3.6	4.2
(Sample N)	(92)	(81)	(77)	(26)

Source: See Table 9.1.

Note: Some percentages may not total 100 due to rounding.

Cubans or Mexican-Americans to consume liquor. For instance, Puerto Rican
young males who drink liquor can expect to consume almost six drinks
containing liquor per day. This pattern is contrasted against Mexican-American females aged 45–74 who average two drinks containing liquor per day.
   The data presented in these four tables indicates a pattern of a higher
prevalence of general alcohol consumption among Mexican-Americans, but
higher *levels* of wine and liquor consumption among Puerto Ricans. These
findings represent interesting differences in both the rates and levels of
alcohol consumption among Hispanic subgroups that merit further study to
determine the possible beneficial or detrimental effects of such consumption
upon morbidity and mortality. Moreover, the high levels of wine and liquor
consumption help explain the high mortality rates from cirrhosis of the liver
among Puerto Ricans (see Rosenwaike, 1987).

Table 9.7
Weight Status Among Hispanics, by Age and Sex, United States
(In percentages)

Weight	Male		Female	
Status	20-44	45-74	20-44	45-74
	A. Mexican			
Underweight	3	3	3	2
Normal	77	69	66	46
Obese	20	28	31	52
(Sample N)	(560)	(346)	(707)	(402)
	B. Cuban			
Underweight	1	2	4	1
Normal	80	74	76	59
Obese	19	24	21	40
(Sample N)	(153)	(239)	(222)	(285)
	C. Puerto Rican			
Underweight	1	4	2	1
Normal	79	70	63	42
Obese	21	27	35	57
(Sample N)	(264)	(222)	(488)	(352)

Source: See Table 9.1.

Note: Some percentages may not total 100 due to rounding.

Table 9.7 shows the weight distribution of the sample subpopulations. Those in the younger age groups are more likely to be within normal weight ranges, as are males. Females, on the other hand, are more likely to be obese. Almost 60 percent of older Puerto Rican women, for example, are classified as obese. A greater percentage of Cubans are of normal weight than are Mexican-Americans or Puerto Ricans. For instance, over 80 percent of young Cuban males are of normal weight. These findings concur with the high mortality rates due to diabetes among Puerto Ricans, Mexican-Americans, and blacks, and the low rates among Cubans and whites (Rosenwaike, 1987). Moreover, these results support the finding that Puerto Rican women (on the island) have a very high rate of obesity (Fernandez, 1975).

Table 9.8 presents levels of blood pressure among the Hispanic subgroups. As the risk of high blood pressure increases with age (Roberts and Rowland, 1981), it is not unexpected that the older age groups exhibit higher blood pressures than do the younger age groups. Further, males usually exhibit higher blood pressures than females. Among the three groups, there are only slight differences, but Puerto Ricans generally have higher blood pres-

Table 9.8
High Blood Pressure[a] Among Hispanics, by Age and Sex, United States
(In percentages)

Blood Pressure	Male 20-44	Male 45-74	Female 20-44	Female 45-74
A. Mexican				
High	3	16	1	13
Normal	97	84	99	87
(Sample N)	(969)	(603)	(1252)	(731)
B. Cuban				
High	2	20	2	14
Normal	98	80	98	86
(Sample N)	(153)	(240)	(226)	(288)
C. Puerto Rican				
High	5	20	1	19
Normal	95	80	99	81
(Sample N)	(269)	(228)	(495)	(360)

Source: See Table 9.1.

[a]Blood pressure is coded as high if the respondent's diastolic blood pressure is over 95 or if the respondent's systolic blood pressure is 150 or higher.

Note: Some percentages may not total 100 due to rounding.

sures than Cubans, and Cubans generally have higher blood pressures than Mexican-Americans. The literature has reported that Mexican-Americans and Anglos have about the same high blood pressure rates, but that Mexican-American males are less compliant in taking blood pressure medications and are therefore less successful in controlling their hypertension (Castro, Baez-conde-Garbanati, and Beltran, 1985).

Diabetes prevalence among Hispanics is shown in Table 9.9. Diabetes is far greater among the old than among the young. Its distribution by sex, however, is similar. There are only slight differences by ethnicity in the prevalence of diabetes between Mexican-Americans and Puerto Ricans. Cubans exhibit a lower propensity toward diabetes, with the prevalence levels at older ages for males and females only half those of the other two groups. These relations support the findings that the prevalence of diabetes is higher for Mexican-Americans than for other whites, and that mortality due to diabetes is twice as high among Mexican-Americans and Puerto Ricans than it is among Cubans and other whites (Rosenwaike, 1987).

Table 9.9

Diabetes Among Hispanics, by Age and Sex, United States (In percentages)

Diabetes	Male		Female	
	20-44	45-74	20-44	45-74
A. Mexican				
Yes	2	13	2	15
No	98	87	98	85
(Sample N)	(1208)	(720)	(1413)	(870)
B. Cuban				
Yes	1	5	2	8
No	99	95	98	92
(Sample N)	(214)	(311)	(293)	(375)
C. Puerto Rican				
Yes	1	10	3	15
No	99	90	97	85
(Sample N)	(354)	(298)	(578)	(457)

Source: See Table 9.1.

Note: Some percentages may not total 100 due to rounding.

DISCUSSION

These findings, which permit comparison of selected health-related characteristics among Hispanic subgroups, are an important addition to the growing literature on health among Hispanics. That lifestyles and health behavior are closely associated with differentials in morbidity and mortality is demonstrated by the different lifestyles and mortality rates between sexes, ages, and various Hispanic ethnicities. But other factors also play a role. Among them are availability and quality of medical care, migration selectivity of healthy people, and differences in socioeconomic status (Rosenwaike, 1988). Future research will be needed so that these interrelated issues can be untangled.

That older individuals are at greater risk of morbid and mortal conditions, especially chronic diseases, is not necessarily because of healthier lifestyles among the young. For instance, the young are more likely to be within normal weight ranges and free of high blood pressure and diabetes, but are more likely to drink and to smoke. Therefore, as younger individuals age, some chronic diseases, especially respiratory diseases, may become more prevalent. Therefore, unhealthy lifestyles during youth may foreshadow chronic diseases in old age.

Females usually engage in fewer risk-taking behaviors. They are less likely than males to smoke or drink heavily (Waldron, 1983). So it would be expected that females would have lower rates of lung cancer and cirrhosis of the liver, an expectation that is borne out from the mortality literature (see Rosenwaike, 1987). On the other hand, females are more likely to be obese and exhibit higher rates for high blood pressure and diabetes than are males.

Certain causes of death are associated with certain behaviors. For instance, coronary heart disease is associated with uncontrolled hypertension, obesity, and smoking; lung cancer with cigarette smoking. Previous studies have documented the low smoking rates and, concomitantly, the low lung cancer mortality rates among Mexican-Americans compared to Anglos and blacks (see Holck et al., 1982). Our results confirm the low cigarette consumption levels among Mexican-Americans, relative to Cubans and Puerto Ricans. Moreover, Cuban men not only smoke more cigarettes than do Puerto Rican or Mexican-American men, but they are also more likely to smoke cigars (percentages not shown in the tables). Such relationships complement the findings that foreign-born Cubans have higher lung cancer mortality rates than do foreign-born Mexican-Americans or island-born Puerto Ricans (U.S. Dept. of Health and Human Services [HHS], 1985; Rosenwaike, 1987).

Compared to Cubans, Mexican-Americans are more likely to drink alcohol, and when they drink, they generally consume more beer, wine, and liquor per day. The high consumption levels may explain why foreign-born Mexican-Americans have higher rates of death due to cirrhosis of the liver and accidents than do foreign-born Cubans. Puerto Ricans are also heavy drinkers, especially of hard liquors, and they exhibit high mortality due to cirrhosis of the liver and accidents (HHS, 1985; Rosenwaike, 1987).

We have found that, compared to Mexican-Americans and Puerto Ricans, a greater proportion of Cubans are of normal weight and do not have diabetes. These findings coincide with the low mortality due to diabetes among foreign-born Cubans, relative to foreign-born Mexican-Americans and island-born Puerto Ricans (Rosenwaike, 1987). Although other factors besides obesity contribute to diabetes, obesity among Hispanics appears to be a fairly accurate indicator.

Our findings characterize selected lifestyle behaviors among the 1982–1984 sample of three adult Hispanic subgroups. Future research is necessary to address the effects of multiple risk-taking behaviors on morbidity and mortality (see, for example, Powell-Griner and Rogers, 1987). Certainly, individuals who smoke, drink, and are overweight are at greater risk than those who are overweight, but do not smoke or drink.

Our results reinforce the view of diversity among Mexican-Americans, Puerto Ricans, and Cubans, stress the need to desegregate relationships by age and sex, and provide new perspectives on the potential health and longevity of each group. These associations suggest possible links with lifestyle, health, and survival, and indicate areas that require further research.

Moreover, such relations indicate areas where culturally relevant public health programs could help reduce risky lifestyles not only for Hispanics as a group, but more importantly, for specific Hispanic subgroups. For instance, Hispanics as a group exhibit high mortality due to diabetes. Cubans, however, have a risk of mortality that is as low if not lower than whites. Therefore, programs that screen for diabetes among Cubans, although worthwhile, would not demonstrate the wisest allocation of resources. Therefore, we have illustrated some of the complexities in linking ethnicity, lifestyle, and health.

CHAPTER 10

Mortality by Violence Among Mexican Immigrants and Mexican-Americans in California and Texas

DONNA SHAI, IRA ROSENWAIKE, AND
RICHARD G. ROGERS

The subject of violent death among immigrants has been given very uneven attention in public health research. Although suicide rates have been widely examined and have been found to vary greatly by country of origin (Burvill et al., 1973; Kushner, 1984), little has been published on differential accident and homicide death rates among migrants (Batta, Mawby, and McCullogh, 1981; Shai and Rosenwaike, 1988; Smith, Mercy, and Rosenberg, 1986). This study partially fills this void by presenting mortality rates for violent causes of death for Mexican immigrants and Mexican-Americans.

In explaining differential mortality among groups, two predominant explanations are migration selectivity (Trovato, 1985) and protective factors associated with strong family networks. These explanations seem reasonable in explaining differences by ethnic group but may be less effective in exploring differences within ethnic group by generation status (Kushner, 1984; Markides, 1981; Trovato and Jarvis, 1986). If immigrants are selectively healthy, then the second generation, whose health is not selected by migration, may show higher rates of violent deaths. Similarly, if the native-born generation is assumed to be less integrated into traditional family networks, then we would also expect to find higher rates of suicide among them. Indeed Burnam et al. (1987), in a study of Mexican-Americans in Los Angeles, found lower prevalence of psychiatric disorder among the foreign-born and elevated rates among the U.S.-born. They argue that these findings are due both to the selection process in which healthier individuals are more likely to migrate to the United States and to frustrations in acculturation experienced by U.S.-born Mexican-Americans. Our work develops this line of research by comparing death rates due to violence among immigrants from Mexico with those of second and higher generations of Mexican-origin persons in the United States in the two states of greatest number, California and Texas.

METHODS AND MATERIALS

The basic data sources employed to measure mortality among populations of Mexican background are California and Texas death statistics for 1980, provided on computer tape by the two health departments, and 1980 Census population counts of residents of these states derived from the 5 percent public use microdata sample (U.S. Bureau of the Census, 1983a).

As other students of Mexican-origin mortality in the United States have noted, the precise measurement of mortality is impeded by the difficulty in accurately classifying the Mexican-American population (Bradshaw and Fonner, 1978; Sullivan et al., 1984). Unfortunately, different classification schemes can yield different mortality rates. We have followed the recommendations of other researchers in designating as Mexican-American those individuals with Spanish surnames (Rosenwaike and Bradshaw, 1988).

The Texas Department of Health codes Spanish surnames on the death record tape. Since the Texas vital statistics data for Spanish-surname persons are confined to whites, for the sake of comparability, tabulations for California also have been limited to the white group. (Our definition of white refers to persons who responded white or who did not check a specific nonwhite category in the census query). Computer coding of Spanish surnames on death certificates in California was performed at the University of Texas School of Public Health with the list of Spanish surnames employed by the U.S. Bureau of the Census (Passel and Word, 1980). This assured reasonable consistency between the Spanish-surname coding of Texas and California records. We excluded from the study persons of Spanish surname who were born in a foreign country other than Mexico.

Deaths were classified according to the Ninth Revision of the *International Classification of Diseases* (ICD) (World Health Organization, 1977) and include homicide (ICD codes E960-E978), suicide (ICD codes E950-E959), and accidents (ICD codes E800-E949). A total of 2,679 native white or Mexican-born residents of California of Spanish surname (2,225 males and 454 females) were tabulated as having died from violent causes (accidents, homicide, suicide) in California in 1980. Of this number, 1,468 were native-born and 1,211 Mexican-born. The number of deaths in 1980 among U.S.-or Mexican-born persons of Spanish surname who were residents of Texas was 2,217 for the selected causes (1,882 males and 335 females). Of this number, 1,512 were native-born and 705 Mexican-born.

The age-adjusted death rates were computed by the direct standardization method, with the age distribution of the total population of the United States five years of age and over in 1980 as the standard (Shryock and Siegel, 1975). Only deaths of persons five years of age and over have been considered here.

A factor that is essential in the evaluation of mortality among Mexican immigrants to the United States is the estimation of the large illegal (undocumented") population. While deaths within the group are reported, the population at risk cannot be well-defined. If deaths among the Mexican immigrants are more completely counted than are individuals, then the base population estimates for the denominator are too small and the resultant rates will be too large, overstating the true risk. This study uses the unadjusted counts published in the 1980 Census, which undoubtedly understate the number of undocumented immigrants. Although little can be done to verify the exact number of illegal immigrants who may have been uncounted in the base population, Census Bureau demographers believe "reasonably complete coverage" of this group occurred (Passel and Woodrow, 1984). If the number of uncounted is extensive, the mortality rates for the foreign-born, based only on census counts, may be too high.

One way to check the data is to compare mortality rates for the immigrant population with those for the native (Mexican-origin) population for causes for which little difference would be anticipated. These might be causes that change slowly or that are related to migration to a new locale. Three such causes are heart disease, cancer, and cerebrovascular conditions. If the immigrant population were seriously undercounted, we would expect a (false) sharp decline in the rates among the native-born for these causes, and for the ratios of the U.S.-born divided by the Mexican-born to be less than unity. The ratios by cause and sex, however, are all close to, but slightly over one, indicating that the undercount probably is not of major significance, at least among the older adult population, where most deaths from these chronic conditions occur.

RESULTS

Homicide

Age-adjusted mortality rates for homicide in 1980 among Mexican-origin persons in California and Texas are presented in Table 10.1. In both states, Mexican-born men show higher rates than U.S.-born men, but in Texas, the differences are especially pronounced. For women, differences by state are slight, but differences by origin are larger. Overall, Mexican-born women exhibit lower homicide rates than U.S.-born women.

The trend in homicide by generation appears to be an accommodation to the trends of the general white population. (Nationwide, the age-adjusted rates for whites are 10.9 per 100,000 men and 3.1 per 100,000 women [Rosenwaike, 1987].) The high homicide rates among the foreign-born and

Table 10.1
Age-Standardized Mortality Rates for Violent Causes of Death for Spanish
Surname Persons of Mexican and U.S. Origin, California and Texas: 1979–81
(Rates per 100,000 population)

Cause of Death and Birthplace	California		Texas	
	Males	Females	Males	Females
Homicide				
Mexican Born	59.5	4.6	102.5	4.8
U.S. Born	40.6	7.4	44.8	7.0
Suicide				
Mexican Born	11.8	2.6	11.7	0.4
U.S. Born	17.1	4.4	19.1	3.3
Accidents, Total				
Mexican Born	97.5	23.9	146.4	20.2
U.S. Born	77.9	27.7	91.7	28.1
Motor Vehicle Accidents				
Mexican Born	61.7	16.8	86.2	13.8
U.S. Born	45.9	15.7	54.4	15.3
All Other Accidents				
Mexican Born	35.8	7.1	60.2	6.4
U.S. Born	32.0	12.0	37.3	12.8

the extreme differences in male and female rates substantiate the findings
of Loya et al. (1986). In Los Angeles—the largest Mexican-American community in the United States—gang violence is an important component of
homicide among Hispanic men 15–24 years old, but becomes increasingly
less important above age 24. With increasing age, other crime-related homicides increase (Loya and Mercy, 1985).

Suicide

An analysis of the age-adjusted rates for suicide (see Table 10.1) shows a
different trend. Mexican-born men have lower suicide rates in California
and Texas than U.S.-born men. Mexican-born women in California and Texas
show the same trends as Mexican-born men, with lower rates than among
the U.S.-born.

Cross-cultural research on suicide has shown marked differences in suicide
rates of migrants from various countries (Burvill et al., 1973), with the presence of social-support networks and traditional ritual being associated with
low suicide rates (Kushner, 1984; Trovato and Jarvis, 1986). A number of
researchers have noted an increase in suicide with length of time in the new
environment due to difficulties in acculturation. Our data support these
findings in that while suicide rates among persons of Mexican origin are low
in general compared to the national rate for whites (21.7 per 100,000 for
men and 12.7 for women (Rosenwaike, 1987), rates are higher for the U.S.-

born Spanish-surname population than for the Mexican-born for both sexes in both states studied. Stress associated with acculturation among the U.S.-born Mexican-Americans may be a contributing factor (Markides, 1981) particularly in regard to low earnings (Chiswick, 1977). Greater alcoholism among more acculturated Mexican-Americans (Yamamoto and Steinberg, 1981), particularly females (Holck et al., 1984), is another indication of stress.

Accidents

Age-adjusted mortality rates for accidents show a pattern similar to homicide (see Table 10.1). In California and Texas, Mexican-born men have higher rates than U.S.-born men, but the difference between these two groups is most notable in Texas. Conversely, in both states, women show higher rates for the U.S.-born than for the Mexican-born.

Research on accident rates among migrants has shown that rates approach that of the host country, as opposed to reflecting the country of origin (Burvill et al., 1973), so that differences among migrants can be expected to converge to that of the mainstream. Mexican immigrants in general are an exceptionally high-risk group for accidental death. (U.S. white men have a lower rate at 70.0 per 100,000; white women have a rate of 25.2 [Rosenwaike, 1987].) In some ways, they offer an interesting parallel to another group that has previously been documented as a high-risk group: Native American Indians, particularly the Hopi (Simpson et al., 1983). Like the Hopi, Mexican-origin persons frequently ride in pickup trucks, increasing the risk of being thrown from the vehicle. In fact, the Texas Mexican-origin population shows an 8 percent rate of carpooling to work in a truck, while the California Mexican-origin population shows only 4 percent (U.S. Bureau of the Census, 1983b, 1983c), with the Texas population having the higher death rate.

Another important factor in explaining motor vehicle accident mortality differentials between population groups is the poor quality of cars in low-income groups. In Los Angeles, the largest settlement of Mexican-origin persons in the United States, a car is considered a necessity due to the city layout and the lack of adequate public transportation. In the *barrio*, many cars are secondhand and often break down. Moreover, drunk driving is a common offense. Cars are a focal point of interest for young Mexican-American men in the Los Angeles *barrio* (Moore et al., 1978). Among illegal immigrants, owning a car is an important social symbol that confers distinction on an individual's whole family (Browning and Rodriguez, 1985). Therefore, the combination of the importance of cars to young men, the limited economic means at their disposal, and the use of inexpensive, old, and poorly maintained cars, may be important factors behind the high accident rates. Moreover, older cars are more likely to be associated with fatal accidents (National Highway Traffic Safety Administration, 1980). The lower mortality rates for the native-born may reflect their better socioeconomic situation, with less dependence on pickup trucks and their use of larger, newer-and better-maintained cars.

Overall, among Mexican-Americans the rate of deaths due to both motor vehicle and nonmotor vehicle accidents are more similar geographically for men and women for the U.S.-born than for the foreign born.

DISCUSSION

Demographic differences between the two states can partially explain differences in rates of violent death. California has attracted large numbers of Mexican immigrants as well as U.S.-born Mexican-Americans due to its superior economic environment relative to Texas, including the widespread availability of jobs, high wages, and good working conditions (Jones, 1984). For example, in Los Angeles the average wage for a "laborer" is double that of San Antonio. In addition, California lacks the degree of racial discrimination found in Texas, with stronger unions (particularly in the farmworker, laborer, and service worker categories) and more legal support for educating the children of illegal immigrants (Jones, 1984).

The continuous influx into Texas of Mexican immigrants with low educational levels serves to keep the Texas Mexican population conservative and traditional (Jaffe, Cullen, and Boswell, 1980). Mexican-origin persons in California are better educated and have higher incomes than those in Texas. At the 1980 Census, 38.1 percent of Mexican-origin persons in California were high school graduates as opposed to 33.4 percent in Texas. The median family income of Mexican-origin persons in Texas is about 80 percent of the income in California. The attraction of California in recent years is reflected in the fact that in this state 36 percent of Mexican-origin persons are foreign-born as opposed to 19 percent in Texas (U.S. Bureau of the Census, 1983b, 1983c). Our data show the complex interplay between migration selectivity, accommodation, acculturation ,and socioeconomic status.

CONCLUSIONS

This study compares homicide, suicide, and accident death rates among immigrant and U.S.-born Mexican-Americans in California and Texas for 1980. A comparison of the age-adjusted death rates by nativity shows that (1) rates among Mexican immigrants are higher than the rates of the general U.S. population for homicide and accidents but lower for suicide; (2) rates among the U.S.-born Mexican-Americans are closer to those of the general population for violent causes, and (3) improved socioeconomic means among Mexican-Americans provides protection against certain causes of death. For males in particular, death rates were much higher in Texas than in California for homicide and accidents.

Our findings on suicide support the findings of Burnam et al. (1987) that the migration from Mexico draws a particularly healthy population from the point of view of mental health, and social stress is much greater among second (or later) generation Mexican-Americans. Nevertheless, a simple model of accommodation to generally prevailing rates is in itself insufficient. Stresses for both the new immigrant and the native-born are apparent and reflected in mortality rates. An environmental or acculturation hypothesis may help explain differences in homicide and accidents. Many of the foreign-born are drawn initially to large urban areas, which are centers of poverty, gang-related violence, and drug traffic. Non-motor vehicle accidents in urban areas are usually associated with tenement-type buildings, deteriorating housing, overcrowding, and drinking (Planek, 1982). Motor vehicle accidents, as noted, are associated with inexpensive, old, poorly maintained cars and pickup trucks. The "improvement" in mortality rates among the native-born may not result just from an accommodation to the behavior of the majority population through "acculturation" but may also be due to improved socioeconomic means that provide protection against certain causes of death.

These results demonstrate the subtle changes that occur over generations in causes of death. Hence the changed mortality profile by generation may be, to a certain extent, a shifting of rates from one cause of death to another (Rogers and Hackenberg, 1987). Further research, then, should be aware of potential changes in the distribution of causes of death, and in the dynamics associated with age, sex, ethnicity, and immigrant status.

CHAPTER 11

Mortality Among Puerto Ricans by Nativity in New York State and New Jersey, 1979–1981

IRA ROSENWAIKE AND KATHERINE HEMPSTEAD

INTRODUCTION

Mortality studies of two generations of the same migrant group provide important perspectives on the effects of genetic and environmental factors on mortality. Similar mortality levels between generations suggest genetic factors, while assimilation to the mortality pattern of the host population on the part of the second generation suggests environmental factors.

The present study uses proportional mortality analysis to examine the cause-specific mortality of two U.S. Puerto Rican populations by nativity group (the island-born and the mainland-born) during the three-year period around the 1980 Census. The distribution of mortality by cause for the two Puerto Rican groups is compared with that of New York City blacks and whites.

At the time of the 1980 Census some 2.0 million persons resident in the United States were classified as Puerto Ricans, of whom about 1.0 million were island-born (U.S. Bureau of the Census, 1984c; Bean and Tienda, 1987). Since Puerto Rican migration to the United States is largely a post-World War II phenomenon, both the island-born and the mainland-born genera-tions are relatively young, the latter especially so. Among the island-born, only 5.6 percent were aged 65 years and older in 1980; among the mainland-born the median age was only 11.8 years and fewer than 5 percent were over 45 years of age. Two states, New York and New Jersey, contained 60 percent of the Puerto Rican population in the United States in 1980 (U.S. Bureau of the Census, 1984c; Bean and Tienda, 1987).

Mortality data are now available for mainland-born Puerto Ricans, as many states began to include an ethnicity query on their death certificates in the late 1970s (Trevino, 1982). Prior to this, mortality statistics were available only for the island-born population (Rosenwaike, 1983).

This study examines mortality by selected causes, particularly "social pathologies" or lifestyle-related causes such as homicide, suicide, and accidents. Previous studies of mortality among Puerto Ricans (limited to the island-born) have found that, compared with U.S. whites, Puerto Ricans residing in the United States have exhibited relatively low rates of death from major chronic causes such as heart disease and cancer, although rates for certain cancers, particularly stomach, have been found to be excessive (Rosenwaike, 1983, 1984). The Puerto Rican mortality profile has also been characterized by relatively high rates from certain lifestyle-related causes, particularly homicide, cirrhosis of liver, accidents, and drug dependence (Alers, 1978).

Overall, these two major characteristics (deficits and excesses) of the Puerto Rican mortality pattern tend to cancel each other out. Accordingly, age-standardized death rates for all causes combined for the Puerto Rican-born population do not differ markedly from those for U.S. whites (Rosenwaike, 1987). Within specific age groups, however, there are significant differences. Relative to U.S. whites, the Puerto Rican-born have excessive mortality rates in younger age groups where violent causes predominate, and lower rates at older ages where chronic causes predominate. In comparison with New York City whites, it would be expected that among Puerto Rican groups the proportional distribution of mortality by cause would be more heavily weighted toward lifestyle-related causes. However, for the non-elderly age range examined in the present study, the proportional differences may not be marked, as most deaths under age 45 for all populations are due to accidental or other violent causes (Rogers and Hackenberg, 1987).

A group's mortality profile is often affected by its socioeconomic characteristics. The high proportion of deaths from violent and otherwise preventable causes among Puerto Ricans in the United States is largely a function of their low economic status, for most are concentrated in impoverished urban areas where they are subject to substandard housing, crowding, high crime rates, and limited access to health-care services.

The major purpose of this study is to compare the mortality of mainland- and island-born Puerto Rican residents of New York and New Jersey with each other and with New York City whites and blacks (populations representative of the principal area in which they reside). A comparison of socioeconomic characteristics of the island- and mainland-born Puerto Rican populations of New York and New Jersey can suggest how the mortality profiles of these two groups may differ from one another. Table 11.1 shows selected characteristics of the two groups taken from the 1980 Census. The U.S.-born group shows considerably higher median family income at all ages, lower proportions below the poverty level, higher median years of school completed, and greater proportions of high school graduates. Thus,

Table 11.1
Selected Socioeconomic Characteristics of Puerto Rican-Origin Residents of New
York and New Jersey, by Birthplace, Aged 20–44 Years: 1980[a]

Characteristic and Age	Island-born	Mainland-born
Median family income		
20-24	$7,270	$10,208
25-34	9,170	12,148
35-44	11,770	14,713
Percent below poverty level		
20-24	41.6	29.6
25-34	35.3	22.7
35-44	31.6	17.7
Median years of school completed		
20-24	10.3	11.3
25-34	10.5	11.5
35-44	9.1	11.3
Percent high school graduate		
20-24	43.2	61.1
25-34	45.1	68.2
35-44	32.6	60.4

Source: 1990 Census, Public-Use Microdata Sample 5(%) A File.

it would be expected that the somewhat higher socioeconomic status of the
U.S.-born Puerto Rican group would exhibit a mortality profile with lower
proportions of deaths due to violent and otherwise preventable causes, relative to the island-born population.

MATERIALS AND METHODS

Since relatively few U.S.-born Puerto Ricans are aged above 45 years,
there are insufficient numbers of deaths for comparative analysis at older
ages. Further, since relatively few Puerto Rican-born residents of the United
States are at very young ages, decedents under age five have been excluded
as well. Due to small numbers of deaths in the younger age groups for
several causes, the analysis has been limited to a few major causes of death.

New York City whites and blacks were used as standard populations due
to the somewhat distinct mortality pattern of New York City, which was the
place of residence of approximately 70 percent of all Puerto Rican decedents
in this study. New York City, even more than other highly urban locations,
is characterized by low proportions of mortality from motor vehicle accidents
and somewhat higher proportions of mortality due to homicide, relative to
the United States as a whole. Since the Puerto Rican population in New
York State and New Jersey is overwhelmingly concentrated in central cities,
it is preferable to use standard populations from a comparable environment.
Puerto Ricans in New York State and New Jersey who did not reside in New
York City were more likely than blacks and particularly whites in these two
states to live in other urban locations such as Paterson and Newark. Thus,

New York City blacks and whites serve as more suitable standard populations than would blacks and whites from New York State and New Jersey.

Mortality data for the Puerto Rican decedent population were derived from codes for ethnicity and birthplace on death certificates for 1979–1981 and were provided by the health departments of the states of New York and New Jersey. Mortality data for New York City whites and blacks are from the National Center for Health Statistics Public Use Mortality Tapes for 1979–1981. Denominators are from the 1980 Census.

In 1980, the total Puerto Rican-born population of New York and New Jersey was 610,369 (of whom 405,290 were 5–44 years of age), and the mainland-born population of Puerto Rican origin was 619,560 (of whom 479,220 were 5–44 years). In the two study states, between 1979 and 1981, there were 2,629 reported deaths among island-born Puerto Ricans aged 5–44 years, and 1,052 reported deaths among the mainland-born in this age range.

Reporting of decedents of Puerto Rican origin appears fairly complete for the island-born population. For example, out of 9,270 Puerto Rican-born decedents in New York City during 1979–1981, 92.7 percent had their ethnicity reported as Puerto Rican, 3.7 percent were classified as "Other Spanish," and 0.7 percent were in other specific ethnic categories. Only 2.7 percent were coded as either "American" or "Unknown" (New York City Department of Health, 1979–1981). The U.S.-born generation, however, is likely to be underreported, since a considerably larger share of decedents are likely to have been reported as "American" or "Unknown." Between 1979 and 1981, the ethnicity of fully 65.4 percent of U.S.-born white decedents in New York City was coded as "American" or "Unknown." Since the children of immigrants represent a large part of New York City's population, this figure undoubtedly includes many who should have been classified to particular ethnic groups, Puerto Ricans among them.

There is reason to believe that relatively few Puerto Ricans (first or later generation in the United States) were improperly classified in the census. This is because, unlike the open-ended query on the death record, the census item on Spanish/Hispanic origin (including Puerto Rican as one of the specified categories) had a check box format. Those who did not respond were allocated to a particular category.

Underreporting of Puerto Rican ethnicity for U.S.-born decedents downwardly biases death rates for this population. Accordingly, in this study, death rates were not calculated, and proportional mortality analysis was used to compare the relative distributions of mortality by cause for the two Puerto Rican populations. These distributions also were compared with those of New York City whites and blacks. Proportional mortality analysis reflects relative differences in the distribution of deaths by cause but not differences in absolute levels of mortality. For the two Puerto Rican populations, standard confidence interval tests of statistical significance were performed on the differences in proportions at the five percent level (Kleinman, 1977).

RESULTS

Tables 11.2 and 11.3 show the proportional mortality distribution by cause for four age groups among the island- and U.S.-born Puerto Rican males and females. Significance tests performed at the 5 percent level reveal few significant differences in these distributions. U.S.-born males have significantly higher proportions of mortality due to non-motor vehicle accidents at age groups 15–24 and 25–34 years. The mainland-born group has significantly lower proportions of total mortality due to homicide for both males and females at age group 35–44. However, at age groups 15–24 and 25–34 years, homicide ranks as the leading cause of death for each population. U.S.-born males have significantly lower proportions of mortality due to suicide than do the Puerto Rican-born in age groups 15–24 and 25–34 years. Generally, however, the mortality distributions of the two nativity groups differ very little, although it should be noted that no inferences can be made regarding absolute levels of mortality from these observed similarities in the proportional distribution of mortality by cause.

Further perspective can be gained on the Puerto Rican mortality distributions by comparison with those for whites and blacks in New York City. Table 11.2 indicates that Puerto Rican males have mortality distributions somewhat more similar to that of blacks than of whites. Relative to New York City whites, both the Puerto Rican and black populations have high proportions of deaths due to homicide (over 30 percent at ages 15–24 and 25–34 years) and slightly lower proportions due to suicide and motor vehicle accidents. A unique characteristic of the Puerto Rican mortality distribution is the exceptionally high proportion of deaths due to cirrhosis of liver (over 20 percent at ages 35–44 years) and drug dependence (especially among the U.S.-born), as well as homicide.

Among the female populations shown in Table 11.3, differences between groups are somewhat less consistent. In general, the Puerto Rican groups have relatively high proportions of total mortality due to homicide, drug dependence and cirrhosis of liver.

Table 11.4 shows the proportion of mortality due to the "social pathologies," here defined as homicide, suicide, cirrhosis, drug dependence, motor vehicle, and all other accidents (Rogers and Hackenberg, 1987) among the four populations. The figures for males indicate that, in each population, the proportion of mortality due to social pathologies peaks in the age group 15–24. This trend is least pronounced for the mainland-born Puerto Rican group, for whom the difference in the proportion of mortality due to social pathologies between ages 15–24 and 25–34 is negligible, and for whom the decline

Table 11.2

Proportional Mortality of Island-born and Mainland-born Puerto Rican Residents of New York and New Jersey, and New York City Blacks and Whites, Males: 1979–81

Age and Cause of Death	Puerto Rican Island-born	Puerto Rican Mainland-born	Blacks	Whites[a]
5-14				
Total deaths (N)	36	123	198	275
Cancer	[b]0.14	0.11	0.15	0.19
Motor vehicle accidents	[b]0.17	0.27	0.16	0.22
All other accidents	[b]0.14	0.19	0.24	0.19
Homicide	[b]0.08	0.11	0.13	0.06
All other	0.47	0.32	0.32	0.34
15-24				
Total deaths (N)	341	371	1263	1543
Cardiovascular	[b]0.02	[b]0.02	0.03	0.02
Cancer	[b]0.03	0.05	0.02	0.05
Motor vehicle accidents	0.06	0.07	0.08	0.15
All other accidents	*0.04	*0.10	0.07	0.11
Suicide	*0.09	*0.04	0.05	0.09
Homicide	0.47	0.48	0.57	0.31
Drug Dependence	0.05	0.05	0.02	0.05
All other	0.24	0.19	0.16	0.22
25-34				
Total deaths (N)	744	219	2048	2331
Cardiovascular	0.05	[b]0.03	0.08	0.06
Cancer	0.03	[b]0.04	0.02	0.07
Motor vehicle accidents	0.05	[b]0.03	0.03	0.08
All other accidents	*0.02	*0.09	0.06	0.09
Cirrhosis	0.08	0.11	0.09	0.08
Suicide	*0.08	*[b]0.04	0.04	0.10
Homicide	0.37	0.31	0.35	0.20
Drug Dependence	*0.08	*0.16	0.10	0.09
All other	0.24	0.19	0.23	0.24
35-44				
Total deaths (N)	871	51	2354	2135
Cardiovascular	0.15	0.22	0.18	0.24
Cancer	0.08	[b]0.04	0.10	0.14
Motor vehicle accidents	0.05	[b]0.06	0.03	0.04
All other accidents	0.01	[b]0.02	0.04	0.04
Cirrhosis	0.20	0.22	0.18	0.13
Suicide	0.06	[b]0.06	0.02	0.07
Homicide	*0.19	*[b]0.06	0.15	0.10
Drug Dependence	*0.03	*[b]0.14	0.05	0.02
All other	0.23	[b]0.18	0.25	0.21

[a]New York City White group excludes the Puerto Rican-born.

[b]Based on less than ten deaths.

*Significantly different from other Puerto Rican group at the .05 percent level.

Note: Causes not listed where less than .05 in all cells.

at age group 35–44 is less sharp than for the other three male groups. The proportion of mortality due to social pathologies is similar among all groups at ages 15–24 and 25–34, but the two Puerto Rican groups exhibit the highest levels at ages 35–44. Among females the same general pattern holds, except in the case of the mainland-born group, for whom the proportion of mortality due to social pathologies does not peak at age group 15–24 years. In every

Table 11.3

Proportional Mortality of Island-born and Mainland-born Puerto Rican Residents of New York and New Jersey, and New York City Blacks and Whites, Females: 1979–81

Age and Cause of Death	Puerto Ricans Island-born	Puerto Ricans Mainland-born	Blacks	Whites[a]
5-14				
Total deaths (N)	31	61	149	149
Cardiovascular disease	[b]0.03	[b]0.04	[b]0.06	[b]0.03
Cancer	[b]0.13	[b]0.11	0.11	0.18
Motor vehicle accidents	[b]0.13	[b]0.15	0.13	0.12
All other accidents	[b]0.10	0.25	0.16	0.08
Homicide	[b]0.16	[b]0.10	0.12	0.13
All other	0.48	0.39	0.42	0.46
15-24				
Total deaths (N)	76	123	418	557
Cardiovascular disease	[b]0.08	[b]0.04	0.06	0.04
Cancer	[b]0.09	[b]0.03	0.07	0.10
Motor vehicle accidents	[b]0.09	[b]0.06	0.06	0.12
All other accidents	[b]0.03	[b]0.05	0.04	0.07
Suicide	[b]0.08	[b]0.06	0.05	0.09
Homicide	0.24	[b]0.24	0.24	0.15
Drug dependence	[b]0.04	[b]0.03	[b]0.02	0.03
All other	*0.35	0.49	0.47	0.40
25-34				
Total deaths (N)	172	76	847	828
Cardiovascular disease	[b]0.05	[b]0.08	0.10	0.08
Cancer	*0.11	*[b]0.04	0.09	0.18
Motor vehicle accidents	[b]0.02	[b]0.05	0.02	0.06
All other accidents	[b]0.02	[b]0.04	0.05	0.06
Cirrhosis of liver	0.07	[b]0.11	0.14	0.05
Suicide	0.08	[b]0.04	0.03	0.11
Homicide	0.15	[b]0.17	0.13	0.09
Drug dependence	0.10	[b]0.13	0.07	0.04
All other	0.40	0.34	0.37	0.33
35-44				
Total deaths (N)	319	28	1349	1055
Cardiovascular disease	0.21	[b]0.11	0.21	0.17
Cancer	0.24	[b]0.21	0.23	0.37
Motor vehicle accidents	[b]0.03	[b]0.07	0.02	0.03
All other accidents	[b]0.02	[b]0.11	0.02	0.03
Cirrhosis of liver	0.10	[b]0.14	0.13	0.07
Suicide	[b]0.02	[b]0.14	0.01	0.06
Homicide	*0.05	[b]0.00	0.04	0.02
Drug dependence	0.10	[b]0.04	0.02	[b]0.01
All other	0.30	[b]0.18	0.32	0.24

[a]New York City White group excludes the Puerto Rican-born.

[b]Based on less than ten deaths.

*Significanlty different from other Puerto Rican group at the .05 percent level.

Note: Causes not listed where less than .05 in all cells.

Table 11.4
Proportion of Mortality Due to "Social Pathologies"[a] for Puerto Rican Residents
of New York and New Jersey, by Birthplace, and New York City Blacks and
Whites: 1979–81

Race or Nativity Group, by Sex	Age Group			
	5-14	15-24	25-34	35-44
Island-born Puerto Ricans				
Total	0.39	0.67	0.65	0.47
Male	0.39	0.73	0.69	0.56
Female	0.39	0.48	0.44	0.26
U.S.-born Puerto Ricans				
Total	0.55	0.67	0.67	0.56
Male	0.57	0.75	0.74	0.58
Female	0.53	0.48	0.54	0.54
New York City Blacks				
Total	0.48	0.69	0.61	0.38
Male	0.53	0.78	0.68	0.47
Female	0.42	0.40	0.43	0.24
New York City Whites				
Total	0.42	0.65	0.57	0.35
Male	0.47	0.71	0.63	0.41
Female	0.34	0.46	0.41	0.22

[a]Homicide, suicide, cirrhosis of liver, drug dependence, motor vehicle accidents, and all other
accidents.

population, females had lower proportions of deaths due to social pathologies
than did males.

DISCUSSION

The proportional mortality analysis suggests that the distribution of mortality by cause differs little between the two nativity groups, indicating that
the mainland-born Puerto Rican population has not assimilated to the mortality pattern of New York City whites. Both Puerto Rican nativity groups
showed similarly high proportions of mortality due to violent, accidental,
and otherwise preventable causes of death.

A cautionary note clearly is necessary. The proportional mortality distribution is based on the mortality data by cause taken from ethnic identification
on death certificates. As discussed above, there is good reason to suspect
underreporting of Puerto Rican ethnicity for mainland-born Puerto Rican
decedents. To consider the proportional mortality distribution calculated in
this study for the mainland-born group to be representative of that population
it is necessary to assume that the distribution of mortality by cause for
mainland-born Puerto Rican decedents who were not coded as "Puerto Rican" on death certificates approximates that among those who were so coded.
This may be a somewhat heroic assumption, as mainland-born Puerto Rican
decedents coded as "American" or "Unknown" rather than "Puerto Rican"
(and hence not included in the proportional mortality distribution) may well

have been more assimilated—in life as well as in cause of death—to the host population than were those coded as "Puerto Rican."

The substantial socioeconomic differences (Table 11.1) between the two Puerto Rican groups suggest that the mainland-born Puerto Rican population should have a mortality distribution that corresponds more closely to that of New York City whites. In particular, one would expect that the proportion of mortality due to "social pathologies" would be somewhat lower among the U.S.-born relative to the island-born population. Yet this expectation was not borne out by the proportional mortality data presented in this study. Although it is possible that underreporting of Puerto Rican ethnicity on death certificates for U.S.-born decedents has affected the proportional distribution of mortality by cause for this group in a nonrandom manner, it is doubtful that adjustment for underreporting would substantially alter the findings observed here.

PART FIVE

Surname Methodology

CHAPTER 12

The Use of Surname Data in the Analysis of Mortality Rates of U.S. Mainland-born Puerto Ricans

IRA ROSENWAIKE, KATHERINE HEMPSTEAD, AND RICHARD G. ROGERS

INTRODUCTION

A population's mortality rates are significant indicators of its health and socioeconomic status. In calculating mortality rates, it is assumed that the denominator and numerator refer to the same population, but the construction of accurate mortality rates for Hispanic-origin populations has been complicated by problems in reporting Hispanic ethnicity on death records. The need of researchers and policy makers for reliable mortality data for persons of Hispanic origin residing in the United States was recently addressed by the Task Force on Black and Minority Health (U.S. Department of Health and Human Services, 1985). At about the same time, the National Center for Health Statistics (NCHS) included for the first time an item on Hispanic origin in the U.S. Standard Certificate of Death that was implemented in the states in 1989 (Freedman et al., 1988). Yet, further research is necessary before the potential usefulness of the new Hispanic ethnicity item can be fully understood (Estrada, 1987).

To assess the usefulness of the new ethnicity item, one valuable approach is to examine the experiences of states that added a query on ethnic origin to their death certificates during the 1980 census period (Trevino, 1982). Rosenwaike and Bradshaw (1988) analyzed ethnic reporting on death certificates in the five Southwestern states where Mexicans are the major group in the Hispanic population. In the present study, we look at possible underreporting of Puerto Rican origin on death records in two Northeastern states, New York and New Jersey, where the majority of the U.S. mainland's

Puerto Rican population resides. Underreporting of deaths has significant consequences because it underestimates mortality rates, and consequently, may provide an inaccurate picture of differential mortality among distinct components of the Puerto Rican population, such as the mainland-born and island-born groups. After calculating age-specific death rates by sex for both island- and mainland-born Puerto Ricans with the original vital statistics data, we present evidence which suggests that the unadjusted rates for the mainland-born group are underestimated due to underreporting of Puerto Rican ethnicity on the death certificate. We then adjust the numerators for these rates by using a list of Spanish surnames to allocate Spanish-surnamed decedents believed to be mainland-born Puerto Ricans whose ethnicity was coded as "American" or "Unknown," rather than as Puerto Rican. The adjusted and unadjusted mortality rates are compared to rates for island-born Puerto Ricans in New York and New Jersey and to rates for U.S. whites.

The three conventional ways to determine Hispanic ethnicity have been self-identification, surname identification, and identification by place of birth. Surname identification has not been previously used in a mortality study of a Puerto Rican population, although the procedure has been often used in studies of Mexican-Americans in the Southwest (Bradshaw and Fonner, 1978; Bradshaw and Frisbie, 1983; Hernandez, Estrada, and Alvirez, 1972; Powell-Griner and Streck, 1982; Roberts and Askew, 1972; Schoen and Nelson, 1981; Sullivan et al., 1984; Hayes-Bautista and Chapa, 1987). In fact, before the U.S. Bureau of the Census queried ethnic identification in the Current Population Survey in 1969 and in the 1970 decennial census, the use of Spanish surname data was the major approach to identifying Hispanic populations in the Southwest. We take this approach one step further, however, by examining mortality among Puerto Ricans.

Until recently, there has been little need for an alternative identifier for examining the mortality of the Puerto Rican population on the U.S. mainland, since most decedents could be identified through the birthplace query. But the mainland-born Puerto Rican population is growing rapidly, and there is increasing interest in the mortality experience of this group. The Census Bureau's pre–1980 Spanish surname lists were far less sensitive in selecting persons of Puerto Rican origin than they were in selecting persons of Mexican origin, since many Spanish surnames common among Puerto Ricans were excluded (Passel and Word, 1980). The Census Bureau prepared a new and expanded list of Spanish surnames for use with the 1980 Census. Thus, whereas 37 percent of respondents self-reported as Puerto Rican origin in a 1971 sample of persons selected from the Current Population Survey did not have a Spanish surname according to the 1970 list (U.S. Bureau of the Census, 1975), an analogous study based on a 1976 sample which used the 1980 list found that only 15 percent did not have a Spanish surname (Passel and Word, 1980). Passel and Word (1980) argue that the new procedures are "extremely" successful in selecting names belonging to persons of Puerto

Rican descent. Clearly the revised list has provided new possibilities for the study of Puerto Rican populations through surname analysis.

EVIDENCE OF UNDERREPORTING

We initially calculated age and sex-specific mortality rates for the island- and mainland-born Puerto Rican population of New York and New Jersey, using as numerators mortality data made available by the health departments of the two states. Denominators were obtained from the 1980 Census Public Use Microdata Sample A (5 percent) file (U.S. Bureau of the Census, 1980). We used 10-year age groups for the population above age 5. Because of small numbers of deaths at older ages among mainland-born Puerto Ricans, the decedent group was limited to those under 35 years of age. (Due to the limited size of the sample, the possibility of sampling error must be kept in mind.) Rates for the island-born population below age 5 were not calculated, due to the small numbers of deaths at these ages.

Table 12.1 shows age-specific death rates calculated for the island- and mainland-born Puerto Rican population in New York and New Jersey and comparable figures for the standard population, U.S. whites. For both sexes combined, mainland-born Puerto Ricans have death rates that average between 56 and 71 percent of those of the island-born. The mortality rates of the mainland-born Puerto Rican population (males and females) are also lower than those for U.S. whites, except for the age groups 0–4 and 25–34 years. Mortality rates for the island-born group are invariably higher than those for the standard population. Indeed, island-born Puerto Ricans have mortality rates at age 25–34 that are almost 90 percent higher than the U.S. white population.

Direct evidence that ethnic reporting for island-born Puerto Rican decedents is fairly complete can be obtained from cross classification of the birthplace and ancestry items. For example, out of 9,270 island-born decedents in New York City during 1979–1981, 92.7 percent had their ethnicity reported as Puerto Rican. Only 2.7 percent had records coded as either "American" or "Unknown" (New York City Department of Health, 1979–1981). The ethnicity of the mainland-born Puerto Rican population, however, is more likely to be underreported, because 65.4 percent of all white U.S. mainland-born decedents in 1979–1981 were reported as "American" or "Unknown" (New York City Department of Health, 1979–1981). Since the children of immigrants represent a large part of New York City's population, this figure undoubtedly includes many individuals who should have been classified to particular ethnic groups. Puerto Ricans are one such ethnic group.

The figures in Table 12.1 provide only indirect evidence of underreporting of deaths of U.S.-born Puerto Ricans. More direct evidence is provided by comparing our (unadjusted) mortality data for 1979–1981 to the data in a

Table 12.1

Age-Specific Mortality Rates of Puerto Rican-Origin Residents of New York and New Jersey, by Birthplace, and U.S. Whites: 1979–81 (Rates per 100,000 Population)

Sex and Age	Mainland-born (1)	Island-born (2)	U.S. Whites (3)	Ratio: Mainland-born to Island-born (1)/(2)	Ratio: Mainland-born to U.S. Whites (1)/(3)	Ratio: Island-born to U.S. Whites (2)/(3)
Both sexes						
Under 1	1075.0	–	1087.3	–	0.99*	–
0-4	279.7	–	279.5	–	1.00*	–
5-14	26.2	46.8	29.1	0.56*	0.90*	1.61*
15-24	98.5	168.0	109.2	0.59*	0.90*	1.54*
25-34	156.8	219.6	117.7	0.71*	1.33*	1.87*
Male						
Under 1	1227.8	–	1216.7	–	1.01*	–
0-4	325.1	–	312.9	–	1.04*	–
5-14	34.7	51.0	35.3	0.68*	0.98*	1.44*
15-24	154.7	294.9	162.5	0.52*	0.95*	1.81*
25-34	251.2	419.2	169.8	0.60*	1.48*	2.47*
Female						
Under 1	920.5	–	951.0	–	0.97*	–
0-4	233.2	–	244.2	–	0.95*	–
5-14	17.5	42.8	22.6	0.41*	0.77*	1.89*
15-24	47.0	57.3	54.4	0.82*	0.86*	1.05*
25-34	75.3	71.8	65.4	1.05*	1.15*	1.10*

Note: Rates not shown for island-born population under five years due to small numbers of deaths. Death rates under 1 year are based on census figures and differ from Infant Mortality Rate (based on number of live births).

*Significantly different from 1.0 at the .05 level.

recent study of infant mortality in New York City, where birth and death certificates were linked for the years 1980–1983 (Chavkin, Busner, and McLaughlin, 1987). For New York City-born Puerto Rican infants whose mothers were born in Puerto Rico, Chavkin and her colleagues found the infant mortality rate to be 12.7 per thousand; for those Hispanic infants (almost entirely Puerto Rican) whose mothers were born on the U.S. mainland, 13.8 per thousand. These rates which relate only to singleton births and exclude death certificates for which a corresponding birth certificate could not be located are considerably higher than that shown for the total population of mainland-born Puerto Rican infants in Table 12.1, namely, 1075.0 per 100,000, or 10.8 per 1,000. Although it is possible that some of the observed difference stems from the use of birth and death certificates in the Chavkin study versus the use of death certificates and census records in our calculations, and the inclusion of Puerto Ricans in New Jersey and upstate New York in our study, such a large difference in rates is unlikely. We believe that our mortality rate for the mainland-born Puerto Rican population under one year of age is artifactually underestimated due to underreporting of Puerto Rican ethnicity for mainland-born decedents.

THE SURNAME ANALYSIS PROCEDURE

In response to this apparent underreporting of Puerto Rican ethnicity on the death certificates of mainland-born decedents, we adjusted age-specific death rates through the use of surname analysis, an attempt to reallocate Spanish-surnamed decedents coded as "American" or "Unknown" but believed to be Puerto Rican.

We employed a New York City Health Department mortality computer tape which lists the surname and ethnic identity of all decedents in New York City in 1979–1981. The surnames were coded "Spanish" or "non-Spanish" according to the 1980 Census list of Spanish surnames (Passel and Word, 1980). This resulted in a distribution of U.S.-born decedents by surname (Spanish or non-Spanish) and ethnicity.

The objective of the procedure was to retrieve those Spanish-surnamed decedents coded as "American" or "Unknown" who were actually mainland-born Puerto Ricans. We assumed that all mainland-born Puerto Rican decedents who were not coded as Puerto Rican were classified as "American" or "Unknown," a reasonable assumption as indicated in Table 12.2, which shows the distribution of ethnic categories (excluding "American" and "Unknown") for mainland-born Spanish-surnamed decedents. It was unlikely that many Spanish-surnamed decedents who were actually of Puerto Rican ethnicity were coded as "Mexican," "Cuban," or "Other Spanish." Similarly, the "All Other" category (all non-Hispanic ethnic groups) for age and sex groups accounts for a relatively small proportion of Spanish-surnamed deaths. (If the "American" and "Unknown" categories were included in this distribution, the proportion in the "All Other" category would be even smaller.)

We first calculated the proportion of all Spanish-surnamed decedents (except those coded as "American" or "Unknown") coded as "Puerto Rican." Table 12.2 presents the proportion of Spanish-surnamed decedents who were coded as Puerto Rican, by age and sex. The proportions who are Puerto Rican range from 65 to 86 percent. Overall, the proportion that is Puerto Rican is slightly lower for females than for males, and is lowest in the youngest age group. The low proportion in the youngest age group may reflect growing numbers of Dominican and other Latin American groups whose migration to New York City has climbed in recent years, since the proportion "Other Spanish" is also relatively high for young Spanish-surnamed decedents. We then multiplied the proportion Puerto Rican among all Spanish-surnamed decedents by the total number of decedents in the "American" or "Unknown" categories, to allocate Spanish-surnamed decedents classified in these two groups to the "Puerto Rican" category.[1] We made another adjustment to account for the relatively few non-Spanish-surnamed Puerto Rican decedents

Table 12.2
Percent Distribution of Mainland-born Spanish Surname Decedents by Ethnic
Origin, New York City: 1979–81

Sex and Age	Total (No.)	American	Unknown	Specific Ethnic Origins				
				Total		Puerto Rican	Other Hispanic	All Other
				No.	%			
Male								
Under 5	712	113	106	493	100	74	21	5
5–14	98	9	4	85	100	82	14	4
15–24	365	54	9	302	100	86	9	5
25–34	262	40	9	213	100	78	12	9
Female								
Under 5	532	101	72	359	100	65	29	6
5–14	58	7	1	50	100	78	22	0
15–24	123	19	5	99	100	80	17	3
25–34	100	23	2	75	100	71	13	16

who were coded as "American" or "Unknown." This procedure amplified
the allocated number by the proportion of U.S.-born Puerto Rican decedents
having non-Spanish surnames. This proportion varied by age and sex, but
was generally quite small, usually between 10 and 15 percent.[2]

To adjust our numerator, we reallocated some of the Spanish-surnamed
decedents who were coded as "American" or "Unknown" to Puerto Ricans.
The entire procedure to determine the new allocations took the following
arithmetic form:

PRSS/(ALLSS − AMSS) × AMSS × ALLPR/PRSS = NEW ALLOCATION
Where:
PRSS   = Spanish-surnamed decedents originally coded "Puerto Rican."
ALLSS = All Spanish-surnamed decedents.
AMSS = Spanish-surnamed decedents coded "American" or "Unknown."
ALLPR = All decedents originally coded "Puerto Rican."

Data on surnames were only available for New York City. To adjust mortality statistics for New Jersey and for the balance of New York State, it was
necessary to assume that the degree of underreporting of ethnicity on death
certificates was similar to that in New York City. Since a large proportion
(approximately 75 percent) of all deaths to U.S.-born Puerto Ricans in the
states of New York and New Jersey occurred in New York City, reporting
is known to be consistent for at least three-quarters of all deaths. Nevertheless, the reader should be aware of this assumption.

To illustrate the technique, let us take the case of males under age 5. As
shown in Table 12.2, there were 493 Spanish-surnamed decedents (ALLSS)
in this category. Of these, 370, or 74 percent, were originally coded as
Puerto Rican (PRSS). This 74 percent (PRSS/ALLSS) is multiplied by the
number of Spanish-surnamed decedents in the "American" and "Unknown"

Table 12.3

Number of Deaths Among Mainland-born Puerto Rican Residents of New York and New Jersey, 1979–81, Before and After Spanish Surname Adjustment

Sex and Age	Original Number	Proportional Increase	Adjusted Number
Total			
Under 5	1058	1.46	1545
5–14	184	1.16	213
15–24	494	1.22	603
25–34	295	1.26	372
Male			
Under 5	622	1.44	896
5–14	123	1.15	141
15–24	371	1.21	449
25–34	219	1.23	269
Female			
Under 5	436	1.48	645
5–14	61	1.16	71
15–24	123	1.24	153
25–34	76	1.33	101

categories (AMSS), of whom there were 219 in this example (Table 12.2). Seventy-four percent of 219, or 162, is the initial allocation.

Next we wish to incorporate non-Spanish-surnamed Puerto Rican decedents. To do this we take the ratio of all Puerto Rican decedents to those with Spanish surnames (ALLPR/PRSS). (These numbers are not shown in the tables.) In the present case, the ratio was 1.15, which we then multiplied by the initial allocation. In this example, 162 multiplied by 1.15, or 186, is the final allocation of decedents to the Puerto Rican category. When we add this 186 to the original numerator (ALLPR), which in this case was 420, the adjusted numerator becomes 606. These calculations, as noted above, are based on New York City data. To adjust the number of deaths for this age group and sex for the states of New York and New Jersey, we multiply the ratio of the new to the old numerator from New York City, 606 divided by 420, or 1.44, by the total number of deaths from the states of New York and New Jersey. As can be seen from Table 12.3, this initial number is 622. When multiplied by 1.44, the adjusted number of deaths is 896, which is also shown in Table 12.3.

THE ADJUSTMENT OF MORTALITY DATA

Table 12.3 shows the extent to which the surname analysis procedure increases the number of deaths originally reported for mainland-born Puerto Ricans. Since the greatest proportionate increase occurs at ages 0–4 years for both males and females, underreporting is assumed to be the highest in this age interval. Such results are supported by the findings of Chavkin, Busner, and McLaughlin (1987). These underestimates at young ages may

Table 12.4
Adjusted[a] Age-Specific Death Rates, Mainland-born Puerto Rican Residents of
New York and New Jersey, and Ratios of Adjusted Rates to Rates for Island-
born Puerto Rican Residents of the Same States and U.S. Whites: 1979–81
(Rates per 100,000 population)

Sex and Age	Adjusted Rates Mainland-born	Adjusted Ratio Mainland-born to Island-born	Mainland-born to U.S. Whites
Both sexes			
Under 1	1601.7	-	1.47*
0-4	408.3	-	1.46*
5-14	30.4	0.65*	1.04
15-24	120.2	0.72*	1.10*
25-34	197.6	0.90*	1.68*
Male			
Under 1	1829.4	-	1.50*
0-4	468.1	-	1.50*
5-14	40.0	0.78*	1.13*
15-24	187.2	0.63*	1.15*
25-34	309.0	0.74*	1.82*
Female			
Under 1	1380.8	-	1.45*
0-4	345.1	-	1.41*
5-14	20.3	0.47*	0.90
15-24	58.3	1.02	1.07
25-34	100.2	1.40*	1.53*

[a]Based on Spanish surname analysis.

*Significantly different from 1.0 at the .05 level.

have occurred because a substantial proportion of infant and child decedents
had mainland-born parents who probably provided the ethnic classification
on the death certificate, and may have been more likely to identify their
child as "American" than would parents born in Puerto Rico.

Table 12.4 shows adjusted age-specific death rates for the mainland-born
Puerto Rican group and the adjusted ratios of mainland-born to island-born,
and mainland-born to U.S. white mortality. The rates differ from those in
Table 12.1 because the death rates for the mainland-born Puerto Rican group
have now been adjusted through the use of surname analysis. As can be
seen, the adjusted ratios of mainland- to island-born mortality rates are
higher than are the unadjusted ratios. The change is somewhat greater for
females than for males, although it should be noted that there are relatively
few female deaths in the age group 25–34 years. The mainland-born Puerto
Rican group now has death rates which are generally high relative to those
of U.S. whites, particularly for the age group 25–34 years.

CONCLUSION

This research has provided a detailed example of the use of surname
analysis to adjust mortality data for Puerto Ricans living in the conterminous

United States. The surname procedure provided mortality estimates which we believe are more reasonable than those calculated with the unadjusted data for the mainland-born Puerto Rican population of New York and New Jersey, 1979–1981. These adjusted estimates must be regarded as illustrative rather than definitive. Nevertheless, our results provide an initial assessment of the quality, accuracy, and utility of vital statistics data in areas with large Puerto Rican populations and highlight the need to attend to technical issues in Hispanic, especially Puerto Rican, mortality research. In the 1990 census period, new analytical possibilities will emerge for mortality estimates. Our findings show new applications of the ethnic group identifier, but also provide a cautionary note as to the indiscriminate use of such data. The potential of surname analysis is great, since it provides a new opportunity to enhance the exploration of the relationship between nativity, environment, and mortality for selected Hispanic populations.

NOTES

1. A possible bias inherent in this procedure is the assumption that all Spanish-surnamed decedents coded as "American" or "Unknown" are either Puerto Rican, Mexican, Cuban, "Other Spanish," or "All Other." Some decedents in these two categories probably acquired Spanish surnames as spouses or as children of exogamous marriages, and are no longer of a classifiable ethnicity. Unfortunately, this bias is unavoidable. Since the surname analysis procedure assumes that a certain proportion of the decedents in these two categories are actually Puerto Rican. The effect of this may be an overstating of the proportion of decedents who are Puerto Rican, yet the bias is believed to be relatively small.

2. This adjustment was made by multiplying the number of Spanish-surnamed decedents allocated into the "Puerto Rican" category from the "American" or "Unknown" categories by the ratio of the total number of decedents originally in the "Puerto Rican" category to those with Spanish surnames.

PART SIX

Overview

CHAPTER 13

An Overview of Age-adjusted Death Rates Among Three Hispanic Populations in Their Home Countries and in the United States

DONNA SHAI AND IRA ROSENWAIKE

The objective of this volume has been to describe the mortality patterns of Hispanic population groups in the United States and in their home countries. These studies have shown that the three major Hispanic groups—Mexicans, Puerto Ricans, and Cubans—have distinct mortality profiles with variations in the rates of death from specific causes of death. To help determine whether distinct mortality patterns are due to genetic differences or lifestyles, comparisons of the mortality rates for each subpopulation of immigrants in the United States with rates for the home country may provide some clues (Krueger and Moriyama, 1967).

This chapter presents an overview of mortality among the immigrant sector of the three major Spanish-origin groups in the United States and mortality in their home countries. This overview begins with a comparison of the mortality for major causes of death for each individual Hispanic population, and concludes with a summary for the major causes of death for all groups.

Death rates previously prepared for each Hispanic subpopulation in the United States were compared with data from the home area. Mortality data for Puerto Rico for the years 1979–1981 were developed from death record tapes provided by the Puerto Rican health department. Data for Cuba for 1981 came from published sources (The World Health Organization), and data for Mexico for 1980 came from official published and unpublished tabulations. Age-, sex-, and cause-specific death rates were calculated for each population using census figures as denominators. Since age-standardized rates for the U.S.-born migrant groups had been calculated using the 1980 census total population of the United States above age 5 (to exclude infants, who are unlikely to be foreign born) as the standard, this standard population was retained. A summary of the results for all causes and leading causes is presented in Table 13.1.

PUERTO RICANS

In comparing the death rates for Puerto Ricans on the U.S. mainland and Puerto Ricans on the Island, it is important to keep in mind the extensive exchange of population between the two localities. Many Puerto Ricans on the Island have been exposed at some point in their lives to the mainland environment and vice versa (Fitzpatrick, 1987). In addition, return migrants to the Island are substantially older than other migrants, a fact which may elevate rates on the Island from certain causes of death. Moreover, just as the heavy concentration of Puerto Ricans in the New York City/New Jersey area has been extensive enough to provide for the maintenance of many cultural elements from the Island, including diet, language, attitudes and lifestyle, over time Puerto Rico itself has been considerably "Americanized," further diminishing sharp differences between the two populations (Garcia-Palmieri et al., 1965).

A comparison of the age-adjusted death rates in the two Puerto Rican groups reveals both similarities and differences. There are almost no differences in the overall death rates, although males on the mainland have slightly higher rates than males on the Island, while mainland females have a slightly lower rate than those on the Island. This similarity is not surprising, given the overlap in population between the two locations. Cancer rates for both groups are very similar, which suggests the influence of inherited characteristics and shared lifestyle. There is little difference in rates for accidents, chronic obstructive pulmonary disease, cirrhosis of the liver, and suicide.

Rates for homicide were especially low on the Island compared to those on the mainland, whereas mainland rates for cancer of the cervix, cancer of the ovary, and cancer of the bladder among women were twice those of the Island. Among mainland Puerto Ricans, greater drug abuse is no doubt due to the stress of migration as well as factors of availability. Although not shown in Table 13.1, the high rates for drug dependence in the United States (2.9 per 100,000 persons of both sexes, 4.9 per 100,000 males and 1.1 per 100,000 females) are to some extent artifactual, since drug dependence is coded differently in various registration areas due to practices of the local medical examiner's offices (Gottschalk et al., 1979). In particular, the very high rates for Puerto Ricans in New York City (e.g., 1.28 per 100,000 males) may not be comparable to rates on the Island. Therefore, the low rates on the Island (0.1 per 100,000) may not necessarily reflect an insignificant problem of death by drug dependence, but rather different coding practices.

Compared to the mainland groups, Puerto Ricans on the Island have relatively high rates for cerebrovascular disease, pneumonia and influenza,

Table 13.1

Age-Adjusted Death Rates for Selected Causes of Death Among the Puerto Rican-, Mexican-, and Cuban-born in the United States as Compared with Their Home Countries: 1979–81 (Rates per 100,000 population)

Cause of Death	Puerto Rican-Born (U.S.)	Puerto Rico	Mexican-Born (U.S.)	Mexico	Cuban-Born (U.S.)	Cuba[a]
All causes, Total	872.8	879.9	819.3	1051.4	689.4	855.5
Male	1121.1	1068.6	1012.0	1207.7	900.7	955.8
Female	680.5	708.6	637.9	897.3	526.8	752.0
Diseases of heart, Total	338.8	252.6	272.4	200.0	252.8	280.2
Male	400.7	289.1	328.8	209.7	320.8	308.5
Female	292.8	219.2	224.2	189.4	200.4	251.1
Malignant neoplasms, Total	150.5	148.6	146.9	97.5	155.1	166.7
Male	193.8	189.8	173.1	93.7	198.0	199.9
Female	122.1	111.8	126.7	101.3	126.7	131.8
Cerebrovascular diseases, Total	56.7	69.7	72.3	61.5	47.7	88.7
Male	59.5	73.1	75.5	59.7	48.6	88.6
Female	54.3	66.5	69.4	62.7	46.5	89.0
Accidents and adverse effects, Total	38.7	35.7	67.4	47.8	36.1	80.2
Male	64.6	59.7	107.8	159.5	58.2	104.7
Female	16.5	13.7	23.1	38.2	16.8	55.4
Chronic obstructive pulmonary diseases, Total	24.1	23.9	15.4	34.3	14.6	10.5
Male	30.5	27.3	22.8	39.8	23.4	11.5
Female	20.0	20.8	9.6	29.2	9.0	9.5
Pneumonia and influenza, Total	30.7	41.9	25.1	57.2	16.0	60.4
Male	39.2	50.9	31.4	60.9	21.7	66.8
Female	25.1	33.9	20.0	53.3	12.3	53.8
Chronic liver disease and cirrhosis, Total	38.1	35.3	18.3	47.6	13.4	9.1
Male	66.0	58.1	27.4	75.0	17.1	10.7
Female	15.7	14.7	9.8	21.6	10.5	7.5
Suicide, Total	12.9	11.5	7.2	2.1	14.6	24.7[b]
Male	24.2	20.6	11.7	3.5	26.3	27.9[b]
Female	3.5	3.3	2.4	0.7	4.8	21.3[b]
Homicide, Total	39.9	18.2	34.8	25.6	33.6	4.5[b]
Male	75.6	34.0	60.4	47.5	63.1	6.3[b]
Female	8.4	3.8	5.0	4.2	7.9	2.5[b]
Diabetes mellitus, Total	29.6	41.1	28.8	59.2	14.7	19.1
Male	26.7	35.7	24.7	53.6	15.7	14.1
Female	31.0	45.8	32.2	63.9	13.9	24.4
All other causes, Total	112.9	201.5	130.5	368.5	90.7	147.5
Male	140.3	230.3	148.4	404.8	107.9	157.1
Female	91.9	175.2	115.4	332.7	78.0	129.7

[a]1981
[b]1977

diabetes, infectious/parasitic diseases, cancers (of the esophagus, stomach, liver, uterus, and prostate), arteriosclerosis, senility and ill-defined conditions, motor vehicle accidents, and undetermined injury. Since many of these conditions are especially likely to affect the elderly, the return migration to the Island may inflate the rate of death from these causes. The higher rates of death from motor vehicle accidents on the Island (not shown) may be related to differences in the level of automobile use. Since New York City has an extensive public transportation system, the New York City population, particularly those from lower socioeconomic levels, are at relatively lower risk of motor vehicle accident. On the other hand, San Juan has no subway system, and driving is essential for commuting over the entire island. Therefore, the higher rates of death by motor vehicle accident may reflect increased exposure to risk.

In general, the Island population has higher rates for causes of death more common in developing countries, such as pneumonia, influenza, and infectious and parasitic diseases. The mainland population has somewhat higher rates for causes common in more developed nations, such as cancer of the colon, breast cancer among women, and heart disease. Despite the similarity in the environments, differences reflect the more industrialized, urban nature of the mainland, especially New York City.

MEXICANS

A comparison of mortality of Mexicans and the Mexican-born in the United States shows only a few causes of death for which rates are similar. These are cerebrovascular diseases, homicide, and motor vehicle accidents, all slightly higher among the Mexican-born.

In general, the higher death rates in Mexico from various causes may be due to the "healthy migrant effect." Studies of immigrant mortality have observed that migration is not a random process, and migrants are often a highly select group with regard to health (Marmot, Adelstein, and Bulusu, 1984). Mortality rates in Mexico are higher for accidents, chronic obstructive pulmonary diseases, pneumonia, influenza, and infectious and parasitic diseases. These are all causes associated with per capita income (Kagamimori, Libuchi, and Fox, 1983), and their prevalence in Mexico may reflect economic differences between the two countries. Mexico also has higher mortality rates for liver cirrhosis, which may indicate differences in drinking practices in the two populations.

Death rates for senility and ill-defined conditions, in particular, are higher in Mexico. The proportion of deaths assigned to this classification is often used as an indicator of the completeness of death reporting: countries with the most complete records of death have relatively few cases assigned to ill-defined conditions (Shryock and Siegel, 1975). The proportion of all deaths in 1980 attributed to senility and ill-defined conditions was 7 percent in

Mexico as compared to 1.8 percent among the Mexican-born in the United States. This strongly suggests less complete reporting in Mexico.

Conversely, the higher rates found among Mexicans in the United States for most forms of cancer, including all cancers, esophageal, colon, rectal, liver, lung, breast, and bladder cancer, may be due to the more complete reporting in the United States. Since diagnosis of these causes depends on the quality of medical care, it is possible that these causes may be under-diagnosed in Mexico due to less complete medical care. The higher rates for colon and rectal cancer among the Mexican-Americans may also be due to acculturation to an industrialized society and its higher standard of living (including a richer diet), since these cancers are associated with these factors. The higher mortality rates from heart disease are also typical of persons at higher socioeconomic levels (Kagamimori, Libuchi, and Fox, 1983), although the differential is higher for males than for females.

Overall, the major finding is that the Mexican-born in the United States have unusually low rates of death compared with Mexicans in their home country. There are several possible reasons for this differential. As suggested earlier, it may be due to the "healthy migrant effect." Since Mexicans cannot travel as easily to the mainland United States as Puerto Ricans can, the decision to migrate may select against persons in poor health. Differences in health services may also account for the differentials in mortality for several causes. In fact, the differential may be understated: to the extent that the population of the U.S. Mexican-born may be undercounted (especially among younger males), death rates for all causes may be overestimated, and this would particularly apply to causes such as homicide and accidents.

CUBANS

As is typical of a population of higher socioeconomic status, Cubans in the United States show lower mortality from almost every leading cause of death than do their counterparts in Cuba. The exceptions are cirrhosis of liver (perhaps due to greater levels of alcohol consumption in the United States) and most particularly, homicide, which is several times higher among emigrants. Cubans in the United States had higher rates for colon cancer and female breast cancer, which is typical of industrialized countries. They also had higher rates for chronic obstructive pulmonary disease (among males), liver cancer, and leukemia. On the other hand, Cubans in the home country have higher rates for heart disease, cerebrovascular diseases, accidents, pneumonia and influenza, diabetes (among females), and many cancers, including esophageal, stomach, rectal, lung, cervical, uterine, and prostate.

The Cubans who migrated to the United States prior to 1980 are a highly select group, representing a substantial share of Cuba's higher social class. That Cubans in the United States have lower age-adjusted mortality than do persons in Cuba is in accord with differential mortality by social class.

Table 13.2

Mortality Patterns in Hispanic Populations, 1979–81: Age Specific Death Rates, Selected Ages, All Causes of Death (Rates per 100,000 population)

Population Group	Males			Females		
	15–24	45–54	65–74	15–24	45–54	65–74
Puerto Rican Born (U.S.)	237.9	913.0	3,440.6	51.2	369.4	2,151.8
Puerto Rico	157.6	782.5	3,264.2	41.5	341.6	2,040.8
Cuban Born (U.S.)	179.6	527.2	2,847.3	49.6	242.9	1,459.8
Cuba (U.S.)	120.8	545.1	3,166.8	107.9	419.6	2,227.4
Mexican Born (U.S.)	311.3	486.7	3,250.5	46.3	254.3	2,046.5
Mexico	266.9	1,017.8	3,630.8	103.8	567.7	2,766.9
U.S. (Whites)	162.5	698.0	3,992.4	54.4	372.1	2,036.7

On the other hand, the very high rates of death by homicide among the Cuban-born in the United States seem to be due in part to the Mariel migration, which unlike previous migrations had fewer middle-class persons and included a core of individuals with criminal backgrounds.

MORTALITY PATTERNS BY AGE

In accordance with Brouard and Lopez's age categories (1985), age groups 15–24, 45–54, and 65–74 were selected for special study, since they are "periods of life when the composition of the leading causes of death is likely to change" (386). Table 13.2 shows the age-specific mortality rates by sex for the six Hispanic populations under consideration, as well as those of the general U.S. white population.

For males aged 15–24, mortality is higher for all three U.S.-resident Hispanic populations than for U.S. white males. The rate for U.S.-resident Mexican males is especially high. Of the countries of origin, mortality rates are highest for young men in Mexico and relatively low for young men in Cuba. Among middle-aged men the pattern changes. For males aged 45–54, mortality rates are relatively high for the U.S. resident Puerto Rican-born, but lower for the Cuban- and Mexican-born, who have rates below those of U.S. white males. Among the countries of origin, Mexico has the highest rate at these ages, and Cuba has the lowest. The rate in Puerto Rico is somewhat higher than the U.S. white rate. Among males aged 65–74 years, all of the Hispanic subpopulations have relatively low mortality rates, with the U.S. resident Cuban-born having the lowest rates.

Overall, the pattern for Hispanic men has a "balance" (following Brouard and Lopez's terminology) among the Puerto Rican-born males between higher mortality at ages 15–24 and 45–54 years and low mortality at the older ages relative to U.S. whites. Among the Mexican-born there is especially high mortality for young adults balanced by relatively low mortality at ages 45–54 and 65–74 years. Among the Cuban-born there are distinctly lower rates at all three age groups. In the countries of origin, the mortality experience of Puerto Rican males follows closely that of the U.S. white male population with slightly lower rates at the younger years, somewhat higher rates at middle-age and lower rates at the older ages. Mexico has relatively high mortality rates in both the younger and at middle age, with lower mortality at the older ages. Cuban males, on the other hand, have lower mortality at all three ages.

With regard to females, all three immigrant Hispanic groups in the United States have relatively low mortality at the younger and middle-aged years. At the oldest age group, the mortality of both Puerto Rican-born and Mexican-born females exceeds that of white women in the United States. Cuban-born women residing in the U.S. have lower rates at all three ages. In the countries of origin, young women in Puerto Rico have lower mortality than do U.S. white women, but those in Cuba and Mexico have rates that are nearly twice the rate for U.S. white women. Middle-aged women in Puerto Rico have slightly lower rates than among their U.S. white counterparts, but women in Mexico and Cuba have higher rates. Finally, at the oldest ages, mortality among all three Hispanic groups exceeds the comparative rate, although the rate among women in Puerto Rico is only slightly higher.

The similarity in rates between women in Puerto Rico and white women in the United States may reflect the fact that Puerto Ricans travel easily between the mainland and the Island and thus share in many of the medical benefits available on the mainland. The higher mortality in both Mexico and Cuba in the three age groups for women suggests lower economic status in the countries of origin, as well as the selection that takes place among migrants to the United States, favoring healthier women. The very high rate for Cuban women at ages 15–24 years points to the need for special attention to health risks in this age group.

CAUSES OF DEATH

Among each of the three Hispanic subgroups (with the exception of U.S. resident Puerto Rican-born males), all-cause mortality was higher in the country of origin. Heart disease was higher among the U.S. residents, except for Cuban-born females, who had lower rates in the United States. Cancer rates were higher for the U.S. residents among both Mexicans and Puerto Ricans. However, it should be noted that the differences were substantial only in Mexico. Higher rates are observed for cerebrovascular diseases in the home countries for Puerto Ricans and Cubans. Only in Mexico were rates lower than among the U.S. residents. Accidents were higher for Mex-

icans and Cubans in their home countries. Puerto Rican residents of the
United States have higher accident rates among both males and females.
Rates for pneumonia and influenza are lower among the U.S. residents than
are those in the home country. Cirrhosis of liver is higher among U.S.
residents for both Puerto Ricans and Cubans; however, Mexican men and
women have higher rates in their home country. Suicide is higher for both
sexes among Mexicans and Puerto Ricans who are U.S. residents, whereas
the Cuban rate for suicide is higher in the home country. Homicide is
distinctly higher for all three U.S. resident groups. Rates for diabetes are
higher in the home countries among Mexicans and Puerto Ricans of both
sexes. Among Cubans this holds only for females, although the rate for males
among the Cuban-born is only slightly higher.

CONCLUSION

For each migrant population group, age-adjusted mortality is lower than
that for the population in the home country. This is not unexpected for a
number of reasons: the healthy migrant effect, the fact that some migrants,
for example, Cubans, have been disproportionately drawn from the higher
social classes, and in the case of Mexican migrants, the relatively higher
quality of medical care in the United States. It is interesting to observe
however, that the difference in the all-cause death rate for Puerto Ricans
living on the U.S. mainland and the rate for those on the Island is only
minimal. In general, there are distinct patterns for each of the Hispanic
groups studied. The pattern of lower mortality rates among the U.S. residents is the most pronounced among Mexicans, whose mortality profile is
much more favorable for U.S. residents than for those in the home country.
There are only two causes of death that show consistent patterns across all
three populations: (1) pneumonia and influenza, for which death rates are
lower among the U.S. resident groups, both males and females; and (2)
homicide, for which death rates are higher among the U.S. resident groups.
Death rates tend to be lower among the U.S. residents for causes such as
diabetes and accidents, except for Puerto Ricans. In general, rates for heart
disease, cancer, cirrhosis of liver, and suicide are generally higher among
the migrants to the United States.

These findings support the picture usually found in transitions to more
industrialized environments: high rates of death from the degenerative diseases and low rates of death from infectious diseases. The findings also
confirm the usual pattern when migrants (Puerto Ricans and Mexicans in
this instance) move into relatively low socioeconomic areas of urban centers—higher rates of death due to accidents. Homicide is the only cause of
death that is higher among all U.S. resident migrant groups. Among Mexican
migrants suicide is the cause that rises most sharply with residence in the
United States, but the difference could be artifactual if suicide is deliberately

underreported in Mexico. Similarly, the elevated levels of mortality from heart disease and malignant neoplasms among Mexican migrants may be due, in part, to differences in reporting between the two countries. (As noted, compared to the United States, Mexico reports a much higher proportion of deaths due to senility. Some of these deaths are probably due to heart disease.)

References

Alba, Francisco. 1977. *La Poblacion de Mexico: Evolucion y Dilemas*. Mexico, D.F.: El Colegio de Mexico.

Alers, J. O. 1978. *Puerto Ricans and Health: Findings from New York City*. New York: Hispanic Research Center.

Antonovsky, A. 1981. "Implications of Socioeconomic Differentials in Mortality for the Health System." *Population Bulletin of the United Nations*, No. 13 (U.N., New York), pp. 42-52.

Arbona, Guillermo, and Annette B. Ramirez de Arellano. 1971. *Regionalization of Health Services*. Preliminary Version Prepared for the Eighth Meeting of the International Epidemiological Association.

Bach, Robert L., Jennifer B. Bach, and Timothy Triplett. 1982. "The Flotilla 'Entrants': Latest and Most Controversial." *Cuban Studies*, Vol. 11–12;2–1:29–48.

Batta, I. D., R. I. Mawby, and J. W. McCullogh. 1981. "Crime, Social Problems and Asian Immigration: The Bradford Experience." *International Journal of Contemporary Sociology* 18:135–168.

Bean, Frank D., and Marta Tienda. 1987. *The Hispanic Population of the United States*. New York: Russell Sage Foundation.

Becerra, Rosina M., and David Shaw. 1984. *The Hispanic Elderly: A Research Reference Guide*. Lanham, MD: University Press of America.

Benitez-Zenteno, Raul, and Gustavo Cabrera-Acevedo. 1967. *Tablas Abreviadas de Mortalidad de la Poblacion de Mexico: 1930, 1940, 1950, 1960*. Mexico, D. F.: El Colegio de Mexico.

Benjamin, Medea, Joseph Collins, and Michael Scott. 1984. *No Free Lunch: Food and Revolution in Cuba Today*. San Francisco: Institute for Food and Development Policy.

Boswell, Thomas D., and James R. Curtis. 1984. *The Cuban-American Experience: Culture, Images and Perspectives*. Totowa, NJ: Rowman and Allanheld.

Bradshaw, Benjamin S. 1976. "Potential Labor Force Supply, Replacement, and

Migration of Mexican American and Other Males in the Texas-Mexico Border Region." *International Migration Review* 10:29–45.

Bradshaw, Benjamin S., and Edwin Fonner, Jr. 1978. "The Mortality of Spanish-Surnamed Persons in Texas: 1969–71." In F. D. Bean and W. P. Frisbie (Eds.), *The Demography of Racial and Ethnic Groups*. New York: Academic Press, pp. 261-282.

Bradshaw, Benjamin S., Edwin Fonner, Jr., and Charles Wright. 1979. "The Ranking of Causes of Death among Mexicans, Mexican Americans and Anglo Americans." Paper presented at Southern Regional Demographic Group meeting, Myrtle Beach, SC.

Bradshaw, Benjamin S., and W. Parker Frisbie. 1983. "Potential Labor Force Supply and Replacement in Mexico and the States of the Mexican Cession and Texas: 1980–2000." *International Migration Review* 17: 394–409.

Bradshaw, Benjamin S., W. Parker Frisbie, and Clayton W. Eifler. 1986. "Excess and Deficit Mortality Due to Selected Causes of Death and Their Contribution to Differences in Life Expectancy of Spanish Surnamed and other White Males—1970 and 1980." In *Report of the Secretary's Task on Black and Minority Health*, Vol. 2. Washington: U.S. Department of Health and Human Services.

Brouard, Nicolas, and Alan Lopez. 1985. "Cause of Death Patterns in Low Mortality Countries: A Classification Analysis." In *International Population Conference, Florence, 1985*. Liege: International Union for the Scientific Study of Population, Vol. 2, pp. 385-406.

Browning, Harley L., and Nestor Rodriguez, Jr. 1985. "The Migration of Mexican Indocumentados as a Settlement Process: Implications for Work." In George J. Borjas and Marta Tienda (Eds.), *Hispanics in the U.S. Economy*. Orlando: Academic Press, pp. 277-297.

Buechley, Robert, John E. Dunn, Jr., George Linden, and Lester Breslow. 1956. "Excess Lung Cancer Mortality Rates among Mexican Women in California." *Cancer* 10:63–66.

Buell, Philip E., Winfred M. Mendez, and John E. Dunn. 1968. "Cancer of the Lung among Immigrant Women in California." *Cancer* 22:186–92.

Bullough, Vern L., and Bonnie Bullough. 1982. *Health Care for the Other Americans*. New York: Appleton-Century-Crofts.

Burnam, M. Audrey, Richard L. Hough, Marvin Karno, Javier I. Escobar, and Cynthia A. Telles. 1987. "Acculturation and Lifetime Prevalence of Psychiatric Disorders among Mexican Americans in Los Angeles." *Journal of Health and Social Behavior* 28:89–102.

Burvill, P. W., M. G. McCall, N. S. Stenhouse, and T. A. Reid. 1973. "Deaths from Suicide, Motor Vehicle Accidents and All Forms of Violent Deaths among Migrants in Australia, 1962–66." *Acta Psychiatric Scandinavia* 49:28–50.

Camposortega Cruz, Sergio. 1987. "Mortality Decline in Mexico, 1940-1980." Paper presented at Annual Meeting of the Population Association of America, Chicago, IL.

Camposortega Cruz, Sergio. 1988. "Mexico: Retos y Perspectivas Demograficas." Unpublished paper.

Carnivali, Judith, and Leida Martinez. 1986. "Tendencias y Patrones de la Mortalidad por Homicidios en Puerto Rico." Paper Presented at the Twentieth Anniversary of the Program of Demography, School of Public Health, Medical Sciences Campus, University of Puerto Rico, December 10.

Carnivali, Judith, and Lilliam Torres-Aguirre. 1986. "De que Mueren los Puertorriquenos? Datos Conflictivos sobre las Causas Muerte." Paper presented at the Twentieth Anniversary of the Program of Demography, School of Public Health, Medical Sciences Campus, University of Puerto Rico, December 10.

Castro, Felipe G., Lourdes Baezconde-Garbanati, and Hector Beltran. 1985. "Risk Factors for Coronary Heart Disease in Hispanic Populations: A Review." *Hispanic Journal of Behavioral Sciences* 7:153–75.

Centers for Disease Control. 1987. "Cigarette Smoking among Blacks and Other Minority Populations." *Morbidity and Mortality Weekly Report* 36(25):404–7.

Chavkin, W., C. Busner, and M. McLaughlin. 1987. "Reproductive Health: Caribbean women in New York City, 1980–1984." *International Migration Review* 21:609–25.

Chiswick, Barry R. 1977. "Sons of Immigrants: Are They at an Earnings Disadvantage?" *American Economic Review* 67:376–80.

Cockerham, William C. 1988. "Medical Sociology." In Neil Smelser (Ed.), *Handbook of Sociology*. Beverly Hills: Sage Publications.

Collver, O. Andrew. 1965. *Birth Rates in Latin America: New Estimates of Historical Trends and Fluctuations*. University of California, Berkeley, Institute of International Studies.

Comite Estatal de Estadisticas. 1981. *Analisis Mortalidad en Cuba: 1943–1953*. Havana.

———. 1983a. *Censo de Poblacion y Viviendas de 1981, Republica de Cuba*, Vol. XVI, No. 1. Havana.

———. 1983b. *Censo de Poblacion y Viviendas de 1981, Republica de Cuba*, Vol. XVI, No. 2. Havana.

———. 1984. *Anuario Demografico 1984*. Havana.

Corona, Rodolfo. 1987. "Estimacion del Numero de Indocumentados a Nivel Estatal y Municipal." Paper Presented at the Binational Symposium on Population Issues at the United States-Mexico Border, Tijuana, June 8–11.

Costas, Raul, Jr., Mario R. Garcia-Palmieri, Paul Sorlie, and Ellen Hertzmark. 1981. "Coronary Heart Disease Risk Factors in Men With Light and Dark Skin in Puerto Rico." *American Journal of Public Health* 71:614–19.

Crimmons, Eileen M. 1981. "The Changing Pattern of American Mortality Decline, 1940–77, and its Implications for the Future." *Population and Development Review* 7:229–54.

Davis, Cary, Carl Haub, and Joann Willette. 1983. "U.S. Hispanics: Changing the Face of America." *Population Bulletin* 38:1–43.

De la Osa, Jose A. 1987. "Infant Mortality: 13.6!," *Granma Weekly Review*, February 1.

Departamento de Salud de Puerto Rico. 1981. *Informe Anual de Estadisticas Vitales, 1980*.

———. 1985. *Informe Anual de Estadisticas Vitales, 1984*.

Departamento del Trabajo. 1967. *Ingresos y Gastos de las Familias, 1963, Informe 2*. San Juan.

Departamento del Trabajo y Recursos Humanos. 1981. *Ingresos y Gastos de las Familias, 1977, Informe 2*. San Juan.

Devesa, S. S., and E. L. Diamond. 1980. "Association of Breast Cancer and Cervical Cancer Incidences with Income and Education among Whites and Blacks." *Journal of the National Cancer Institute* 65:515–28.

Devesa, S. S., and D. T. Silverman. 1978. "Cancer Incidence and Mortality Trends in the United States: 1935–74." *Journal of the National Cancer Institute* 60:545–71.

Diaz, Guarione M. (Ed.). 1980. *Evaluation of Policy Issues in the Cuban Community*. Miami: Cuban National Planning Council.

Diaz-Briquets, Sergio. 1983. *The Health Revolution in Cuba*. Austin: University of Texas Press.

Diaz-Briquets, Sergio, and Lisandro Perez. 1981. "Cuba: The Demography of Revolution." *Population Bulletin* 36, April.

———. 1982. "Fertility Decline in Cuba: A Socioeconomic Interpretation." *Population and Development Review* 8:513–37.

Drury, T. F., K. M. Danchik, and M. I. Harris. 1984. "Sociodemographic Characteristics of Adult Diabetics." In *Diabetes in America*, NIH Publication No. 85–1468, DHHS.

Ellis, John M. 1959. "Mortality Differentials for a Spanish-surname Population Group." *The Southwestern Social Science Quarterly* 39:314–21.

———. 1962. "Spanish Surname Mortality Differences in San Antonio, Texas." *Journal of Health and Human Behavior* 3:125–27.

Escobedo, Luis G., and Patrick L. Remington. 1989. "Birth Cohort Analysis of Prevalence of Cigarette Smoking Among Hispanics in the United States." *The Journal of the American Medical Association* 261:66–69.

Estrada, L. F. 1987. "Mortality Research on Hispanics: Challenges and Opportunities." *National Center for Health Statistics: Proceedings of the 1987 Public Health Conference on Records and Statistics*, pp. 465-467.

Evans, J. 1987. "Migration and Health." *International Migration Review* 21:v-xiv.

Fagen, Richard R., Richard A. Brody, and Thomas J. O'Leary. 1968. *Cubans in Exile: Disaffection and the Revolution*. Stanford University Press: Stanford, CA.

Fernandez, Nelson A. 1975. "Nutrition in Puerto Rico." *Cancer Research* 35:3272–3291.

Fitzpatrick, J. P. 1987 *Puerto Rican Americans: The Meaning of Migration to the Mainland*. Englewood Cliffs, NJ: Prentice-Hall.

Freedman, M. A., G. A. Gay, J. E. Brockert, P. W. Potrzebowski, and C. J. Rothwell. 1988. "The 1989 Revisions of the U.S. Standard Certificate of Live Births and Deaths and the U.S. Standard Report of Fetal Death." *American Journal of Public Health* 78:168-72.

Frey, S. 1982. "The Socioeconomic Distribution of Mortality Rates in Des Moines, Iowa, 1974." *Public Health Reports* 97:545–49.

Garcia-Palmieri, M. R., R. Costas, M. Cruz-Vidal, et al. 1970. "Risk Factors and Prevalence of Coronary Heart Disease in Puerto Rico." *Circulation* 42:541–49.

Garcia-Palmieri, M. R., M. Feliberti, R. Costas, Jr., et al. 1965. "Coronary Heart

Disease Mortality—A Death Certificate Study." *Journal of Chronic Diseases* 18:1317–1323.

Gee, Susan C., Eun Sul Lee, and Ron N. Forthofer. 1976. "Ethnic Differentials in Neonatal and Postneonatal Mortality: A Birth Cohort Analysis by a Binary Variable Multiple Regression Method." *Social Biology* 23:317–25.

Goldberg, D., R. Lowenstein, and L. Habel. 1988. "Comparisons of Leading Causes of Death and Trends in Death Rates in Older Persons in New York City and the United States, 1980–1984." Paper presented at the Annual Meeting of the American Public Health Association, Boston, Mass.

Gonzalez, Q. Fernando, and Jorge Debasa. 1970. "Cuba: Evaluation y Ajuste del Censo de 1953 y las Estadisticas de Nacimientos y Defunciones Entre 1943 y 1958. Tabla de Mortalidad por Sexo 1952–1954." Santiago, Chile: Centro Latinoamericano de Demografia, Series C, No. 124.

Gordon, Antonio M. 1982. "Nutritional Status of Cuban Refugees: A Field Study on the Health and Nutriture of Refugees Processed at Opa Locka, Florida." *The American Journal of Clinical Nutrition* 35:582-90.

Gordon, T., M. R. Garcia-Palmieri, A. Kagan, et al. 1974. "Differences in Coronary Heart Disease in Framingham, Honolulu and Puerto Rico." *Journal of Chronic Diseases* 27:329–44.

Gottschalk, L. A., F. L. McGuire, J. F. Heiser, et al. 1979. "A Review of Psychoactive Drug-Involved Deaths in Nine Major United States Cities." *International Journal of the Addictions* 14(6):735–58.

Graham, S., and C. Mettlin. 1979. "Diet and Colon Cancer." *American Journal of Epidemiology* 109:1–20.

Hayes-Bautista, David E. 1980. "Identifying 'Hispanic' Populations: The Influence of Research Methodology upon Public Policy." *American Journal of Public Health* 70:353–56.

———. 1983. "On Comparing Studies of Different Raza Populations." *American Journal of Public Health* 73:274–76.

Hayes-Bautista, D. E., and J. Chapa. 1987. "Latino Terminology: Conceptual Bases for Standardized Terminology." *American Journal of Public Health* 77:61–68.

Hazuda, Helen, S. M. Haffner, M. P. Stern, and C. W. Eifler. 1988. "Effects of Acculturation and SES Status on Obesity and Diabetes in Mexican-Americans." *American Journal of Epidemiology* 128:1289-1301.

Hernandez, J., L. Estrada, and D. Alvirez. 1972. "Census Data and the Problem of Conceptually Defining the Mexican American Population." *Social Science Quarterly* 53:671–87.

Hill, Kenneth. 1983 "An Evaluation of Cuban Demographic Statistics, 1938–80. "In Paula E. Hollerbach and Sergio Diaz-Briquets (Eds.), *Fertility Determinants in Cuba*. National Research Council, Committee on Population and Demography. Washington, D.C: National Academy Press.

Holck, Susan E., Charles W. Warren, Roger Rochat, and Jack C. Smith. 1982. "Lung Cancer Mortality and Smoking Habits: Mexican-American Women." *American Journal of Public Health* 72:38–42.

Holck, Susan E., Charles W. Warren, Jack C. Smith, and Roger Rochat. 1984. "Alcohol Consumption among Mexican American and Anglo Women: Results of a Survey Along the U.S.-Mexican Border." *Journal of Studies on Alcohol* 45:149–54.

Hollerbach, Paula E., and Sergio Diaz-Briquets. 1983. *Fertility Determinants in Cuba*. National Research Council, Committee on Population and Demography, Washington, DC: National Academy Press.

Howe, G. M. 1976. "The Geography of Disease." In C. O. Carter and J. P. Peel (Eds.), *Equalities and Inequalities in Health*. London: Academic Press, pp. 45-64.

Howson, C. P., T. Hiyama, and E. L. Wynder. 1986. "The Decline in Gastric Cancer: Epidemiology of an Unplanned Triumph." *Epidemiologic Reviews* 8:1-26.

Humble, Charles G., Jonathan M. Samet, Dorothy R. Pathak, and Betty J. Skipper. 1985. "Cigarette Smoking and Lung Cancer in Hispanic Whites and Other Whites in New Mexico." *American Journal of Public Health* 75:145-48.

International Labour Office. 1986. *Economically Active Population: 1950-2025*, Vol. III, Latin America. Geneva.

Jaffe, A. J., Ruth M. Cullen, and Thomas D. Boswell. 1980. *The Changing Demography of Spanish Americans*. New York: Academic Press.

Janofsky, Michael. 1987. "In Cuba, Call is Out for Less Smoke, More Action." *New York Times*, May 4, p. 18.

Jolliffe, Norman, Robert S. Goodheart, Morton Archer, Hady Lopez, and Flavio Galban Diaz. 1958. "Nutrition Status Survey of the Sixth Grade School Population of Cuba." *Journal of Nutrition* 64:355-98.

Jones, R. C. 1984. *Patterns of Undocumented Migration between Mexico and the United States*. Totawa, NJ: Rowman and Allanheld.

Kagamimori, S., Y. Libuchi, and J. Fox. 1983. "A Comparison of Socioeconomic Differences in Mortality Between Japan and England and Wales." *World Health Statistical Quarterly* 36:119-24.

Kautz, Judith H., Benjamin S. Bradshaw, and Edwin Fonner, Jr. 1981. "Trends in Cardiovascular Mortality in Spanish-surnamed, Other White, and Black Persons in Texas, 1970-1975." *Circulation* 64:730-35.

Kicza, J. E. 1981. "Mexican Demographic History of the Nineteenth Century: Evidence and Approaches." In J. W. Wilkie and S. Haber (Eds.), *Statistical Abstract of Latin America*, Vol. 21. Los Angeles: University of California Latin American Center, pp. 592-609.

Kitagawa, E. M., and P. Hauser. 1973. *Differential Mortality in the United States: A Study in Socioeconomic Epidemiology*. Cambridge, MA: Harvard University Press.

Kleinman J. C. 1977. "Mortality." *Statistical Notes for Health Planners*, 3: National Center for Health Statistics.

Kristofersen, L. B. 1979. "Occupational Mortality in Norway, 1970-1973." *The Fifth Scandinavian Demographic Symposium (Hurdalssjoen, Norway)*, The Scandinavian Demographic Society, Oslo.

Krueger, Dean E. and I. M. Moriyama. 1967. "Mortality of the Foreign Born." *American Journal of Public Health* 57:496-503.

Kushner, Howard I. 1984. "Immigrant Suicide in the United States: Toward a Psycho-Social History." *Journal of Social History* 18:3-24.

Lee, Eun Sul, Robert E. Roberts, and Darwin R. Labarthe. 1976. "Excess and Deficit Lung Cancer Mortality in Three Ethnic Groups in Texas." *Cancer* 38:2551-2556.

Lerner, M., and R. N. Stutz. 1977. "Have We Narrowed the Gaps between the Poor and the Nonpoor? Part II." *Medical Care* 15:620–35.

Loya, Fred, Philip Garcia, John D. Sullivan, Luis A. Vargas, James A. Mercy, and Nancy Allen. 1986. "Conditional Risks of Types of Homicide Among Anglo, Hispanic, Black and Asian Victims in Los Angeles, 1970-1979." In *The Secretary's Task Force on Black and Minority Health*, Vol. 5. Washington DC: Department of Health and Human Services.

Loya, Fred, and James A. Mercy. 1985. *The Epidemiology of Homicide in the City of Los Angeles 1970–1979*. Department of Health and Human Services, Public Health Service, Centers for Disease Control.

Luzon, Jose Luis. 1987. *Economia, Poblacion y Territorio en Cuba (1899–1983)*. Ediciones de Cultura Hispanica, Instituto de Cooperacion Iberoamericana, Madrid.

Marcus, Alfred C., and Lori A. Crane. 1984. "Smoking Behavior among Hispanics: A Preliminary Report." *Progress in Clinical and Biological Research* 156:141–51.

———. 1985. "Smoking Behavior among U.S. Latinos: An Emerging Challenge for Public Health." *American Journal of Public Health*. 75:169–72.

Markides, Kyriakos S. 1981. "Death-Related Attitudes and Behavior among Mexican-Americans: A Review." *Suicide and Life-Threatening Behavior* 2:75–85.

———. 1983. "Mortality Among Minority Populations: A Review of Recent Patterns and Trends. *Public Health Reports* 98:252–60.

Markides, Kyriakos S., and Jeanine Coreil. 1986. "The Health of Hispanics in the Southwestern United States: An Epidemiologic Paradox." *Public Health Reports* 101:253–65.

Markides, Kyriakos S., Jeanine Coreil, and L. A. Ray. 1987. "Smoking among Mexican Americans: A Three-Generation Study." *American Journal of Public Heath*. 77:708–11.

Markides, Kyriakos S., and Helen P. Hazuda. 1979. "Ethnicity and Infant Mortality in Texas Counties." *Social Biology* 27:261–71.

Marmot, M. G., A. M. Adelstein, and L. Bulusu. 1984. "Lessons from the Study of Immigrant Mortality." *Lancet*, June 30, pp. 1455–1457.

Martin, Jeanne, and Lucina Suarez. 1987. "Cancer Mortality Among Mexican Americans and Other Whites in Texas." *American Journal of Public Health* 77:851–83.

Martinez, I. 1969. "Factors Associated with Cancer of the Esophagus, Mouth and Pharynx in Puerto Rico." *Journal of the National Cancer Institute* 42:1069–1094.

Martinez, I., R. Torres, and Z. Frias. 1975. "Cancer Incidence in the United States and Puerto Rico." *Cancer Research* 35:3265–3271.

McKeown, Thomas. 1979. *The Role of Medicine: Dream, Mirage, or Nemesis?* Princeton, NJ: Princeton University Press.

McMichael, A. J., and J. M. Hartshorne. 1982. "Mortality Risks in Australian Men by Occupational Groups, 1968-1978." *The Medical Journal of Australia* 1:253–56.

Melville, Margarita B. 1988. "Hispanics: Race, Class, or Ethnicity." *Journal of Ethnic Studies* 16:67–83.

Mesa-Lago, Carmelo. 1981. *The Economy of Socialist Cuba: A Two Decade Appraisal*. Albuquerque: University of New Mexico Press.

Mexico. 1980. Dirección General de Estadistica. ND. Tabulacion 5, "Defunciones generales por entidad federativa de residencia habitual del fallecido segun lista basica de causa de muerto (incluye titulos de grupos), grupos quinquenales de edad y sexo."

———. 1985. *Annuario Estadistico de los Unidos Mexicanos, 1984*.

———. 1986. Instituto Nacional de Estadistica, Geografia e Informatica. *Estadisticas Historicas de Mexico*.

Miller, G. H., and Dean R. Gerstein. 1983. "The Life Expectancy of Nonsmoking Men and Women." *Public Health Reports* 98:343–49.

Moore, Joan W., Robert Garcia, C. Garcia, L. Cerda, and F. Valencia. 1978. *Homeboys: Gangs, Drugs and Prison in the Barrios of Los Angeles*. Philadelphia: Temple University Press.

Morales, Zoraida. 1982. *Regional Differences in Economic Growth, Urbanization and Labor Force Trends: The Case of Puerto Rico*. Ph.D. dissertation, University of Pennsylvania.

Morales Del Valle, Zoraida, and Judith Carnivali. 1985. "Cambios en la Mortalidad de Puerto Rico Mediante el Analisis de la Tabla de Vida, 1765–1980." *Center for Demographic Research (CIDE), Demography Program*, No. V.

Moriyama, I. M., D. E. Krueger, and J. Stamler. 1971. *Cardiovascular Diseases in the United States*. Cambridge, MA: Harvard University Press.

Nangle, B., J. E. Brockert, and M. Levy. 1985. "Mortality Patterns and Projections by Educational Attainment: Utah, 1978–1982 and 1990." *Proceedings of the 1985 Public Health Conference on Research and Statistics*, DHHS Pub. No. (PHS) 86–1214, pp. 271–74.

National Center for Health Statistics. 1985a. *Vital Statistics of the United States: 1980, Vol. II, Mortality, Part A*. Washington: U.S. Government Printing Office.

———. 1985b. "Plan and Operation of the Hispanic Health and Nutrition Survey, 1982–84." *Vital and Health Statistics*. Series 1, No. 19. DHHS Pub. No. (PHS) 85-1321. Hyattsville, MD: U.S. Government Printing Office.

———. 1986. *Report of the Panel to Evaluate the U.S. Standard Certificate*. Hyattsville, MD (Unpublished report).

———. 1988. *Hispanic Health and Nutrition Examination Survey, 1982–1984*. Public Use Data Tape and Documentation. Issued by the Inter-university Consortium for Political and Social Research.

National Highway Traffic Safety Administration. 1980. *Fatal Accident Reporting System 1980*. Washington DC: U.S. Department of Transportation.

New York City Department of Health. 1979–1981. *New York City Death Record Tapes for 1979–1981*. New York City Department of Health, New York, NY.

Ortiz, V. 1986. "Changes in the Characteristics of Puerto Rican Migrants from 1955 to 1980." *International Migration Review* 20:612–28.

Pamuk, E. 1985. "Social Class Inequality in Mortality from 1921 to 1972 in England and Wales." *Population Studies* 39:17–31.

Pan American Health Organization. 1974. *Health Conditions in the Americas, 1969–1972*. Washington, DC.

———. 1978. *Health Conditions in the Americas, 1973–1976*. Washington, DC.

————. 1982. *Health Conditions in the Americas, 1977–1980*. Washington, DC.
————. 1986. *Health Conditions in the Americas, 1981–1984*. Washington, DC.
Passel, J. S. and K. A. Woodrow. 1984. "Geographic Distribution of Undocumented Immigrants: Estimates of Undocumented Aliens Counted in the 1980 Census by State." *International Migration Review* 18:642–71.
Passel, J. S. and D. L. Word. 1980. "Constructing the List of Spanish Surnames for the 1980 Census: An Application of Bayes' Theorum." Paper presented at the annual meeting of the Population Association of America, Denver.
Pearce, N. E., P. B. Davis, A. H. Smith, and F. H. Foster. 1985. "Social Class, Ethnic Group, and Male Mortality in New Zealand, 1974–8." *Journal of Epidemiology and Community Health* 39:9–14.
Pedraza-Bailey, S. 1985. *Political and Economic Migrants in America: Cubans and Mexicans*. Austin: University of Texas Press.
Perez, Lisandro. 1986. "Immigrant Economic Adjustment and Family Organization: The Cuban Success Story Reexamined." *International Migration Review* 20:4–20.
Peterson, William. 1986. "Politics and the Measurement of Ethnicity." In William Alonso and Paul Storr (Eds.), *The Politics of Numbers*. New York: Russel Sage Foundation, pp. 187-233.
Planek, Thomas W. 1982. "Home Accidents: A Continuing Social Problem." *Accident Analysis and Prevention* 14:107–20.
Portes, Alejandro, Juan M. Clark, and Robert L. Bach. 1977. "The New Wave: A Statistical Profile of Recent Cuban Exiles to the United States." *Cuban Studies* 7:1–32.
Portes, Alejandro, and Cynthia Truelove. 1987. "Making Sense of Diversity: Recent Research on Hispanic Minorities in the United States." *Annual Review of Sociology* 13:359–85.
Powell-Griner, Eve, and Richard G. Rogers. 1987. "Strong Compounding Effects of Multiple Risks During Pregnancy on Birthweight and Infant Survival." *Sociology and Social Research* 72:49–54.
Powell-Griner, Eve E., and D. Streck. 1982. "A Closer Examination of Neonatal Mortality Rates Among the Texas Spanish Surname Population." *American Journal of Public Health* 72:993–99.
Preston, Samuel H. 1976. *Mortality Patterns in National Populations*. New York: Academic Press.
Ramirez de Arellano, Annette B. 1981. "The Politics of Public Health in Puerto Rico, 1926–40." *Revista de Salud Publica de Puerto Rico*. Vol. 3.
Remington, Patrick L., Michele R. Forman, Eileen M. Gentry, James S. Marks, Gary C. Hogelin, and Frederick L. Trowbridge. 1985. "Current Smoking Trends in the United States: The 1981–1985 Behavioral Risk Factor Surveys." *Journal of the American Medical Association* 253:2975–2978.
Rivera de Morales, Nydia. 1970. *Mortalidad en Puerto Rico, 1888–1967*. Biostatistics Section, School of Public Health, Medical Sciences Campus, University of Puerto Rico.
Roberts, Jean, and Michael Rowland. 1981. "Hypertension in Adults 25–74 Years of Age: United States, 1971–1975." *Vital and Health Statistics*. DHHS Publication No. PHS 81–1671, Series 11, No. 221. Hyattsville, MD: U.S. Government Printing Office.

Roberts, Robert E., and Cornelius Askew, Jr. 1972. "A Consideration of Mortality in Three Subcultures." *Health Services Reports* 87:262-70.

Robinson, J. G. 1987. "Evaluation of Coverage of the 1980 Census of Puerto Rico Based on Demographic Analysis." Paper Presented at Annual Meeting of the Population Association of America, Chicago, IL.

Rogers, Richard G., and John Crank. 1988. "Ethnic Differences in Smoking Patterns: Findings from NHIS." *Public Health Reports* 103:387–93.

Rogers, Richard G., and Robert Hackenberg. 1987. "Extending Epidemiological Transition Theory: A New Stage." *Social Biology.* 34:234–43.

Rogler, Charles C. 1972. "The Morality of Race Mixing in Puerto Rico." In Eugenio Fernandez Mendez (Ed.), *Portrait of a Society.* San Juan: University of Puerto Rico Press, pp. 57-64.

Rosenwaike, Ira. 1983. "Mortality among the Puerto Rican Born in New York City." *Social Science Quarterly* 64:375–85.

———. 1984. "Cancer Mortality among Puerto Rican-Born Residents of New York City. *American Journal of Epidemiology* 119:177–85.

———. 1987. "Mortality Differentials among Persons Born in Cuba, Mexico, and Puerto Rico Residing in the United States, 1979–81." *American Journal of Public Health* 77:603–6.

———. 1988. "Cancer Mortality among Mexican Immigrants in the United States." *Public Health Reports* 103:195–201.

Rosenwaike, Ira, and Benjamin S. Bradshaw. 1988. "The Status of Death Certificates for the Hispanic Population of the Southwest." *Social Science Quarterly* 69:722–36.

———. 1989. "Mortality of the Spanish Surname Population of the Southwest: 1980." *Social Science Quarterly* 70:631–41.

Rosenwaike, Ira, and Donna Shai. 1989. "Changes in Mortality Among Cubans in the United States Following an Episode of Unscreened Migration." *International Journal of Epidemiology* 18:152–57.

Rudolph, James D. 1985. *Mexico, a Country Study,* 3rd ed. Washington, DC: Headquarters, Department of the Army.

Samet, Jonathan M., Charles R. Key, D. M. Kutvirt, et al. 1980. "Respiratory Disease Mortality in New Mexico's American Indians and Hispanics." *American Journal of Public Health* 70:492–97.

Samkoff, J. S., and S. P. Baker. 1982. "Recent Trends in Fatal Poisoning by Opiates in the United States." *American Journal of Public Health* 72:1251–1256.

Schoen, Robert, and Verne E. Nelson. 1981. "Mortality by Cause among Spanish Surnamed Californians, 1969–1971." *Social Science Quarterly* 62:259–74.

Schoenborn, Charlotte A., and Veronica Benson. 1988. "Relationships between Smoking and Other Unhealthy Habits: United States, 1985." *Advance Data from Vital and Health Statistics.* DHHS Pub. No. (PHS) 88–11250. No. 154. National Center for Health Statistics, Hyattsville, MD.

Schur, Claudia L., Amy B. Bernstein, and Marc L. Berk. 1987. "The Importance of Distinguishing Hispanic Subpopulations in the Use of Medical Care." *Medical Care* 15:627–41.

Scott, C.S. 1981. "Health and Healing Practices among Five Ethnic Groups in Miami, Florida." In G. Henderson and M. Primeaux (Eds.), *Transcultural Health Care.* London: Addison-Wesley.

Seidman, H. 1970. "Cancer Death Rates by Site and Sex for Religious and Socio-economic Groups in New York City." *Environmental Research* 3:234–50.

Shai, Donna, and Ira Rosenwaike. 1988. "Violent Deaths among Mexican-, Puerto Rican- and Cuban-born Migrants in the United States." *Social Science and Medicine* 26:269–76.

Shopland, Donald R., and Clarice Brown. 1987. "Toward the 1990 Objectives for Smoking: Measuring the Progress with 1985 NHIS Data." *Public Health Reports* 102:68–73.

Shryrock, Henry S., J. S. Siegel et al. 1975. *The Methods and Materials of Demography.* Washington, DC: U.S. Government Printing Office.

Simpson, Sylvia G., Raymond Reid, Susan P. Baker, and Stephen Teret. 1983. "Injuries among the Hopi Indians: A Population-Based Study." *Journal of the American Medical Association* 249:1873–1876.

Smith, Jack C., James A. Mercy, and Mark L. Rosenberg. 1986. "Suicide and Homicide among Hispanics in the Southwest." *Public Health Reports* 101:265–70.

Sorlie, Paul D., Mario R. Garcia-Palmieri, Raul Costas, Mercedes Cruz-Vidal, and Richard Havlik. 1982. "Cigarette Smoking and Coronary Heart Disease in Puerto Rico." *Preventive Medicine* 11:304–16.

Spencer, Gregory. 1984. "Mortality Among the Elderly Spanish-surnamed Population in the Medicare File: 1968 to 1979." Paper presented at Population Association of America meeting. Minneapolis.

Stern, Michael P., Benjamin S. Bradshaw, Clayton W. Eifler, Donald S. Fong, Helen P. Hazuda, and Marc Rosenthal. 1987. "Secular Decline in Death Rates due to Ischemic Heart Disease in Mexican Americans and non-Hispanic Whites in Texas, 1970–1980." *Circulation* 76:1245–1250.

Stern, Michael P., and Sharon Parten Gaskill. 1978. "Secular Trends in Ischemic Heart Disease and Stroke Mortality from 1970 to 1976 in Spanish-Surnamed and Other White Individuals in Bexar County, Texas." *Circulation* 58:537–43.

Stockwell, E. G., J. W. Wicks, and D. A. Adamchak. 1978. "Research Needed on Socioeconomic Differentials in U.S. Mortality." *Public Health Reports* 93:666–72.

Sullivan, Teresa A., Francis P. Gillespie, Michael Hout, and Richard G. Rogers. 1984. "Alternative Estimates of Mexican-American Mortality." *Social Science Quarterly.* 65:609–17.

Susser, Mervyn, William Watson, and Kim Hopper. 1985. *Sociology in Medicine.* Third Edition. New York: Oxford University Press.

Thomas, D. B. 1979. "Epidemiological Studies of Cancer in Minority Groups in the Western United States." *In Second Symposium on Epidemiology and Cancer Registries in the Pacific Basin.* National Cancer Institute Monograph 53:103–13.

Tienda, Marta, and Vilma Ortiz. 1986. " 'Hispanicity' and the 1980 Census." *Social Science Quarterly* 67:3–20.

Trevino, Fernando M. 1982. "Vital and Health Statistics for the U.S. Hispanic Population." *American Journal of Public Health* 72:979–81.

Trovato, Frank. 1985. "Mortality Differences Among Canada's Indigenous and For-

eign-Born Populations, 1951–1971." *Canadian Studies in Population* 12:49–
80.

Trovato, Frank, and George K. Jarvis. 1986. "Immigrant Suicide in Canada: 1971
and 1981." *Social Forces* 65:433–57.

United Nations. 1986. *World Population Prospects: Estimates and Projections as
Assessed in 1984.* Department of International Economic and Social Affairs,
Population Studies, No. 98 (ST/ESA/Ser.A/98), New York.

———. 1988. *World Demographic Estimates and Projections, 1950–2025*, Department of International Economic and Social Affairs, New York.

U.S. Bureau of the Census. 1953. *Census of Population: 1950. Vol. II. Characteristics
of the Population, Part 53, Puerto Rico.* Washington, DC: Government Printing Office.

———. 1963. *Census of Population: 1960. Vol. 1. Characteristics of the Population.
Part 53, Puerto Rico.* Washington, DC: Government Printing Office.

———. 1975. "Comparison of Persons of Spanish Surname and Persons of Spanish
Origin in the United States," by E.W. Fernandez, Technical Paper No. 38.,
Washington, DC: Government Printing Office.

———. 1980. *Census of Population and Housing, 1980.* Public-Use Microdata Sample 5(%)A, New York and New Jersey, machine-readable data file, prepared
by the Bureau of the Census, Washington, DC.

———. 1982. *Census of Population: 1980. Vol. 1, Chapter A. Number of Inhabitants.
Part 53, Puerto Rico.* Washington, DC: Government Printing Office.

———. 1983a. *Census of Population: 1980. Vol.1, Characteristics of the Population;
Chapter D, Detailed Characteristics, Part 34, New York.* Washington, DC:
Government Printing Office.

———. 1983b. *Census of Population: 1980. Vol.1, Characteristics of the Population;
Chapter B, General Characteristics, Part 53, Puerto Rico.* Washington, DC:
Government Printing Office.

———. 1983c. *Census of the Population: 1980. Public Use Microdata Sample, Technical Documentation.*

———. 1983d. *Census of the Population: 1980. Summary Tape File 5A.* The Bureau
Producer and Distributor.

———. 1983e. *Census of Population: 1980. Vol. I. Characteristics of the Population;
Chapter B, General Population Characteristics, Part I, U.S. Summary.* Washington, DC: Government Printing Office.

———. 1984a. *1980 Census of Population. Detailed Population Characteristics:
Puerto Rico. PC80–1-D53.* Washington, DC: Government Printing Office.

———. 1984b. *Census of Population: 1980. Vol. I, Characteristics of the Population;
Chapter D, Detailed Characteristics, Part 1, U.S. Summary.* Washington,
DC: Government Printing Office.

———. 1984c. *1980 Census of Population. Characteristics of the Population, General
Social and Economic Characteristics: U.S. Summary, PC80–1-C1.* Washington, DC: Government Printing Office.

———. 1984d. *1980 Census of Population. Characteristics of the Population, General
Social and Economic Characteristics: Part 6, California. PC80–1-C6.* Washington, DC: Government Printing Office.

———. 1984e. *1980 Census of Population. Characteristics of the Population, General*

Social and Economic Characteristics: Part 45, Texas. PC80–1-C45. Washington, DC: Government Printing Office.

―――. 1984f. *Census of Population: 1980. Foreign-born Persons in the United States (Special Tabulation).*

U.S. Department of Health and Human Services. 1985. *Report on the Secretary's Task Force on Black and Minority Health.* Washington DC: Government Printing Office.

Valdivieso, Rafael, and Cary Davis. 1988. "U.S. Hispanics: Challenging Issues for the 1990s." *Population Trends and Public Policy.* 17:1–6. Population Reference Bureau.

Vazquez Calzada, Jose L. 1988. *La Poblacion de Puerto Rico y su Trayectoria Historica.* Escuela Graduada de Salud Pública, Recinto de Ciencias Médicas, Universidad de Puerto Rico.

Vazquez Calzada, Jose L., Iris Parrilla Boria, and Luz E. Leon Lopez. 1986. *El Efecto de Los Partos por Cesarea Sobre la Esterilization Femenina en Puerto Rico.* Escuela Graduada de Salud Pública, Recinto de Ciencias Médicas, Universidad de Puerto Rico.

Vazquez Calzada, Jose, and Zoraida Morales Del Valle. 1982. "Female Sterilization in Puerto Rico and Its Demographic Effectiveness." *Puerto Rico Health Sciences Journal* 1(2).

Waldron, Ingrid. 1983. "Sex Differences in Illness Incidence, Prognosis and Mortality: Issues and Evidence." *Social Science and Medicine.* 17:1107–1123.

Warren, Charles W., Charles F. Westoff, Joan M. Herold, et al. 1986. "Contraceptive Sterilization in Puerto Rico." *Demography* 23:351-65.

Weisburger, J. H. 1979. "Mechanism of Action of Diet as a Carcinogen." *Cancer* 43: 1987-95.

Wilson, Kenneth L., and Alejandro Portes. 1980. "Immigrant Enclaves: An Analysis of the Labor Market Experiences of Cubans in Miami." *American Journal of Sociology* 86:295–319.

World Health Organization. 1977. *International Classification of Diseases (Ninth Revision). Manual of International Statistical Classification of Diseases, Injuries, and Causes of Death.* Geneva.

―――. 1986. *World Health Statistics Annual 1985.* Geneva.

Yamamoto, Joe, and Alan Steinberg. 1981. "Ethnic, Racial and Social Class Factors in Mental Health." *Journal of the National Medical Association* 73:231–40.

Yang, S., and B. Pendleton. 1980. "Socioeconomic Development and Mortality Levels in Less Developed Countries." *Social Biology* 27: 220–29.

Yeracaris, C. A., and J. H. Kim. 1978. "Socioeconomic Differentials in Selected Causes of Death." *American Journal of Public Health* 68:342-51.

Index

About the Editor and Contributors

BENJAMIN S. BRADSHAW is an Associate Professor of Demography at the School of Public Health, University of Texas Health Science Center at San Antonio.

SERGIO DIAZ-BRIQUETS currently is a Research Director, Commission for the Study of International Migration and Cooperative Economic Development, Washington, D.C. Previously he was associated with Duquesne University.

KATHERINE HEMPSTEAD is a graduate student in the Department of History, and the Population Studies Center, University of Pennsylvania.

KAREN A. LIESE is a Research Associate, School of Public Health, University of Texas Health Science Center at San Antonio.

ZORAIDA MORALES DEL VALLE is a Professor in the Demography Program and Director of Office of External Resources, Graduate School of Public Heath, University of Puerto Rico Medical Sciences Campus.

RICHARD G. ROGERS is Research Associate in the Population Program and Assistant Professor, Sociology Department, University of Colorado.

IRA ROSENWAIKE is Research Specialist, School of Social Work, and Research Associate, Population Studies Center, University of Pennsylvania.

DONNA SHAI is Associate Professor of Sociology at Villanova University.